Charmaine Hale, youngest of five siblings, was born and grew up in Hatfield, Hertfordshire. She still resides in Hatfield and lives with Jase. They have a son and a daughter and five grandchildren. This is Charmaine's first book and she wants to leave this true family story as a legacy to her grandchildren and future generations at home and abroad.

To my deceased sister Tara Evelyn Knight, for all her hand written memories of her childhood and of growing up.

To my cousin Brigitte Knight, for her French input into my uncle Alfie's life in France.

To my cousin Darren Vivian, in Canada, with the Knights family tree of my long-lost cousins and relatives.

Charmaine Hale

THE LIFE AND TIMES
OF THE KNIGHTS

AUSTIN MACAULEY PUBLISHERS™

LONDON • CAMBRIDGE • NEW YORK • SHARJAH

A CIP catalogue record for this title is available from the British Library.

ISBN 9781398499614 (Paperback)
ISBN 9781398499621 (ePub e-book)

www.austinmacauley.com

First Published 2023
Austin Macauley Publishers Ltd®
1 Canada Square
Canary Wharf
London
E14 5AA

To my genealogist, Mathew Homewood, who gave me all my vital information into the history of my ancestors, and information about Alfred's army records.

To my sister, Carol Reeley, for her help with grammar and editing my book.

To my brother, Philip Knight, who helped me with the protocol with life in the army along with the army song.

To my daughter, Maria Leto, for her help getting me on the correct app, for writing my book.

To my son, Marcus Hale, who gave me help with my computer details and problems.

Prologue

One cold winter's afternoon in January, I was relaxing sitting in my lounge, gazing out of the window watching the birds feeding on the nuts in our garden. I was just daydreaming when something strange started to happen to me, suddenly the window became misty, then slowly cleared; whether I dozed off or not I don't know! I rubbed my eyes and tried to focus on the window. I seemed to have been transported back in time, for I saw myself walking down an unfamiliar street.

I realised I had gone back in time, to the year 1866, eighty-one years before I was born! Do you ever feel like you have been somewhere before and you know full well you never have? Then I suddenly saw a road sign that read BACK KINGSTON ROAD, YEOVIL. I continued to walk on, passing many small cottages built very close together. As I passed, I could not help but glance inside. Then further along, I saw a bright light shining in one of the cottage windows. I walked slowly towards it, there I stopped and looked inside.

I saw a young man sitting at a table, cutting up some leather, with his tools beside him. On the other side of the room, I saw a lovely lady sitting rocking a beautiful oak cradle. The baby was wrapped in white linen, I could just see the top of the baby's tiny head. Some instinct told me, "I know these people." I was just about to knock on the front door when everything went blank and I found myself back in my own front room rather dazed! Did I imagine it all or was I dreaming?

My husband then entered the room asking, "What's for Dinner Tonight?"

Introduction to the
Hancock Family

EVELINE ROSE HANCOCK: Eldest sister Eveline was born on 31 December 1929 in Somerset England. Eveline married David John Heming in 1950 at Gloucester. She had three children while living in Evesham, two sons and one daughter. They emigrated to Australia in 1960 and had two more sons there. Eveline sadly passed away on 12 May 2013. David John Heming passed away in Australia in 2017.

MICHAEL SIMON DICKER HANCOCK: Eldest brother Michael Knight was born on 26 March 1936 in Shoreham-by-sea (changed name by deed poll in 1961 to Michael Knight). Michael never married and passed away in 2015.

CAROLINE JUNE JANE THELMA HANCOCK: Sister Caroline was born on 5 June 1939 in Hatfield. Married in 1958 to William Edward Reeley in Evesham, Worcester at the Catholic Church. They had three sons. In later life, they moved to live in Spain. Eleven years later, they moved again to live in France. William passed away in 2019, then Carol moved back to Worcester to be with her family.

PHILIP DAVID DERRICK ARTHUR HANCOCK: Brother Philip was born on 25 August 1942 in Hatfield. He moved to Australia, changed his name by deed poll to Philip Knight, still living happily there with his wife Eeva.

CHARMAINE RIO-LINDA HANCOCK: Youngest sister Charmaine was born on 22 February 1947 in Hatfield; I still reside there. Charmaine married Jeffrey Peter Hale in May 1969. They have a son and daughter.

Our brother Michael suddenly died of a stroke in 2015, aged 78. Michael had carried on living in Selwyn, where my brother Philip and I were born and brought up. Michael was a bachelor and lived alone after our mother passed away in 1979. My sister Carol and myself were left with the daunting task of clearing his three-bedroom house, which Michael had carried on renting from a private landlord since our parents moved there in 1940.

My brother Philip and Sister Eveline had long ago moved to Australia and settled there with their families. Carol, who was living in southern France, came over to help me clear the house. The landlord wanted the house cleared within two weeks. While going through Michael's effects, I was reminded of the day when I had that vision of going back in time when finding a small old diary among piles of Michael's correspondence; it was dated 1948. It belonged to our late grandfather, Alfred Frederick John Knight.

Reading through this tiny diary gave me the enthusiasm to look into our family history. Oh! Little did I know then what it would lead to, what mystery and intrigue I was going to discover. I felt that I must write a book about our grandfather's extraordinary life. I found myself a good genealogist, then I began to research the Knight's family history with relations from many places in the world, including France, Canada and Australia.

Chapter One

George Knight was born in 1844 in Yeovil Somerset England, like his Father Thomas Knight before him. Thomas Knight's parents came from Hallow in Worcestershire; they moved to Somerset in about 1822. George was raised in the village of Yeovil by his parents, Thomas and Mother Mary, who dearly loved their son. He was a strong, healthy boy, happy and content; he had many friends who lived in the village. His father only wanted the very best education for his son and sent him to a very good school.

Thomas worked as a local handyman and generally kept busy doing various jobs for the villagers around his town. He was well-liked, always finishing his jobs on time. He never overcharged his customers, known all around the village for his fine workmanship and his happy disposition. The villagers would sometimes call on him in the middle of the night; Thomas never complained, made a fine living and loved his job. His lovely wife Mary always kept a clean, comfortable home.

They had a little garden at the back, where Mary would love to potter around; she grew roses, violets and primroses and other sweet-scented flowers. She would often cut a bunch, bringing them into the house, arranging them in an ornate lilac vase, which once belonged to her mother. She would place the vase in the middle of the dining room table, which would fill the room, smelling of fresh flowers. Mary had a lovely singing voice, she could often be heard singing Cornish and Irish folk songs like *The Sweet Primroses, The Sweet Nightingale* and *Sweet Alice Ben Bolt*.

The years passed by, soon George would be fourteen and leaving school. On the school leaver's last day, it was expected for the parents to come into school to talk to the Headmaster about the future of each boy or girl leaving their school and also to receive their Final Exams reports.

The Headmaster Mr Brown taking Thomas into his office said, "Mr Knight, George was always a clever boy, quick to learn, his attendance has been good; he has always been well behaved in school. You should be very proud as I present you with George's final exam results, he has passed all subjects with excellent high grades." He also went on to say, "He is very good with his hands, this year in his woodwork class, he made this." Mr Brown unwrapped a beautifully polished wooden cross and gave it to Thomas, "I would like you to keep it."

"My, it's very fine work, Mr Brown." Thomas could not believe the workmanship, he said, "George never mentioned to me that he was good at woodwork. Thank you, Mr Brown, it's a lovely memory of his school days, for the family to keep."

"Mr Knight, before you depart, I would also like you to know that George's class teachers have told me that George has always been very helpful in the classroom; he would often give up his play time, helping pupils in his class if they were falling behind with their lesson. His teachers have also told me that George was liked by his fellow students and was a pleasure to teach. I am sure George has a fine future ahead. Does he have a trade or profession he would like to pursue, Mr Knight?"

"Well, not exactly, but he does help me with my building work, he did mention once that he would like to run his own company, but we shall see."

"Mr Knight, George has been an excellent scholar. I wish him all the best in whatever trade or profession he takes in life. I am sure he will do very well indeed. Goodbye, Mr Knight."

"Goodbye, Mr Brown and thank you again." George was waiting outside the Headmaster's office, when Thomas came out he was smiling, saying, "Son, you have done me and your mother proud, let's go home and tell her and show her your excellent results and your work of art."

Thomas and Mary were pleased and so very proud of their son. Mary said, "Now, we know you are great at working with wood George, you can make a frame for your Exam certificate for the hall to show everyone just how proud we are."

George laughed and said, "Oh, you liked the wooden cross I made for you, Ma?"

"Oh, yes son, it's beautiful, we both love it. George why did you never tell us, you were so good at woodwork?"

"Oh, I didn't think it was that good, Ma."

"George, it's more than good, it's a work of art! I shall hang it above our bed, first thing tomorrow morning," his smiling mother replied.

George often helped his father, trying to learn his trade. Thomas would reward him with a little pocket money. If his father gave him a penny, George would spend ha'penny and

save the other half. But George did not want to become a builder. He had other ideas, *I will look for something that will be more profitable*, he thought about perhaps going into business on his own. One warm afternoon in August, Thomas had finished a local guttering job early, he had been well paid.

He started to walk home and paused outside the local village pub, he felt the need for a long cool drink and popped in for a pint of cider. While he sat at the bar chatting to the barmaid, a smart-looking gentleman walked in and sat next to him. Thomas turned his head to look, smiling. Thomas nodded saying politely, "Good afternoon sir."

The man stood up, smiled and offered his hand. "Pleased to meet you, my good man. I'm John White at your service, would you care for another pint."

"Thank you kindly, sir. I'm pleased to meet you, John White; my name is Thomas Knight."

As they shook hands John said, "Are you from around here Thomas?"

"Yes, a matter of fact, I live locally."

They soon became acquainted. After talking and laughing, John told Thomas that he was married to his lovely wife Ann; they had six children, Johnny, William, Hannah, Frederick, Susannah and Amelia. He told him he was in the leather trade business, Occupation Glover. They made and sold gloves and other goods. He was now expanding his business to make all types of leather goods. He went on to say that two of his sons worked with him, Johnny and William Two of my daughters Hannah and Susannah work in the Machine Shop. I also employ manual workers on my staff.

He said he was now looking for a strong young lad to train up and join the team in his leather business. Thomas could not believe his luck, he then explained to John that his son George had just left school with excellent reports, George was now looking for a good working trade.

"Well now," said John, "That is a fine thing, I will gladly take him on, give him an apprenticeship if that is what he wants! I'll give him an interview, to see if (he be) what I am looking for. If I think he is suitable, I am willing to give him a month's trial. Tell George to be at my small outbuilding next to the large outbuilding at Belmont Road at 9 o'clock sharp on Monday morning."

"Thank you, sir, good day." They shook hands and departed.

Thomas marched home with a spring in his step, he could not wait to relate this good news to his wife and son. He washed his face and hands at the pump, hanging up his work jacket and cap, as he entered the house. Mary was just about to serve up the evening meal, she turned to her husband and said, "Hello, Tom. You're late, why, you look very pleased with yourself!"

"Sorry for being late, Mary." He turned to his son who was sitting reading his history book, *Life And Times Of Henry VIII And His Six Wives*.

He looked up and said, "Evening, Pa."

"Evening, Son."

They all sat down to eat, then Tom related his good news. George was delighted and Mary was overjoyed for her son. They all retired to bed chatting and laughing, George could hardly get to sleep that night. On the morning of the interview, George was a little nervous and left the house in plenty of time. He arrived just before nine and knocked on the outhouse door.

It opened and a smell of urine hit him, the man introduced himself as Johnny, "I'm Mr White's son," he said offering to shake George's hand.

"Very nice to meet you, Johnny White."

"My father is with a client at the moment, he will be with you shortly. If you will follow me, I'll take you to my Father's office." He took George into another small brick building. "This is Father's Office, I will tell him you have arrived," he told George to take a seat in the waiting room. Ten minutes later Mr White came out of his office, with a very distinguished-looking elderly gentleman, they shook hands, said goodbye and the gentleman smartly walked out of the door.

He then called George into his office, Mr White introduced himself while shaking hands, "George, do take a seat," Mr White said. "I am sorry for keeping you waiting, the gentleman who left was one of my important clients. I am happy to say, the gentleman has left me with a very large order."

George replied, "That's fine, Mr White, thank you for giving me an interview."

After they had gotten acquainted, Mr White started by explaining that the work is gruelling but very rewarding. He went on to tell George that he would like him to learn all aspects of the Leather trade. Eventually becoming a qualified Leather Draper. I would also like you to learn all about the running and selling in our Leather goods shop.

John White then said to George, "Come with me and I will show you around." He took him into the larger outbuilding, then started explaining to George all the procedures needed, to take place with the animal skins.

"Firstly, the skins arrive on the cart, then all the animal hides are dehaired. Then they have to go through the process of tanning, which is a mixture of strong chemicals which can be toxic. We have to be careful and wear gloves when handling the skins, which will then be put into tanks, for up to a week, so as to make the leather more durable and less susceptible to decomposition. After the tanning process, the leather is hung up and dried. My two sons work as a team in this smaller warehouse."

Mr White took George across to another larger outhouse, John continued, "This warehouse is where we carry on the next process when the leather is completely dry. The hides are then brought in here ready to be cleaned, the leather is now a good colour (Any flesh left on the hide is removed). The leather is then softened and polished. The hides are split in two, one side is for the best leather goods, the other for cheaper goods.

The Machine cuts the leather, then it's made into a variety of leather clothing or bags. My two daughters run the Machine Shop. I also employ three other ladies that also work with them. We also have a barn where we keep our pony and cart, which we use to pick up the hides and deliver the goods to our customers. I have already extended the business, we are now in production of making all sorts of garments for ladies and gentlemen to wear.

I am willing to take you on a month's trial, to see if you are suitable. If you like the job, I will take you on as an apprentice, George, you can start work in two weeks' time. Now if you come back to my office with me, I will give you the monthly wage details."

George was optimistic, but replied, "It would be an honour to work for you Mr White. I will work hard, I'll try my best to become a good Leather Draper."

"Excellent, George; be at the small outhouse on 17 August at 7 o'clock."

"Thank you, Mr White, I look forward to starting my new Job."

Mr White and George shook hands, "George, we will supply all overalls, which you will take home and clean daily; until our next meeting. Good day, George."

"Good day, Mr White. I do appreciate your time."

"Until we meet again, George. I wish you a pleasant day."

George walked home thinking about all the procedures involved. He also thought that Mr White was a very nice gentleman.

After the first couple of months, George had settled in, he picked up the work very quickly, he liked his job and the surroundings. All the staff were nice and friendly. Mr White was a very pleasant manager, who was always giving George praise for his work. George was happy and enjoyed working here, he would take pride in what he did, and his wages were good too.

He also had a very good relationship with Mr White's sons, Johnny and William. They laughed and played jokes on each other while at work. Sometimes after work, they would go to the local pub together, where they would play cards, gamble a bit, drink a pint or two and chatter to the ladies. They were all very handsome-looking gentlemen.

After six months, Mr White called George into his office to tell him that he was offering to take George on a permanent contract and give him an apprenticeship. George was so happy and thanked him, "Mr White, you are very kind, my parents will be so proud of me."

Over the next year, George worked his way up in the business showing signs of becoming an excellent "Leather Draper."

One day, Mr White asked George if he would like to learn all the aspects of running and selling in their High Street Shop. "George, full training will be given."

George said he would very much like to learn about the running and selling of the shop. Mr White said, "I shall give you three weeks' training, starting tomorrow."

Mr White started training George the next day. George liked this side of the business much more, after his three weeks of training, Mr White realised that George had the right attitude needed to make a very good salesman. He would acknowledge all his customers, with a smile and confident manner.

After a month, Mr White took George into his office and said, "George, you have done a very fine job of running my shop. I am very pleased with your salesmanship, you are a great asset to my company. "Well done." I have decided to give you an increase in your wages from next week. George, in a week's time, I am planning to take my dear wife Ann on a two-week summer vacation to Weymouth. You would be in full charge of the accounts, running and selling in my absence. I trust you will make me proud George. What do you say?"

"Mr White, I would be proud to take over the running of your shop. I love working in the shop and meeting the customers. You can rest assured Mr White, I will work hard to make lots of sales for your business. I hope you both have a lovely holiday in Weymouth."

Chapter Two

One sunny morning, a beautiful lady came into the shop and ordered a pair of Leather boots, while she was being measured up, they got talking and there was an instant attraction between them, she told him she lived locally, "I would like the boots made as soon as possible, as I will be going away at the end of the week with my parents to Weymouth for a holiday. While we are away, I am intending to have Horse Riding Lessons; my father's best friend owns a large farm, just outside Weymouth."

She said, "I would like them ready before the end of the week as we will be departing early Saturday morning. I would be very much obliged if you could possibly have the boots made ready by Friday afternoon." In her West Country accent, she said, "I'll call back in seven days to see if they Are Ready."

George smiled and replied, "That I will, madam, do my best and I will start work on them tomorrow."

George and William worked tirelessly, to get the boots finished by the end of the week. With other orders from customers, they are kept busy all that week! The lady returned at the end of the week to see if her boots were ready. George said, "Yes, madam, your boots are ready."

He bent down behind the counter and passed them to her when she saw them, she was delighted and tried them on. "Why. They are a perfect fit," she exclaimed! "and soft too." The lady thanked him wholeheartedly, "You, sir, have done an excellent job."

"You were lucky, madam, we have been extremely busy this week. I managed to get help from the manager's son William."

"Please thank him for me? Now, how much will they be?" He gave her a fair price. "That's a very reasonable price," she was happy to pay, while she was paying, he casually asked her, "How long, madam, do you intend to be away?"

"Why do you ask, sir"?

George smiled, "Well, I, er, wanted to ask you if you would like to walk out with me when you return home?"

"Oh! I intend to be away for at least two weeks." The lady smiled at him, her eyes lit up, she replied, "I would be delighted to walk out with you, George."

"Oh! You know my name."

"Of course, I know your name," she said, "You have been working for my father, John White and my two brothers, Johnny and William, for a long time now."

George was lost for words, after a moment he replied, "I never knew that your father had such a beautiful daughter."

"You flatter me, sir," she said blushing.

"May I be so bold as to ask you your Christian name?"

She beamed at him and said, "it's Amelia."

They walked towards the door, he opened it slowly saying, "Shall we arrange to meet each other, outside the shop at 6 o'clock on Saturday 24th in two weeks' time, Amelia?"

"Yes, George, that will be fine. Well, I'll bid you a good day and I will see you in a fortnight."

George gave her a big smile and said, "Enjoy your holiday, Amelia, see you in a fortnight, goodbye," he closed the door behind her, with nice thoughts.

The days passed quickly, George was kept very busy, trade was good, he took orders for waistcoats, bags, gloves, belts, shoes and many other items. New items like leather ties were starting to become fashionable. Orders came in from the gentry, local farmers, many from nearby towns and villages.

Soon the two weeks were up and George was now looking forward to his date with the lovely Amelia. He put on his best shirt and tie, his best brown suit and his brand new brown leather shoes. He wanted to look dapper for his first date, walking out with this beautiful lady Amelia. Amelia kept her promise, she turned up with a beautiful tan and she just looked stunning.

The first thing George said when he saw her was, "Amelia, you look so beautiful tonight."

She smiled and said, "Thank you, George, you look very dashing yourself."

"Shall we take a walk, Amelia?"

"Yes."

"I thought it would be nice to go to 'Uncle Tom's Cabin' after, for a drink and some food."

George took her arm and they walked off, enjoying the lovely warm summer evening. They had to get a cab to the Pub as it was in Wincanton, a little too far for them to walk.

"How was your holiday, Amelia."

"Oh, it was really lovely, George. The weather was beautiful, we went for long walks along the beach, played ball games and swam in the sea. We stayed on my father's friend, James Walker's farm. Mama and I had some Horse Riding lessons, but Mama hated bouncing up and down. I also did not enjoy it much, so I think I'll give it a miss next time. By the way, George, I found the boots were very comfortable!"

The date went well, they talked and laughed. He told her about the tricks her brothers, Johnny and William, loved to play on him sometimes. He told her how they would hide his tools, they would both swear blind, they hadn't seen them. Then he would find them hidden behind a cupboard and they would both fall about laughing.

Amelia also laughed saying, "Those naughty brothers of mine, they used to tease me too while I was growing up."

When they returned to Yeovil, he walked her to her front door. He said, "Amelia, will you come out with me again next Saturday afternoon, maybe we could have a picnic in the park."

"Yes, George, that would be splendid; call for me at about 1 o'clock, I will bring a picnic lunch basket. Goodnight, George; thank you for a lovely evening."

"Goodnight, Amelia."

On Saturday George walked quickly, he couldn't wait to see Amelia again, he arrived at Amelia's house a little early and knocked on the door. Mrs Ann White opened the door and said, "Good afternoon, George, please do come in; Amelia is just putting the food in the picnic basket, she will be with you shortly."

"Thank you, Mrs White. I am so glad it's not raining today."

"Yes, you've both picked a fine day, it's meant to be heavy rain tomorrow."

Amelia joined them and they headed off to the park. "Mother has kindly made us some gingerbread. I hope you'd like gingerbread, George."

"Like it, I Love it!"

They have a lovely afternoon, enjoying the sunshine and each other's company. Amelia said, "George, there is a dance taking place in the Village Hall tomorrow night with a live band, it might be fun, would you like to be my escort?"

He looked at Amelia aghast! "But Amelia, I can't dance."

"Oh, then I will have to teach you a few simple steps."

"Come with me, we will find a secluded spot behind the trees."

"No, I don't think so."

"Yes, George," she grabbed his hand and pulled him up saying, "don't worry, George, it will be fine, no one will see us. Anyway, it will only take fifteen minutes for you to learn a few basic steps."

Reluctantly, he went along. After ten minutes, he had learnt how to hold Amelia, he soon picked up the one, two, three, steps. Amelia was satisfied, he would not make a fool of himself on the dance floor. "Remember, George, we will be dancing to live music, so you will have to learn to move with the rhythm; if you are not happy, then we will just sit and listen to the band play. OK!"

"OK, Amelia."

At the dance Hall, he felt a bit uneasy, there were so many people, they found two seats together, then the band started to play and he felt the rhythm and turned to Amelia and said, "Would you care to dance my dear."

She smiled at him, "It would be a pleasure, sir."

After courting for nearly nine months, they were falling deeply in love. On their next date, he got down on one knee and took her hand and said, "Amelia, I love you, will you marry me, my darling"?

He looked up at her beautiful smiling face and she said, "Oh! George, I love you too. Yes, I will marry you."

He gently kissed her hand. He stood up, took her into his arms and kissed her most passionately. One week later while at work during his half-hour lunch break, George had found enough courage to knock on the office door. Mr White opened the door and said, "Hello George, what can I do for you?"

"I would like to talk to you, Mr White."

"Yes, of course, George, come in and take a seat."

"Well, Mr White, I have been courting Amelia for over nine months now. I love her dearly and she loves me, I would like to ask you for your daughter Amelia's hand in marriage."

Mr White was delighted, he liked George and thought he would make a good caring husband and father. "Yes, George, I give you both my blessing."

They had a beautiful Wedding, with no expense spared. They married in the local Chapel in South Street Yeovil. They moved into a little cottage in "Back Kingston Road, Yeovil." When George and Amelia settled, they were both very happy.

The following year, Amelia was expecting a baby; she gave birth to a healthy baby boy on the ninth day of the ninth month 1866. They named him Alfred Frederick John. George and Amelia were delighted, they could not have been happier. After celebrating the birth of their beautiful baby boy, George had a gift for Amelia. He placed it in her hand. It was a very delicate gold locket and chain, he said, "Amelia darling, it opens up."

Inside Amelia saw there was a place for two miniature pictures, "I would like you to have the locket inscribed on the back, with Alfred's full name and his date of birth, we will need two miniature pictures, one of our lovely baby boy on one side and one of you, my darling Amelia, on the other."

Amelia was overwhelmed, "Oh! George, it's lovely; turn around my lovely, let me fasten it for you, now go and see my darling, how it looks around your pretty neck."

She went to the dressing table mirror, to admire this lovely gold locket, that she would keep the locket forever. She went over to George, kissed him passionately with love and devotion. "George I will go into town first thing tomorrow and have it inscribed at the Jeweller's shop."

"I, my dearest, must take a picture of baby Alfred and also one of you, with your antique camera, small enough to fit inside your locket."

Ann and John White bought them a beautiful Rocking Oak Cradle for their grandson. They are both overwhelmed by their generosity, they cannot thank them enough. George and Amelia were very happy and adored baby Alfred, he was so cutely loveable and they both adored him.

Amelia was not a very good cook like her Mama as she never watched her Mama when she was growing up. But she did improve when her nosey neighbour Mary gave her an old worn out Mrs Beaton's Cookery book she was throwing out.

Amelia never really liked her next-door neighbour Mary Sweet, although Amelia always tried to be nice and pleasant to her, she found her to be loud, uncouth and a gossip. Her husband was a night porter and during the day, she could often hear them arguing. Her son was known to be a bully to other children in the street and was troublesome, Amelia could often hear Mary reprimanding him.

It was about two and a half years later when Amelia and George's marriage started going wrong. Amelia had not been happy at home for some time, she was not getting the love and attention anymore from George. He seemed distant, Amelia tried hard to overlook this until he started coming home late. When she asked him why? He told her he had to work extra hours as they were so very busy. Amelia accepted this and questioned him no more.

One morning while Amelia was hanging out the washing in the yard, her neighbour Mary came out and asked her, "Why are you looking so damn miserable and unhappy lately?"

Amelia snapped at her saying, "Mind your own business. What's it got to do with you, Mary, you always was a nosey parker."

Mary started to shout and her, "How dare you say such a thing?"

While in dispute, Mary's son aged 13 came out and threw a bucket of water at Amelia. When she went to remonstrate with him, she was set upon by Mary who tore at her hair and pummelled her with a broom. Mary's husband came out and pushed Amelia away, shouting abusive language at her. Amelia ran indoors and decided at that moment to take Mary Sweet to court for assaulting her. She did not tell George about the incident or that she was taking her neighbour Mary Sweet to court for assault.

On the day of the court hearing, Amelia was very nervous. Amelia had previously asked her mother Ann if she would look after Alfred that day, she told her that she had to go to the hospital for a check-up. Ann was more than happy to look after her Grandson that day, she adored baby Alfred. Mary Sweet was summoned to court for assaulting Amelia Knight on 4 July.

On the day in question, the evidence of the complainant was that it appears that Mary Sweet the defendant's son threw a pail of water in Amelia's face. She went over to remonstrate with him when she was set upon by the defendant, who tore at her hair and pummelled her with a broom. Defendant's husband also came over and pushed Amelia, shouting abusive language. The complainant Amelia, had no witnesses to corroborate her statement.

A cross-summons charging Amelia Knight with assaulting Mary Sweet was next heard. Mary Sweet the defendant said that Amelia Knight threw water at her and Mary Sweet defendant held the brush at her in self-defence. Mary Sweet, the defendant said that Amelia had threatened her child with death and used fearful oaths towards her. Defendant said that Amelia Knight took hold of her by the hair, dragging her into her yard. Corroborative evidence was given by two neighbours.

The case against Mary Sweet was dismissed and Amelia Knight was fined 2 shillings 6 pence, including costs. Amelia left the court very despondent, she just could not believe why both her neighbours had given false evidence against her. Now, all she wanted to do was move as far away from this street as possible! When George came home from work, she broke down and cried, "What is the matter, Amelia, why on earth are you crying so?"

Amelia felt very upset and between tears, she started to explain to George what had been going on with their neighbour Mary Sweet. That she had to go and appear in court today.

"Why on earth didn't you tell me all this when it all happened Amelia?"

"Because I thought you would be cross with me. I didn't want to get you involved, George."

"I'm your husband, of course, I should be involved when it concerns my wife."

He started to shout at her, "You should have told me at the time, look at all this unnecessary trouble you have caused, don't you realise that this incident will be printed in the local newspapers." George stormed out and slammed the front door! Amelia went up to her room and cried, thinking about the trouble she had caused her husband. It was only when she heard Alfred cry, she went and picked him up. As she cuddled him, it made her feel a bit better, she laid him in his cradle and rocked him back to sleep; she then got herself ready for bed.

When eventually George returned home late that evening, he found Amelia upstairs lying on the bed with the saddest look he had ever seen on Amelia's face. He went over, took her in his arms and kissed her saying, "I really am so sorry, Amelia. I should be more understanding, but please in future my darling if ever you are in dispute with the neighbour again, please tell me straight away."

"I will George, I will."

The next day she asked George if they could move away from the area, he said, "No, Amelia, I do not want to move away, you must say sorry and make it up with Mary. I am not moving, as my place of work is here and this is where we will stay."

As the months passed, their relationship became distant. George was slowly falling out of love with Amelia. He thought about leaving her, but George stayed with Amelia for Alfred's sake, he could not bear to leave his son, he loved him so much.

Chapter Three

One day while busy in the shop, business was booming. In the late afternoon, the shop became quiet for a while, then a very attractive-looking lady came into the shop. George looked up and said, "Can I help you, madam?"

"I do hope so, I have lost a button off my leather glove, it must have fallen off somewhere; would it be at all possible to have a button made to replace the missing one?"

The lady was charming with the most lovely blue eyes he had ever seen; he could not take his eyes off her. "Of course, we can match up a button for you, madam. If you would like to take a seat, I can make one while you wait, it will take about fifteen minutes."

"That will be fine," as the lady passed him her glove, their eyes met and something stirred within George. When he gave her back her finished glove, she said, "Thank you so much, that's a very fine job, it matches perfectly."

After being paid George said, "Madam, I don't mean to be presumptuous, but would you do me the honour and walk out with me tonight?" George had already noticed she was not wearing an engagement or wedding ring.

"I am afraid that is not possible. I am going to the Hospital tonight to see my grandmother who is ill, they think she has consumption."

"How about tomorrow then?"

"Yes, I shall be free tomorrow evening."

"That's good, er, what time would be suitable for you madam?"

"Let's say 6 o'clock then."

"Yes, that would be perfect. Oh pardon me, madam. I should introduce myself, I'm George Knight and you are?"

"My name is Frances Taylor, but I like to be called Fanny, George."

"Well, Fanny, I will meet you outside the Old Coaching Inn, just outside of town at six tomorrow evening."

"Indeed, I shall look forward to meeting you there, good day, George."

"Fanny, I do hope your grandmother is feeling a little better."

She turned, "I hope so too," then closed the shop door behind her.

On the night of their first date, George told Amelia that he was going to meet up with William to play Bridge. All she said was, "Don't be late home, George."

"Oh, don't bother waiting up for me, these games can go on for some time."

When he met up with Fanny, they had found a nice secluded part of the pub. "What would you like to drink, Fanny?"

"I'll have a gin and lemonade please, George."

He ordered the drinks at the Bar, then brought them back to the table. He sat down opposite Fanny and said, "Fanny, tell me a little about yourself."

"Well, I was born on 10 June 1846 in Mudford Somerset. My mother's name is Elizabeth and my father's name is Thomas Taylor, I was an only child. My father is an accountant and my mother is a seamstress. I work with my mother at home; now, George, it's your turn to tell me all about you."

George then begins to tell Fanny about his life since leaving school. He then slowly goes on to explain that he has been married almost four years to his wife Amelia, they had a son called Alfred, who was almost three years old. He said, "Our marriage has been over for a long time, Fanny. I have been thinking about leaving my wife for quite a while, but I just could not walk away from my son Alfred. I don't think I could ever leave him, I love him so much."

Fanny looked at him and said, "George, I did not know you were married. I really should not be sitting here with you tonight."

Frances went to get up. "Fanny, please just listen to me before you walk away. I do not love my wife anymore. Our marriage is truly over, I will honestly be leaving Amelia and my home very soon."

George and Frances started meeting in secret, at first for short periods of time. Then their meetings were slowly becoming more and more frequent. Their relationship was becoming stronger until they started to fall in love, besotted with each other. They carried on seeing each other a few evenings a week. If Amelia asked where he was going, he would say, "I am meeting up with Johnny and William to play Snooker or Bridge," which he did quite often.

Amelia never questioned him. Amelia never really got on with her brothers and very rarely saw them. Johnny and William of course had no idea that Amelia and George's marriage had been slowly breaking down. Amelia accepted this reason and did not question him.

On their next evening out, on his date, he asked Fanny if her Grandmother was any better?

"No, George, she sadly passed away a few days ago. I went to her funeral, it was very sad."

"I am sorry to hear that, Fanny; were you close?"

"Yes, she was very dear to me. Grandmother Sheila was always loving and kind to me. I spent a lot of my childhood with her, I shall miss her; she was 89 when she died."

George was becoming more and more fond of Fanny, desperately wanting to be with her permanently. She made him laugh and feel wanted, she had a loving and kind nature. Frances became special to George in every way. But how could they always be together and take Alfred with them. George would find a way! George spent many days considering what he was going to do. He finally made his decision, he decided to ask Fanny if she would elope with him to Wales, taking Alfred with them.

So when George was out on his next date with Fanny, he asked her if she would be willing to elope with him, also taking his son Alfred with them so they could always be together. Fanny told George that she loved him, with all her heart, she wanted to start a new life with him, "George, surely it could never be, I feel very strongly that your wife Amelia will never willingly part or agree with you taking her son away with you."

"Fanny, don't you worry about that. I will take care of everything."

"George, my love, if Amelia does let you take Alfred, which I very much doubt, I want you to know that I would be willing to foster Alfred."

"Fanny, my love, there is just one thing I ask of you. Amelia never needs to know about you, I think it's best for everyone."

"George, I give you my word, I will never speak her name to anyone."

"Frances, are you absolutely sure that you would be happy to foster Alfred."

"Yes George, when we get to Wales, I will get the legal papers signed up."

They started making their plans, the coach would take them to the Welsh town of Llandrindod Wells. A week later, they were both packed and ready to leave. They had arranged to meet at the Horse and Carriage stop, opposite the Inn on Friday morning 10 May at 10 30 a.m. Departure time was at 11 o'clock It was now into late spring of 1869 and Alfred was almost three years old.

Frances' parents lived in Mudford just outside Yeovil, she had told her parents that she had met a fine gentleman called George Knight. "He is a qualified Leather Draper, he is going to start up his own business, we are soon to become engaged. George and I have been courting for over six months now. We have fallen in love and want to spend our lives together. We plan to move and settle in Worcestershire, but we would like to live in Wales for a while. Father; he is a real gentleman, I know you would approve of him. We intend to leave for Wales very soon. When we find a place to live, we shall get married."

Frances never really got on with her father, Thomas, because he was a strict stubborn man. He never liked any of her boyfriends she brought home, making them feel ill at ease, never once making them feel welcome. They were never good enough for his daughter. So she just stopped bringing them home and met her boyfriends in secret. Her mother Elisabeth was forever nagging her, "Frances, why don't you go out and find a wealthy gentleman and settle down?"

Her father said, "Well, Frances, let's hope gentleman George can keep you in the lifestyle you have been accustomed to."

"Yes, Papa, he certainly will."

All her mother said was, "It's about time, Fanny. I don't think you wanted to end up an old maiden, did you my girl?"

"Not much chance of that now, Mother. I will write to you and keep in touch. Our intentions are to eventually settle in Worcestershire, where George's ancestors once lived. We hope to find a lovely house and have a nice quiet wedding. All my bags are now packed, I shall be leaving tomorrow morning father. If you have gone off to work before I leave, I will say goodbye to you now!"

Her father gave her a hug and said, "Let us know, we may even come to your wedding Frances."

"Goodbye Father, take good care of Mother. I will write when we are settled."

Frances went off to bed, making sure she had packed everything she wanted to take. She would never be coming back home again.

The plans were made, they would elope together on Friday 22 May, taking little Alfred with them. So the following day they were both packed ready to leave. They had already arranged to meet at the Horse and Carriage stop, opposite the Inn at about 10:30 a.m. After saying goodbye to her mother, Frances left her home at 10:15 a.m. and got a cab into town. She sat and waited for George and Alfred. She watched as George was struggling up the street with all his and Alfred's luggage.

Alfred was hanging on to his coattails, carrying his little teddy bear. George greeted Fanny with a kiss and sat down beside her, silently hoping and praying he was doing the right thing by taking Alfred with them. The carriage came in at 10:45 a.m. The friendly coach driver loaded up their luggage. They boarded the carriage, which they had all to themselves. At 11 o'clock departure time, they set off for Wales.

Earlier that morning on 22 May, Amelia could not understand why George was up so very early; he had dressed and gone down for his breakfast, which was so unlike him. When she came downstairs, she noticed that his bags were stacked by the hall door. She came into the kitchen and stood watching him, he sat silently at the kitchen table eating his breakfast, he never looked up and never spoke.

Amelia sat down opposite him and said, "George, is something wrong, why are your bags packed, are you going somewhere?"

After a moment he looked her in the eyes and said, "Yes, Amelia, everything is wrong, our marriage is over, I do not love you anymore. Amelia, you know full well that our marriage has been over for a long time. I cannot endure living here with you anymore, this marriage has become unbearable.

The only reason that I have stayed living with you was for the sake of our son, Alfred, I want you to know Amelia, I will be leaving you forthwith and never coming back, I shall be going far away."

He then went on to say, "Amelia, I am taking Alfred with me, he will be better off with me. I shall take good care of him and he will have the best life I can possibly give him. I know it's going to be heart-breaking for you, but I cannot leave without Alfred and that's final. Go now and say goodbye to Alfred as I am about to depart."

Amelia was totally devastated, she could not believe what he was telling her. Amelia looked at George completely shocked and heartbroken, she knew the marriage had been slowly breaking down for a long time. Although Amelia knew that, she just hoped that they would stay together for Alfred's sake. Amelia burst into tears and she started crying out, "please George, please don't take Alfred. I'm begging you, George, don't take my son away."

She knew then that he would take Alfred. Amelia slowly realised that with no means of support, Alfred would be better off with his father; she did not have the means to take care of Alfred, she knew that George would take good care of him. Amelia also knew just how much George loved Alfred, he would never go hungry and be loved and cared for. She cried bitterly, as she reluctantly let Alfred go.

That night the bed was bare, Amelia prayed that one day Alfred would come back home to her; she cried and cried herself to sleep. Amelia eventually went back to live with her parents, Ann and John White until the end of 1881. After that date, no one saw or heard of her again, she just seemed to disappear. In later years, it became known that Amelia

41

suffered a nervous breakdown. Her parents had no choice but to get medical help. Amelia was put into an institution, suffering from mental health issues. It would be the best option for her own safety.

George and Frances were so happy to be together; at last, George felt good to have his son with him. It was a lovely journey, with lots of views of the Countryside. Alfred was excited and sat happily, looking out of the carriage window, pointing to all the new-born baby lambs and sheep. The next field they passed had lots of cows and calves. He saw horses and ponies and when he tried to say, "Horsey" they both laughed at him.

When they arrived in Wales, George had already booked them into a very smart upgraded place to lodge. Within the week, he had found a little two-bedroom cottage in Ridgebourne, near Llandrindod Wells. George Knight finds himself a temporary job, working as a cobbler in the local village shoe shop. Frances, true to her word, legally fostered Alfred. They all seemed happy enough, getting settled into their new home and surroundings.

In that first year, Frances showed a loving kindness towards Alfred, but sometimes when he was alone with his father, he would ask his papa, "Where is Mama?"

"Son, your Mama loves you dearly, but she became too ill to look after you. Alfred, you will see your Mama again one day."

"Will I see Grandma and Grandpa again too, Papa?"

"Indeed you will, Alfred, in time, in time, my son."

Frances was strict with Alfred, although he did try to be a good boy. If he was naughty, he got a good spanking. The following year Frances was expecting her first child, George was such a happy expectant father. On 21 October 1869, Fanny gave birth to a son; they called him William Thomas, he was a beautiful baby with bright blue eyes and tight fair curly hair. Fanny and George could not have been happier parents.

Alfred would spend a great deal of time happily playing with his baby brother, he would tickle him, make funny faces at him, William would screech with laughter, it formed a bond between them. It was about this time when Frances's attitude seemed to change towards Alfred, she started to resent him, unnoticed by George. When George had gone to work, Frances started to give Alfred jobs to do around the house, giving all her attention to William Thomas.

In time, he slowly began to miss the love and affection he had known with his own Mama; he knew in his heart that one day he would see his real Mama again. Frances kept Alfred busy, he was expected to bring in the logs for the fire, make his own bed, tidy his room, all before he was allowed to go out to play. She would also set him simple early school work to get him ready for starting school the following year. She would reprimand him if he did not do it.

George knew that Frances was a little strict with Alfred, but he thought the discipline would do his son some good. He would often take Alfred fishing at weekends, he loved this time with his Papa; if they caught a fish, they would take their catch home for supper. After supper, he would sit him on his lap, reading him the short stories from Aesop's fables. Alfred loved bedtime when Papa would read stories from *Hans Christian Andersen's children's book of stories*.

He liked it when his father would make a quacking noise when reading *The Ugly Duckling*; others he enjoyed were *The*

Emperor's New Clothes and *The Tinder Box*. The flowing year Alfred started school, he was good at school, quick to learn, but he was not happy when some children started picking on him for his "West Country accent", which would usually end in a fight; he would always get the blame, being sent to the Headmaster's office, where he would be punished. He would be whacked across the bottom with the slipper for being spiteful to the other children, even when he didn't start the fight.

Sometimes Alfred was sent home for his misbehaviour in the classroom to face Frances or instead of facing his foster mother, he would go and sit by the river until home time. He would often pull funny faces in the classroom when the teacher's back was turned, which would make the children giggle or he would stick out his tongue at the boys he did not like. He started to hate this school and was reluctant to go.

One evening, George told the family they would shortly be moving to Worcester in England in a place called Hallow near Martley; he said that his ancestors once lived in the village. Alfred was so excited when his father told him he would be going to a new school. Alfred could not wait, he was so happy to be leaving this school he hated. George found a lovely five-bedroom house just outside Hallow; it had a huge garden, they all love the location being in a quiet area, situated next to a large wood. George bought into a local business, managing the running of a Leather Dressers shop. Which did very well, eventually would make them quite wealthy.

In 1871, George Knight married Frances Taylor. Frances did invite her parents to the Wedding, but they were unable to go due to her mother now finding walking very difficult, after falling over on ice and breaking her leg. They sent them both their love with a wedding gift of a very nice amount of money. Life was good for everyone. Alfred was the happiest of all, he would be going to a new school. The house was just what George and Frances had been looking for.

Alfred was growing into a bright and happy child. He was counting the days he would start his new school in two weeks' time. Alfred was so enjoying his new school, especially as his little brother William would be starting the school very soon. Alfred was looking forward to having his little brother to take care of and look after; they had already become very close, they were happiest when they were playing together.

When William Thomas started school, he liked his teacher, all the teachers were nice and kind to all the pupils. The children at this school were eager to make friends with both of them. Both boys could not wait for the next school day to begin as they would be having physical education, which would involve lots of fields and outdoor games.

Chapter Four

In April 1873, Frances gave birth to her second son and they called him George Henry. Frances went on to give birth to another two sons; Charles, born on 27 July 1877 and Walter, born on 24 June 1881; the last child to be born in England was a daughter, they named her Mary Ellen, born on 30 March 1884. After school, Alfred would take William to play in the woods, they had so much fun together; they would go scrumping apples, climb trees and pick wild blackberries for Frances to make a pie.

Sometimes, they would be naughty; breaking the rules, they would go down to the river and skim stones across the water to see who's stone could travel the furthest. The boys would often play their naughty game "Knock Down Ginger," where they would knock on a door, run and hide out of view, then watch to see the bewilderment on the people's faces when opening the door to find nobody there!

They would roll about laughing. Until the day they picked on old "Mr Grumpy," who the local children called him. He lived down the road, all the children in the street hated him, but when Alfred and William picked on him again, he was waiting for them; he caught them in the act, that was the end of that game because old Mr Grumpy went and complained to

Frances. Well, as always, Alfred took the blame and he was punished.

But one day they were seen stealing the Apples, while William was standing on Alfred's shoulders reaching up, leaning up against the fence to pick the red apples that hung there. The mean owner's teenage son John Milton spotted them, these apple trees backed onto the woods. He knew the boys as they attended the same school. He went and told his father, who then went around to speak to Mrs Knight.

Frances said, "I am very sorry indeed, Mr Milton, this is very serious and I will deal with the boys when they come home. Rest assured, Mr Milton, this will never happen again."

Mr Milton nodded and said, "It better not, Mrs Knight, but I will say no more, good day."

Frances answered, "Good day to you, Mr Milton."

She was livid as she closed the front door, she had never been so cross and angry. When the boys came home, Alfred was in big trouble; Frances shouted at him, giving them both a good hiding, saying, "Alfred, you are the eldest, you should know better," telling them that they could get locked up in prison for stealing. "I am going to teach you both a lesson you will never forget, you naughty boys."

She dragged Alfred by his ear and locked him in the shed for over an hour, she also gave William a good telling off and marched him off to bed without any supper. The boys never ever stole anything ever again. The next day their father made them go around to Mr Milton's house to apologise.

Some three months later, school term had ended. The school summer holidays had now begun. The boys were down by the river having lots of fun, padding their feet in the fast running water. Alfred was leaning over, trying to catch a large

47

fish that swam by when William for fun pushed him into the water. Luckily, it was not too deep near the very edge, but William still had to lean over and help drag him out because the water came over Alfred's shoulders; he was very angry and shouted at William.

They both went home to face Frances, Alfred was soaking wet. He told Frances that he fell in the river, trying to catch a fish for supper; he never got William into trouble, he was very protective towards him. Frances started by giving Alfred a good scolding saying, "How many times have I told you not to go near the edge of the river, don't you understand how dangerous the fast-flowing river can be, you could have been drowned."

She sent Alfred off to bed without any supper. When George came home, he asked her where Alfred was; she told him what had occurred down by the river and that he came home soaking wet and how she had told him so many times not to go near the fast-flowing river without an adult.

"Come on, Fanny, Boys will be Boys. No harm done."

George went upstairs with some bread and soup and gave his sad-looking son a cuddle. "You must say sorry to Fanny, Son," then gave him another hug.

"I'm sorry, pa."

"Never go near the river's edge again without me. I think it's about time, son, I taught you boys how to swim!"

On Alfred's 13th Birthday, Frances and George decided to take the family on a picnic. The children played nicely together, having such fun playing all kinds of ball games and chasing each other. Then William said, "Let's play Hide and Seek."

William started counting up to 100 with his eyes closed. Alfred climbed up a tree, their two brothers ran off and hid in the bushes. William soon found his brothers, except Alfred; he looked everywhere but could not find him, he was just about to give up when he heard a loud shout! The tree branch that Alfred was leaning on broke and Alfred fell, falling on a very large sharp stone; all William could see was blood gushing out of his leg.

He ran to his father saying, "Pa, come quickly. Alfred has fallen from a tree."

George quickly takes off his 'neckerchief, wrapping it as tightly as possible around Alfred's cut leg which was pouring with blood. He quickly carried him home. They now had a maid working for them, she quickly ran to get the local Doctor. Fortunately, there were no bones broken, the wound was very deep and he had to endure painful stitches. He could not go out for several weeks as it was so painful to walk; he was left with a deep scar on his left leg.

Time is a good healer and he returned to finish school. It was his last year, which he totally enjoyed. He was very popular with the other children. Alfred left school at the age of fifteen. Passing his school leaving exams with excellent results.

After school, Alfred would meet William in the woods. They both knew where their secret hideout was, then they would then go off and hunt for wild mushrooms, walk deep into the woods to explore, looking for badger setts, rabbit warrens and squirrels. They would try and name the birds they spotted. In September, they would look for chestnuts to take home. George would roast them in the fire grate, which they all enjoyed eating.

In October, they would hunt for conkers. Alfred would make a whole in the middle with one of Fanny's knitting needles; she would give them some string, which a knot was made in one end, threaded through the conker and held up, then they would take it in turns to try and hit each other to smash their opponents' conker, first one to break a conker was the winner!

Any mischief done in the home or any breakages, Alfred would take the blame and say, it was his fault, always covering up for his step-siblings; they all loved and admired him for it. Now and again, William would say, "Mama, don't blame Alfred; it was my fault, not Alfred's," she would just tell him off saying, "Don't you ever do that again, William, or you will be in big trouble."

He was very rarely ever actually punished, then it would be over. After Alfred had left school, his father told him he had to find a Job and make his own living. He wanted him to carry on the Family Business. After three months working with his father, he told his father that he hated the Job, especially working indoors, he wanted to quit. He said he would be much happier working outside, he was going to try for a Job working for the local Farmer.

George was sorry, he hoped that Alfred would follow on in the family business, but he would not stop him or stand in his way, he wanted him to be happy, whatever job he decided to do. So happily he went off to find a farming Job. He did not have to look far, nor did it take him long; this farm he found was only two miles away, his luck was in, he found that the local farmer had been looking for an extra farm hand to work on his very large farm.

Alfred landed a lovely job working for Mr Oaks, "A happy-go-lucky Farmer"; he had white hair, a white beard and wore a large hat, he had a great sense of humour. After a quick introduction as to the work involved, what his weekly wage would be. Alfred agreed to the terms and conditions and was taken on. Alfred started work at 6 o'clock the next day. Alfred's jobs included milking the cows, feeding the sheep, collecting the chickens' eggs for market, he would muck out the pigs.

He later even learned to ride a horse. He loved Autumn best when it was haymaking time. It didn't matter what kind of farming work he was asked to do. Alfred enjoyed all types of farming work, including learning to drive the tractor, with the help of a trained sheepdog he would go off and round up the sheep, bringing them in for shearing and for lambing time in the spring. Mr Oaks also had other local men working for him. Alfred was now an extremely "Happy Chappy!" The next four years passed very quickly, he would save half his wages and give Frances the other half towards his keep.

While at work, he would often remember the good and bad times of growing up. He always had a good relationship with his step-brother William, remembering the fun they'd had together as young boys; he remembered how Frances would reprimand him, very rarely William. He did not mind too much because if he was sent to bed with no supper, William would discreetly take food like bread and cheese, even a slice of fruit cake or what Alfred liked best was cider apple pie, he would sneak it up to him while his Mama would be busy working on her embroidery.

He loved the free time they spent together during the school holidays, playing games and climbing trees, foraging in the woods, playing jokes on each other. Sometimes, they would try to frighten one another. One of them would hide behind a tree when the other wasn't looking, then suddenly with their 'neckerchief pulled up over their nose would jump out, making the other scream with fright, then they would squeal with laughter.

He then remembered the bad times, Frances locking him in the shed for Scrumping Apples but worse of all, was remembering falling from the tree; the excruciating pain, then the agony of those very painful stitches. He then thought about his large family and himself, did he really want to be a farmer for the rest of his working life? He loved the work and being outdoors, but it just wasn't fulfilling enough; he had a few other ideas for the future, he mulled this over as he walked home.

He studied the options to carry on working as a farm labourer, perhaps one day become a farmer with his very own farm. Or he could have another try at being a leather draper, where he would carry on the family business, where there was big money to be made. He decided he would carry on being a farm hand for the time being, at least he was very happy and enjoyed the work. One day after a hard day's work at the farm, he came home and overheard his father talking to Frances, discussing emigrating to Canada.

Alfred was totally shocked. He loved his country and wanted to stay in England. After a lot of thought, now eighteen years old, he was by no means short of money; saving his money since working on the farm. He thought about going back to Yeovil to try and find his birth mother and grandparents. Alfred stayed awake long into the early

52

hours, thinking it over as to what he should do. By the time, Alfred had closed his eyes, he had made up his mind!

The next day he went to work, he sadly told farmer Oaks that he was leaving Worcester as soon as possible; his parents were planning to leave England to make a new life in Canada.

"I want to stay in England, so I have decided to return to Yeovil in Somerset to live. My main purpose, Mr Oaks, is to try and find my birth mother and find my roots."

Mr Oaks said, "I am sorry you will be leaving us, Alfred; we will all miss you, come into my barn so we can settle up your final weeks' pay that's due. Alfred, you would have made an excellent farmer, may I wish you all the very best in whatever you do, come back and see me someday. Goodbye and good luck, Alfred."

As he gave him a manly hug he said, "Thank you, Mr Oaks, for all your kindness." They shook hands as Alfred sadly said, "Goodbye, Mr Oaks." Alfred felt depressed as he slowly walked home, thinking about what he was intending to do; he made his final decision as he walked home. That evening after supper he said, "I have had a very busy day at work today folks, I am very tired so I am off to bed, Nighty Night."

Everyone was busy doing their own thing. They just said, "Night, Alfred." He went up to his room to pack all his clothes and personal belongings. He counted out his savings, then put pen to paper and wrote a well thought out letter to his father and family.

Dear Father, Frances, William and family,

I am sorry, but I honestly do not want to go and live in Canada. I want to stay here in England. I have given this a lot of thought, I have made up my mind and nothing will change that. My intentions are to go back to Yeovil to find my birth mother and grandparents. I hope the family will all be happy starting a new life in Canada. Don't worry about me, I love England and want to find my roots.

Father, you can write to me at my grandparent's home. I hope they are still with us. Love to you all; tell William Thomas I will never forget the great times we spent together, I will miss him. I do hope to see you all again one day, maybe in Canada. Take care of each other, pray for me, give my love to all the family.
Your devoted son,
Alfred xxx

He left the letter on his dressing table. He knew that his father would occasionally write to his parents Thomas and Mary in Yeovil, just to keep in touch, but George never received a reply from his father Thomas or his mother Mary. Alfred could never understand why even his own birth mother, Amelia, never wrote to him.

He closed his eyes but had a sleepless night.

Chapter Five

Alfred set off at the crack of dawn the following morning and caught a train to Bristol, where he changed at Exeter for Yeovil. When Alfred reached Yeovil, it was late afternoon. He started walking towards the street, where he was born and lived with his mother and father. But he could not quite remember which cottage it was as they all looked exactly the same in this street. He knocked on a door and waited, a little old lady with a walking stick answered the door, "Yes, can I be of help to you?"

"Well," said Alfred, "I am looking for Mrs Amelia Knight's residence, do you know where she lives dear lady?"

"Then 'who you be' young man?"

"I am Alfred Knight, her son."

"Well, the lady you speak of, once lived in this street but been long gone since, but if you be any relation to Mary Knight, she lives in Higher Kingston Road."

"Why yes, Mary is my grandmother, thank you kindly, dear lady."

The lady replied, "You're welcome," and closed the door. After a little searching, he found his grandmother Mary's house, with anticipation he gently knocked on the door. Mary did not recognise him at first; when he told her who he was,

Mary was totally overwhelmed to see her Grandson. "Well, now can it possibly be you, Alfred, after all these years past?"

"Yes, Grandma, it's me."

She gave him a big hug. "My Alfred," she exclaimed, "this is such a surprise, the last time I saw you was as a little boy, must be almost eighteen years ago. Please do come on in." After she got over the shock, she settled him into a comfortable armchair, put the kettle on and made the tea, served with slices of freshly made gingerbread.

They then started telling each other their life stories. Mary said, "Alfred, I don't think your grandfather Thomas ever forgave George for walking out on his dear caring wife Amelia, taking you away from your mother without any knowledge of where he was taking you; it broke her heart and she never got over losing you. Thomas thought it was such a very cruel thing to do. I myself can never forgive George either, it was unforgivable of him. It was not so much him leaving Amelia but to take her son away. Thomas nor I can never forgive or forget what he did."

Mary told him of the sad passing of his dear grandfather Thomas, with a tear in her eye she said, "Do you know, Alfred, it almost broke my heart; he seemed to be so fit and well, but he had started to look a little pale. I was a little concerned so I asked him if he was alright; he said don't worry my dear, I am fine. Thomas died a few days later of a sudden stroke. He never suffered, which was a blessing, he was put to rest in the local Catholic Churchyard."

(Mary never disclosed to Alfred that Thomas Knight and herself, Mary Knight, had both made wills on her death, the inheritance would be split between Alfred and his Step-Brother William Thomas.) Mary found out through George's letters that Alfred was very close to William Thomas. Alfred then asked Mary if she knew the whereabouts of his mother Amelia, "Alfred, I am sorry to tell you that I do not know where your mother can be found; all I can tell you is that after your father took you away, she went back to live with her parents, John and Anne White."

"All the Whites family sold up and moved away, even though their Leather Business had gone, they left their business premises empty. It's strange that nobody seems to know where they have moved to, it's a mystery."

Mary was a lovely lady who was such a happy soul, blessed with a kind heart and a loving nature. Mary said, "Alfred, if you would like to live here with me until you find a house of your own, you would be more than welcome to stay."

Alfred thanked her, "that would be lovely, Grandma Mary, I would be very grateful to live with you until I can find work and rent a place of my own." He said, "I love you, Grandma, thank you," and gave her a big hug.

Mary was a very good cook, baked her own bread, he loved her rich fruit cake; she made the lightest Victoria Sandwich filled with her own homemade blackberry jam, blackberries she had picked herself, the best he had ever tasted. He enjoyed all her meals. One evening she asked Alfred about his childhood, he told her everything, even showed her his scar, how he fell from the tree, on his 13th Birthday.

He told Mary how very strict Frances was with him, but William and I had great fun together, we became very close. Father would take me fishing, he told Mary of all the naughty things William and he got up to, "if we were in trouble with

Frances, she would always punish me, I always took the blame, whatever we got up to."

Mary smiled, "That was very courageous of you, Alfred, but all said and done, BOYS WILL BE BOYS!"

He was happy to live with Mary. The very next day he went out looking for a local farming job, just until he found his vocation in life. That evening while Alfred was talking about the past, he said, "My father told me grandmother that you have a beautiful singing voice, would you sing for me now, my father's favourite song, *My Darling Clementine*."

"Oh, I don't know, Alfred, my voice is probably a bit croaky now. I haven't sung for such a very long time, but if you insist, I'll try and remember the words, but only if you join me in the chorus."

When Mary began to sing, it sounded beautiful. She still had a lovely singing voice, Alfred joined in with the chorus. Mary harmonised and they sounded good together. They both clapped for each other, Alfred said, "Grandmother, that was so lovely, father George and grandfather Thomas would have been very proud."

"Thank you, Alfred, that's a real compliment." They said goodnight and retired to bed.

It was soon to become an important day for Alfred, but he did not know about it just yet! Over the next few weeks, while out looking for farm work, Alfred saw a large poster of Lord Kitchener pointing the finger that said "YOUR COUNTRY NEEDS YOU." Alfred stood and looked at it for some time. He knew then he wanted a career in the Army and to become a Soldier.

When he got home, he told Mary that he wanted to join the British Army and become a Soldier; she thought he was very brave and gave him her blessing. The next day Alfred sent a letter to the Army Headquarters, giving them his details and asked for an interview.

Two weeks later, Alfred received an important letter informing him of an arranged interview date taking place at their Army Headquarters, Prince Albert's Light Infantry Army in Taunton Somerset in two weeks' time! What a good feeling that was!

On the morning of the interview, Mary made him a good breakfast of oats and honey; she then made him a salmon sandwich, added an apple and wrapped them in a linen cloth tied up with string; she put his lunch into his knapsack, for Alfred to eat on his way. He hugged Mary, "Thank you for looking after me so well, Grandma. I love you so much. I will write to you when I am settled in."

Mary sadly said, "Goodbye, Alfred, if I hear any news about your dear Mother, I will let you know." He gave her another big hug before leaving on his way. They waved goodbye until he was over the steep hill and out of sight.

Chapter Six

It was a cold brisk morning with frost on the ground, today was 14 January 1885, the day for Alfred's Enrolment. All he could think about was his future career in Prince Albert's Light Infantry Army. He pressed on his merry way towards Taunton in Somerset. He stopped along a high ridge, to enjoy the lovely views across the countryside; he sat on a log while he enjoyed his delicious sandwich and sweet red apple, he got a drink from the stream. He then continued on his way, arriving at headquarters at about 2 o'clock.

On his arrival, he was met by an Army Officer who introduced himself as Officer Shepton. He asked Alfred his full name and age. He told Alfred that he would be having an interview with his Sergeant Major. He was escorted into a large Military Building, down a long corridor until they reached the Sergeant Major's Office.

Officer Shepton knocked on the door, his Sergeant Major's stern voice said, "Enter."

On entry Shepton saluted, then said, "This is Alfred Knight, the new recruit who has come to enlist Sir."

"Dismissed," he replied.

"Yes, sir," he saluted again and left.

The Sergeant Major shook Alfred's hand, then told him to take a seat; the Major then took his place behind his large desk. The Sergeant Major started by firing questions at Alfred, saying, "I want your full name, present address, date of birth, birthplace, age, occupation, reason why you want to become a soldier, what exactly can you contribute to the British Light Infantry Army?"

Slowly but confidently he replied, "Well, sir, my name is Alfred Frederick John Knight. I was born in Yeovil Somerset on 9/9/1866. Age 18 years 9 months. I am a Farm hand by profession. My parents will soon be Emigrating to Canada. I have chosen to stay in England. I am looking for a long-term career in the British Army. I am strong and healthy, quick to learn, I pledge to follow the strict guidelines of army rules and all the regulations that are required of me. What I can contribute to the army is doing my duty to the King and country. I will try my best to become a good British soldier. I look forward to making some good companions with my regiment, Sir."

The Major stood up and said, "I am very pleased with your interview, Mr Knight; tomorrow you will be given a paper questionnaire for you to complete, followed by a written and math's exam. Two full medicals which will take place with the army physician; if you are successful, you will be enlisted. You will then be shown to your barracks, then you will be fitted with the Light Infantry Uniform. Over the next few months, the very hard military training will be given with guns and live ammunition. I hope you will make an excellent soldier, Mr Knight."

Alfred smiled and said, "Thank you, sir." They shook hands and Alfred left the office with his head held high.

Alfred now has the last of his army procedures to complete, he passed his written and math tests. He had almost finished his second medical when the Doctor asked, "How did you get that deep scar on your left leg, Mr Knight"?

Alfred explained to the doctor, bringing back the painful memories of that awful day, "I was thirteen years old, I fell from a tree when the branch broke, I landed on a very sharp stone, doctor."

The doctor said, "Mr Knight, you are very lucky not to have suffered a broken leg; do you have any trouble with your leg now, Mr Knight?"

"No, doctor, there is no pain; it has just left me with this awful scar." The Doctor asked a few more questions and then signed the two medical certificates. He had passed all his medicals and was fit to enlist in the British Army. Alfred signed up on 15/1/1885.

Over the next ten weeks, Alfred had to have his hair cut very short, although all soldiers were allowed to keep or grow their moustaches. All other facial hair had to be shaved each day. The barracks where he would be sleeping was a room with twelve other recruits.

Soldiers had to be up at six each morning and in bed by ten at night. Every morning there would be a barracks inspection, all their gear would be laid out on the bed, if it looked untidy you would be put on a charge. The boots had to be like glass, they called it "spit and polish."

Then the strict military training started; all the new recruits were lined up on the forecourt for the parade, then the Sergeant Major started shouting orders. The rules and regulations had begun. The military training was intense, marching across rough terrain, then hour after hour of nonstop physical exercise, learning to use the guns and ammunition with target practice every day.

Alfred's bunk was the first in the line, next to him was a man called Arthur Daniels, who befriended Alfred; they became best of friends, all through their army career.

The Great Indian Mutiny started on 8/7/1857 against the British East India Company, functional as a sovereign power on behalf of the British Crown. It was to become the most tragic episode in the nineteenth-century. British and also Indian soldiers with wives were being tortured or shot, the war spread all over India.

The Segers massacred and murdered Europeans of the North, these rebels worked upon the uprising being a religious crusade, destroying three cathedrals and twenty-five churches. The British troops fought back, looting and destroying mosques and Hindu temples. The uprising carried on as the sepoys were torn between loyalty and affection to the army on one side, religion and their way of life on the other.

Now, they were fighting for Independence in India. The war came to a halt in May 1858. But it was never settled. Then another uprising started in India. British soldiers who still remained in India were at war again, as they were being shot by the rebels. Alfred was now a British soldier in the Light Infantry Army, he was ready for any war that lay ahead.

The Major General informed all the troops what had been officially informed to him by Her Majesty's Government that all British Light Infantry troops were to be sent out to India immediately! The rebels were fighting and killing many of our British troops who still remained in India.

He wrote one last letter from his barracks in England to Grandma Mary, telling her he would be leaving England for India. His departure was imminent.

I will send you the new army address when they reach base camp. All infantry troops are being sent out to fight the rebels, as the uprising war continues. Take care of yourself. Lots of love Grandma.

Alfred xxx

The British Light Infantry soldiers were sent out to India on a Military ship. When they arrived in India, most of the troops found the heat unbearable; after a few weeks they gradually became acclimatised to the hot climate.

The British troops had many things to worry about, continuous fighting with the rebels, brave soldiers were being killed every day. If the soldiers were not shot or wounded, some were being bitten by snakes or caught dysentery, Malaria, Typhoid and many other deadly diseases. The most deadly weapons were being used against them. Daggers and swords were used to slaughter their enemy. Many of the soldiers who were badly wounded, who had lost limbs, were sent back to England.

While Alfred was on his late night duty, he would often see their Indian soldiers who were fighting alongside with British troops sitting in a circle in their small groups, smoking from these long pipes, which were connected to a metal stand with a small glass water bowl at the base, a bowl for tobacco at the top, a long pipe was connected to the base with a mouthpiece on the end. It was fascinating to watch, he went over and asked them what they were smoking from.

One Indian soldier spoke in broken English and said, "This officer is a hookah and it helps us relax, then we sleep good, would you like to try hooker, sir?"

"Soldiers, I am on duty, but I will join your group soon as I want you to teach me your Hindi language, maybe I will try your smoking pipe too. Now, I suggest you all return to your sleeping tent, we will be moving ranks tomorrow. It is going to be a busy day. I bid you all goodnight."

They all got up and went back to their tents for the night. A few nights later, Alfred sat in with the Indian soldier's group. He felt a little out of place as they started chanting words he did not understand. He did try the hookah and liked it. He was given a few sentences in Hindi and he wrote them down, they told him to repeat them. Alfred did not know that his best friend Arthur happened to see him sitting with the Indian soldiers that night. Alfred had the best night's sleep, he woke up refreshed and ready to go. After a few months, he could slowly converse with the Indian soldiers in Hindi.

The horrendous fighting continued throughout that year 1886. On 12 December 1886, Alfred was hit in the shoulder by a gunshot; he was quickly sent to the Military Hospital, where he was only slightly wounded and his injury was not too serious. While in hospital, he met a beautiful young nurse, who looked after him. When he was getting better, they started to become good friends; she told Alfred her name was Evelyne Jane De-Roza, that she was Anglo-Indian. Her father was from Goa and her mother was Portuguese Dutch.

Evelyne told him she was born in the region of Chittor, India, in 1867. Alfred thought Evelyne was the most beautiful lady he had ever seen. They would often talk openly about themselves and their childhood days. She told him that her father was at one time Governor of the province of Pulicat and that her dear father was quite a wealthy man.

All the time Alfred spent in hospital, they got to know each other quite well. As time went by, they started to become very fond of each other; so when the time came for Alfred to leave hospital, they both wanted to stay in touch by mail. They would try to see each other, whenever Alfred could get leave. They kept in touch and after nearly a year, only seeing Evelyne for only short periods of time, he wrote Evelyne a letter, which read:

My dearest darling Evelyne,

I am in love with you. I fell in love with you from the first time I saw you in your white nurse uniform. I love you with all my heart. WILL YOU, EVELYNE JANE, MARRY ME? I will be waiting for your decision.
All my love and kisses,
Alfred xxx.

Chapter Seven

After a week, he receives two letters, one from Evelyne and one from his grandmother Mary. He read Evelyne's letter first.

My dearest Alfred, I love you too with all my heart, "OH YES," Alfred, I will marry you!

The next time he saw Evelyne they became Engaged, they had a party at her parent's home, so Alfred could meet her wealthy respectable family. They all got on very well, they thought Alfred a fine gentleman and soldier; they both liked his kind, friendly manner. Alfred also liked them very much. They were both happy with Evelyne's choice of her future husband.

The other letter was from his Grandma Mary:

My dear grandson Alfred.

I received your letter from India; I also received a very distressing letter from Canada. It was from your Step-Brother William Thomas, telling me the very sad news that on the 8 February 1889 your father George Knight died falling from a ladder after working on his roof, while climbing down he slipped. I am so very sorry. I have sent a letter of condolence to the family. I have their address if you want to write to them. I will write it down for you.

I am constantly thinking about you, I still do not know the whereabouts of your mother. But the only information I have was from my friendly neighbour who has lived on this street for many years. She told me that she did hear some gossip around the village about Amelia White being put into an Institution, a very long time ago. As far as she knew, Amelia was living with her parents when she had a nervous breakdown in health.

Amelia could not get over losing her only beloved son. Amelia was put away for her own safety. Mrs Kimble went on to say that The White family sold the business and moved away from this area. Mrs Kimble has no idea where the family moved to. If I do find out where Amelia is now living, I will write and let you know.

I pray you will stay safe, that your wound will soon heal, that you will soon be back to full health again. I was pleased to hear that you are courting a fine lady nurse, who you intend to marry. I send my love to you both and wish you both well. All my love, write soon.

Grandma Mary xxx

P.S.: I enclose William Thomas Knight's Address in Ontario Canada.

Alfred, I made up this little verse, to make you smile:

In Saxon times there lived a King, his war was with the Danes. They tried to invade our Country, A war they fought for Gains.

The Danes were not at all prepared, for what Alfred had in store King Alfred was a fighter and he would win this war.

The men were trained, they fought the Danes, to teach the Danes a lesson that they would never try and take our land for their possession.

The Danes were defeated, by Alfred's men, we'll stand to salute Our GREAT KING ALFRED, Saving country and our land.

But we should all remember, King Alfred makes mistakes While tending to his weapons, He went and burnt the cakes!

The fighting was getting so much worse in the North. The Indian uprising was just going on and on. Soon Alfred's regiment was posted to Northern India, where the fighting continued. He was unable to see Evelyne, but he kept in touch by mail when he could.

Alfred wrote a letter to his family in Canada.

Dear Frances, William and family,

We are saddened to hear that father George has died, we will pray for him; our love and condolences go out to all my family. I will never get the chance ever to see him again. Or for him to meet my future wife, Evelyne, with who I am now engaged, we hope to get married very soon. Give our love to all the family.

Lots of love,
Alfred xxx

Alfred was allowed by his Sergeant Major to get absence of leave to get married. But the day before he left his army base camp, he was suffering from Malaria. He was sent back to the Military Hospital, where he was put into confinement. It was such a relief to be told it was not serious, thankfully he did make a full recovery. Evelyne had attended him, she came to see him without her mask after Alfred was being allowed into the recovery ward. While there, he and Evelyne arranged their Wedding day.

On 2 May 1892, Alfred married Evelyne Jane De-Roza at St Joseph's Catholic Church in Chittoor, India. They had a short honeymoon by the Pulicat Lake on the Coromandel Coast. Alfred would soon have to say goodbye to his wife, as he had to return to his post in Northern India; the fierce fighting continued, sadly it was time to leave his lovely wife and return back to his station. It was a tearful farewell, Alfred told her that he would buy a beautiful house nearer to his station in the north so they could be closer to each other, he would then be able to see Evelyne more often.

The fighting was getting worse, many men were being killed. During a brief break in the fighting, Alfred did somehow manage to get word to Evelyne by letter, letting her know he had managed to find a house way up north in the state of Himachal Pradesh, he sent her the address. Evelyne with the help of her dear father, who owned a large van and with the help of a few close friends, they loaded up her house contents and belongings, as much as she was able to take and moved her up to her new house so she could be nearer her husband.

Evelyne soon found a nursing job, working in another very busy hospital, quite near her home, with a constant abundance of wounded and dying soldiers. In 1895, Evelyne was with child; she gave birth to a girl, Cathleen Lilyan Mary;

sadly she died in Infancy. Alfred was allowed to attend the funeral.

The following year 1896, Evelyne was pregnant again and gave birth to a healthy boy, who they named Alfie Lionel Philip. He was born in Subathu (near Shimla), INDIA. The couple were overjoyed, they could not have been happier.

In 1897, Evelyne gave birth to another son, Arthur Montague Oswald, who also sadly died in Infancy. He was buried next to his sister at the local Catholic Cemetery. It was another very sad time for them both.

Evelyne and Alfred were soon to move again, he wanted to bring back the smile on Evelyne's beautiful face, he would do his very best to make her happy again. So he travelled down to Poona and looked for a fabulous house with a large garden with some land. He soon found just what he was looking for; A stately looking home, with five bedrooms, a large garden and some land. He employed servants to cook and clean, also a gardener.

When the house had been repainted and decorated and furnished, he sent for Evelyne and Alfie Lional. When Evelyne saw the house, she cried with joy, "What a beautiful house, I shall be very content and happy here. Thank you, darling, you have made me smile again, I love you so very much."

The year passed by, Alfred had already worked his way up in the ranks. In 1898, he was made a Corporal. Alfred's army pay had increased and he was now on a very good wage. His Army promotions came about; as he was brilliant in learning many of the dialects, he was now conversing with the Indian troopers in their own languages He could speak fluent Hindi.

He later had another promotion. He now had the title of Lieutenant Colonel! His long service in the British Army had served him well. Alfred was a very proud man, Alfred Frederick John Knight was awarded many Medals and a Sword. WHAT A GREAT HONOUR!

Chapter Eight

After his long service career in the Army, it was a pleasure to settle down to enjoy civilian life with his beloved wife and family. Evelyne was a very good cook and kept the house in very good order. They adored their son Alfie, who was a very contented baby and only cried if he wanted to be fed. On Sundays, Alfred would take his wife to the local Catholic Church. She was a staunch Roman Catholic and they had Alfie Lional baptised in this little Church. Evelyne would never miss Mass unless she was unwell.

When Alfred was five years of age, he started the local school in Poona. In 1901, Evelyne gave birth to a healthy daughter, Agnes Evelyn Maud. The years flew by, Agnes soon joined her brother at school. Four years later in 1905, Evelyne gave birth to another daughter, they named her Blanche Emily Constance Millicent. When Blanche was five years of age, she too joined the infants class at her sister's primary school.

Five years later in 1910, Evelyne gave birth to her last child, a daughter who they named Cecelia Ivy Virginia. When Alfred picked her up at the hospital, she was so tiny, he called her his little "Biddy Knight."

All the children were baptised in the Catholic Church. Alfred had already employed an Ayah to take care of their children. She was to become their friend and confidant. All the children liked her, as she would play games with them and teach them card tricks.

One year later, while at Sunday Mass, Evelyne started having terrible pains in her back and knees; she could hardly get up from her kneeling position. After a week the pain in her spine got worse, Alfred took her to the best Doctor available; tests were done, but the results were not good. Doctors found she had a rare complaint "osteoarthritis," which meant her bones and joints in her legs were degenerating.

With her special treatment, Evelyne was fitted with painful callipers, together with specially fitted boots that had to be worn at all times while walking, one boot was very slightly higher than the other. Alfred never loved her less, he loved her more for being so brave and strong.

Alfie was well educated, Alfred sent him to the best high school in Poona for further education. Alfred had to pay for his son to attend this high educational school. At this school they had an Orchestra, where boys could learn to play an instrument. They were free to join the "Musical Instrument Classes," where the boys could choose from a selection of instruments and learn to play them.

They also had choir practices, where they could learn to sing. These classes were held after school lessons in the main hall twice a week. Alfie's choice was to learn to play the violin, which he loved to play; over the next few years, Alfie had mastered the violin becoming a very fine accomplished player. His teacher would let him have a solo performance.

At the end of the school year, the school would hold a parents' evening where families could come for the school leavers' concert. These gifted boys had a chance to show off their talent, only the best players or singers were chosen to perform. One would play the piano, some would play trumpet or flute. The very best voices would sing solo or in a group where they would harmonise. The orchestra would play and it would be a grand evening's entertainment.

Alfie would often play outside on his terrace at home. The neighbours would gather around the gate, Alfred and Evelyne would invite them in, their memsahibs would serve them food and drink. One of the Anglo-Indian neighbours played the banjo, they would all have a jolly good time, often singing and dancing way into the late evenings.

When Alfie left school, his father wanted him to join the Army, but Alfie had other ideas. He joined the British Marines instead. He became a British Naval engineer. He served in India until he was twenty. Evelyne did write to him, but his letters would sometimes not be returned as Alfie would be on his ship fighting the war at sea. Only when he was based at port, did he receive his mail. His letters to Mama and Papa were far and few between.

Agnes also was a reasonable scholar; she wanted to learn to play the piano and become a concert pianist, but the school she attended did not give music lessons. To get the required training proved to be extremely difficult. When Agnes left Secondary school, she went off to training school where she became a boarder as it was much too far to travel each day. She wanted to become a nurse, like her Mama. To eventually become a Matron of a Hospital.

The war was closing in on them again and it was time to move well away, so Alfred decided to move the family to Bankipore, Bihar, in the North Eastern part of India. They would write to Agnes and tell her what was happening and where they would be moving to. It would also be nearer the children's school which was "St Joseph's Covent Private Boarding School for Girls." The school was run by German Nuns, which was located near the Himalayas, where the children would hopefully be safe.

Alfred's close army friend Arthur Daniels and his wife Jayed had always kept in touch by mail. Alfred knew that they had already moved to Bankipore, so they would have their close friends living nearby.

When the children found out they were moving, they were very upset as they had made good friends locally. They liked their school, especially the teachers. Both girls were doing well with good marks in their three subjects, reading, writing and arithmetic. They also made some nice school friends there! Alfred told the girls it was for their own safety, that he would give them each a lovely surprise if they would cheer up.

Alfred made lots of inquiries for a large house that was for sale in Bankipore. He was notified within a week that there was a vacant deserted house, which could be purchased very cheaply; he was told by the agents that the house had an outbuilding. This property has been empty for a long time, it would need a lot of work done to the exterior and interior to make it liveable.

He travelled up to Bankipore to see what condition this deserted house was in. As soon as he saw and entered the house, although it needed a lot of work, the structure looked sound, but he would get it checked out. He knew it would be the right choice, it was situated in the hills, with stunning views across the valley looking down on plantations and paddy fields. It also came with another small building, which could be turned into servants' quarters.

Alfred loved the very spacious garden with trees and shrubs. He would start by having this five-bedroom house, totally refurbished inside and out, with new doors, windows and fittings. He put in an offer for the property, which was agreed by the agents. After Alfred had bought this large five-bedroom house, he got in touch with builders, painters and decorators to do the work. Alfred agreed on a price, he would pay them in full when the work was completed. They hoped that they could complete the work in four to five months.

When Alfred went to see the progress, it was amazing, the property had been totally transformed. They told Alfred that the decorating work inside would be completed within a month's time. Alfred and Evelyne went shopping to choose all the new curtains and carpets, furniture and beds. They moved into the house four weeks later. The family settled very quickly into their beautiful new home. Mama and the girls loved this big house, they could look down into the valley from their bedroom windows.

Alfred employed six Memsahibs to do all the household chores but was on the lookout for a good gardener; he employed a young Ayah to take care of his children. The girls were so thrilled to have a lovely big bedroom all to themselves. After they had been living in the house for a few weeks, the girls felt like they were the luckiest girls in the world, living in this magnificent home.

Alfred said, "Girls, I have a surprise for you both like I promised," he carried a round basket into the lounge, covered over with a cloth.

"What have you got there, Papa?"

He gave the children a wide smile, "Look Here!"

Inside the basket were two tiny fox terrier puppies, both children screamed with delight, they both gently picked them up and cuddled it. Blanche said "I'm going to call this puppy Jacky," and Biddy said, "Well, I shall name this one Nelly because it's a girl."

They had already written to their friends, Arthur and Jayed Daniels to tell them they had now moved to Bankipore, that they should come for a visit whenever they had a free weekend. They could stay the night as they had plenty of room. They arranged to come on the following weekend. On their arrival, they were so happy to see their dear friends again; they were only living five miles away, to have their friends living so near was just perfect for them all. When they were seated on the terrace, happily chatting away, it was so good to be together again.

Evelyne went back into the house and helped the Memsahibs bring out the food and drinks, as the food and drinks were arriving at the table, Arthur gave Alfred a wrapped gift, he said, "Before you open this present, I want you to think back to your early days in the Army; do you remember sitting in the circle with the Indian soldiers late one evening. I was sent to pick up some medical supplies, I saw you sitting with them; you were smoking a long pipe, well this gift is to remind you of that time."

Evelyne came out with glasses and nibbles, Alfred opened his gift, it was a lovely wooden carved pipe with a packet of tobacco. Alfred was spellbound, "My! what a lovely pipe, I will only smoke it when Evelyne goes to bed. Thank you, dear Arthur, it's lovely; yes it does remind me of the first time I smoked. I just want you to know Arthur that the real purpose of sitting with Indian soldiers was that I wanted to learn to speak the Hindi language, in which I became fluent."

Evelyne picked up the pipe and looked at it, Arthur smiled up at her and said, "Evelyne, I do hope you approve?"

She smiled as she put the pipe down on the table, saying to Alfred, "Now darling, you won't get addicted, will you?"

They all laughed and laughed. "Evelyne, we also have a gift for you." Jayed gave her a beautifully wrapped present; she opened it, inside was a dressing table set, consisting of a Comb Brush and Mirror made of a lovely polish mahogany wood.

"Oh! Jayed and Arthur, what a wonderful gift, you are both so very kind and generous, thank you so much; it is the best gift I have ever had. I will treasure this gift forever," she gave them both the biggest hugs. Then she poured the wine, "Cheers everyone."

Cheers they clinked glasses, enjoying their happy reunion. One warm hazy afternoon, three months later, Mama and Papa together with Jayed and Arthur were relaxing on their terrace, while being served tea with a fine selection of cream cakes by one of their new servants, who already knew their preferences by heart and didn't need to interrupt their conversation.

Alfred said, "Arthur, do you know by chance, of any good gardeners. I am looking for one to tend my huge garden."

"You, my dear boy, are looking at him I would love to sort out your garden. I, my good man pride myself in my knowledge of botany; it happens to be one of my many favourite hobbies."

"Splendid old chap, when do you want to start, Now?" They all started laughing.

Then on to a more serious conversation, they started discussing the latest news of the past few days; unfortunately, it was not good. For the many Army personnel, which had moved away, involved Gandhi and the British Raj. On the vast lawn, the girls were happily playing with their puppies, who were chasing them around the garden. The girls, oblivious of any of this talk going on around them, were having great fun, just playing with their best mates two tiny fox terrier; Jack and Nelly in turn were trying to pull the sash from the girl's sari.

Their parents and friends were now watching them, wondering how long these tranquil scenes were going to last! Arthur, true to his word, took on the job of looking after their vast garden. He would cut the lawn, trim the hedges. He planted colourful flowers and made flower beds, he built pergolas growing plants up them, even made a little pond with a waterfall beside the lovely flower bed, sowed and planted many different shrubs. He also grew a herb garden. Arthur transformed the garden. Alfred paid him well for his dedicated hard work, which in fact all the family appreciated.

Arthur would just smile and say, "Folks this is what I do best!"

Chapter Nine

The girls were now ready to start their new boarding school, with their bags packed and labelled. "Now Biddy darling doesn't forget to give the teachers and girls you meet your real name; from now on, you will be addressed as Ivy, not Biddy, that is just your nickname."

"OK, Mama, I'll remember."

They were just sad about leaving Jacky and Nelly. So Ivy said to Blanche, "We must try hard to focus on making new friends at the convent school. We will see Jacky and Nelly when the school term ends, so we must cheer up."

When they arrived at the station, the train was in; they said their sad goodbye's to Mama and Papa. "We will write to you, take good care of Jacky and Nelly, Papa; they need a long walk every day."

"Yes, girls, you can be sure I will."

The station master blew his whistle, the guard waved his flag and they were off, waving out of the window until they faded out of sight.

The train was full of girls of different age groups, some were returning after school holidays; excitedly relating to friends all about the wonderful things they got up to while on their holidays. But some sat quietly looking out of the train window. Two girls sat opposite Blanche and Ivy, both girls were very pretty, laughing and chatting.

When they saw Ivy smiling at them, one of the girls spoke to them saying, "Are you girls looking forward to starting the Convent school?"

Ivy looked at Blanche who shrugged her shoulders and said, "I think so, what is it like there?"

"Oh, it's very strict, the German nuns will expect you to be on your best behaviour at all times, but you'll get used to the rules; what are your names?"

"Well, I am Blanche Knight, this is my younger sister Ivy, but we call her Biddy, that's her nickname; we live with our parents, our mother's name is Evelyne and our father's name is Alfred, our father has now retired from the British Army. We now live in Bankipore." The girls answered eagerly, as they wanted to make new friends.

"Well, my name is Doreen Armour and this is my younger sister Irene; our father's name is Jack and our mother's name is Jennifer, our father is a ranking British Army Soldier, still fighting in the Northern Provinces; we also reside in Bankipore. We have not seen our father for many months, but he is all right, as we do get mail from him, but our dear mother misses him so very much. We are returning to this school, after our summer vacation," Doreen said.

"I am looking forward to a different class teacher this term. I do not want to spend another day in Miss Stern's class. 'Miss Stern' is what the girls in our class called her because she could be so dreadfully mean to us girls."

Blanche looked at Ivy with a frown, "I hope I don't get 'Miss Stern' for my teacher!"

The girls continued to chatter away on their long journey, they discovered that these girls only lived a few miles away from them. Ivy mentioned that they had two dogs. Doreen said, "We both like dogs, but we do not have any pets."

Ivy said, "In the school holidays, you must both come to our house and meet our lovely dogs, Jacky and Nelly."

The girls thanked them for the invitation, "we would love to come." These girls were soon to become very dear friends, but because they were older, they would not be in the same classes.

This train would only take them just over half the way as their school was near the Himalayas. The train pulled into the station, nearly all the girls rushed to get a good seat on the other train, which would take them up the scenic route. The older girls never got tired of what the new girls were going to see. This train took them up the mountains into the Darjeeling Area. As the train slowly ascended the very steep mountain track, the views became breath-taking, with magnificent and awesome scenery. In the far distance, they could see beautiful mountains with snow on the top; the girls thought it was the most spectacular view in the whole world!

The trip was long, but not boring, when the girls glanced down, they could see Tea-trees being planted around the area by those oblivious to the enormity of their humble task. How would they ever know this was to become a major ongoing industry for the Darjeeling area. Later coffee beans were also grown successfully in the surrounding area.

The school where they were heading had belonged to the Buddhist Monks, who still had monasteries around this part of Darjeeling, who very generously gave up this building to a small community of German Nuns, "THE URSULINE

SISTERS." The Nuns had taken on setting up the school in the earlier days, mainly for the needs of the children, who were in great need of tuition and care in these troubled times. The sisters had worked extremely hard to get this place into some kind of order. They had taken on an enormous task as the children were of all ages and sects.

The Nuns now running the school were lay teachers, who were of the strict Roman Catholic faith; all the children had to abide by their strict rules, at least they had a chance of a decent education. Some fees were subsidised by wealthy parents, donations and grants were given by the Bihar Banks, which helped to keep the school going. Most of the sisters were nice enough, some were very strict, even rather cruel.

On arrival, all the new children were met by the Reverend Mother who welcomed the new arrivals; they were told to follow the Matron Nurse who would supply them with their new uniforms and bedding. Matron said, "follow me girls," and she took them to their dormitories, where she split the girls into age groups so that the girls of the same age would all be together.

The older girls would be in another dormitory next door. The Matron Nurse, who supplied their uniform, asked each girl their size; they were then given their uniform and bedding. They were then shown to their beds where they were told to unpack, they were given one small cupboard and one drawer per child. The girls were then told by the Matron that she would inspect the dormitories every day, they were to be kept tidy and their beds made up. Their dirty washing was to be left in the wicker baskets inside their cupboards with their names on, which they would be given later. Their beds had to be stripped once a week.

The girls each had to give their full name, date of birth and addresses. Then they were told to report to the main hall, where the Reverend Mother would give them a briefing on the school rules. Then the Reverend Mother read out various names, just to get the older children into groups with their new teachers' names and class numbers. Then she read out the younger age group and did the same. Lastly, she read out the new starters' names and placed them with their teachers and class numbers.

The Reverend Mother went on to say, "there will be a prayer service first thing every morning, every child must attend; only if you are sick, will you be allowed to stay in the dormitory."

The Nuns would have liked Mass to be read, but there was no priest in the area, only the Monks in Tibet, they could hardly be helpful in this situation!

The first thing the girls noticed was how extremely cold it was, temperatures always seemed nearer zero for most of their first term. After morning service, they would assemble in the Dining Room next to the main hall for breakfast. After Breakfast, each child was given chores to do. It could be helping clear the breakfast trays, cleaning the tables, tidying and cleaning the dormitories and making their beds, collecting up all the dirty laundry to take to the back kitchen.

All chores had to be done before school started at 9 o'clock. Blanche was always complaining to Ivy about doing her chores, "Blanche, you were born lazy, you never liked doing any jobs even at home." No one ever helped Blanche, she was often late back to the classroom.

The first thing that Blanche noticed about her class teacher was that Sister Helga was very strict. Whenever

Blanche was late for lessons, her teacher made her stand in the corner, facing the classroom wall with her hands behind her back, until the lesson was over or she was made to write a hundred times (I MUST NOT BE LATE FOR CLASS) after the lessons for the day had finished.

Blanche didn't like her teacher, she suddenly remembered what Doreen had said about this very strict teacher "Miss Stern," Blanche, unfortunately, was having to deal with this strict unsmiling teacher, Sister Helga. This Nun always had a permanently stern look on her face, any child who flouted her rules was kept in class after lessons. Nobody knew what punishment they had, they were told not to discuss it with their friends.

Rules were Rules and had to be obeyed. But Blanche did secretly tell Ivy, it was called detention where she had to write a hundred words on good behaviour, any spelling mistakes had to be corrected. One day while in her English lesson, Blanche was writing an essay, her teacher Miss Helga stopped at her desk and said, "What's that word Blanche," she looked up and said, "What word, Miss."

Her teacher pointed to the word with her ruler, "That word is WAPS, Miss."

"The word has an 's', wasp, say wasp, Blanche."

"WAPS."

When she said WAPS again, her teacher whacked her across the fingers with the ruler, "saying not WAPS, WASP, WASP," a whack for each time she said it wrong until she had mastered the word. Her fingers were still stinging and red for the rest of the day.

The only thing that Blanche was good at was sewing. On Friday mornings they had a sewing class with a lovely teacher

Sister Grace, who always had a smile for the girls, giving them all encouragement; she would often give Blanche praise for her good work. She liked her sewing class and looked forward to Fridays.

Ivy was the lucky one, her class teacher Sister Theresa was nice, all the girls in her class liked her, she had a very kind manner. She was also their music teacher, she took Music lessons on Thursday afternoons. Any of the girls with a good singing voice could join their choir from various classes. Sister Theresa had the most beautiful singing voice, she was also a very good pianist. Ivy had the nicest singing voice in her class so she asked Ivy if she would like to join their choir, which Ivy was hoping for. After a few months, Ivy was given the lead to sing solo in morning service. Ivy sang *AVE MARIA* so beautifully.

The year flew by and the summer holidays were upon them, all the children would be going home for the summer vacation.

All the girls caught the same train home. They soon found their friends Doreen and Irene Armour, they had saved a seat for them both, so they could sit together. Blanche said, "You know what teacher I got, don't you? Yes, you were right Doreen, Sister Helga was very strict, not a nice teacher at all. I hope to Heaven that I don't have her again next term!"

Papa was at the Railway Station to meet them, Blanche introduced their new friends Doreen and Irene Armour; just when Papa was saying hello to the girls, the girls saw their parents coming towards them, delighted the girls ran over to see their Mama and Papa, giving them both their biggest hugs and kisses.

Doreen said, "Come over Mama and Papa and meet our new friends, Blanche and Biddy Knight."

They came over and introduced themselves. "I am Jennifer Armour, this is my husband Jack," after shaking hands, Alfred said, "Would you all care to come over to our house for Dinner, next Saturday? I'm sure my wife Evelyne would be delighted to make new friends."

The Armours only lived two miles away, they seemed like very nice people. "Yes, Mr Knight, we would love to come."

Alfred said, "Shall we say next Saturday at around 1:30 p.m.?"

"Lovely, we will look forward to meeting your wife, if there are any problems Mr Knight, just let us know."

"Call me Alfred," he said with a smile. They gave each other their addresses.

Jennifer said, "It's lovely to meet you and your daughters, all being well, we will see you next Saturday, Alfred."

The girls hugged their friends and waved goodbye. Papa was so pleased to see the girls, the house seemed so empty without them. Although they did write one letter to their parents, they wrote about the two girls they had met on the train, they said how nice these new friends Doreen and Irene Armour were. They asked about Jacky and Nelly, they were longing to see them. They mentioned that the nuns kept them very busy, having to do private studies after their evening meals, then there were morning chores to do, not giving them much spare time to write letters to their parents.

When they arrived home, they gave Mama the biggest cuddles, then they told her about the Armour's family, they asked Mama if it was alright for them to come to Dinner on the following Saturday. "Yes, of course, I would be pleased to meet the Armour's, especially looking forward to meeting Doreen and Irene, who you wrote so caringly about. I will look forward to Saturday, we will have the cooks make something special for our guests to eat."

Biddy said, "Mama, we have both missed you so much."

"Girls, I am so glad you're back home again, it's been so lonely without you, thank Heaven we had these for company!"

Mama opened the back door, Jacky and Nelly came bounding in. The girls were so happy to see their dogs again, they spent the rest of the day playing and making a complete fuss of them.

The holidays were in full swing, the girls were so enjoying the lovely weather; they went out every day, walking the dogs; they had picnics on the terrace, chilling out, just enjoying their freedom.

The Armours arrived, they all got on extremely well. Jennifer and Jack were very special people, they had brought Mama a lovely bunch of flowers and Jack gave Alfred a large bottle of red wine. It was an instant friendship. Papa and Jack talked about their army careers, while Mama and Jennifer talked about their hobbies. Jennifer said she loved to draw and paint, Mama talked about how she loved to bake, she would sometimes give the servants ideas about what to cook for their evening meals, she started to write her own recipes for them to follow.

While they were all enjoying themselves, Doreen happened to mention that Biddy was the lead singer in the school choir, "You must hear her sing, Mama."

Jennifer looked at Evelyne and said, "Jack and I would very much like to hear Biddy sing."

Mama turned to Biddy and said, "Will you sing for us, darling?"

Biddy smiled saying, "OK then if I must." She sang *There's No Place Like Home*! Biddy had such a lovely clear tone to her voice. They all clapped and cheered.

The Armours and the Knights had a lovely afternoon together getting to know each other, they enjoyed the special Chicken Pie with vegetables, which was one of Mama's Favourite recipes; the red wine was good too; for dessert they had a mixed fruit trifle. Before leaving they invited the Knights back to their house, whenever they had a free weekend. From then on, they became close friends. Doreen and Irene loved playing with their dogs. The girls told Biddy later that they would ask their Mama and Papa if they would buy them a puppy. This was starting to be the best summer Holidays they had ever had. Their friendship with the Armours lasted a long time.

But unfortunately, all this happiness was not to last!

Chapter Ten

They had only been home a few weeks when one afternoon Blanche Biddy with their young Ayah went for a walk, they did not take the dogs as Nelly had been sick and taken to the vet.

The girls wanted to play Hide and Seek, Ayah was made to close her eyes and count to 50. The girls ran off in different directions. After about half an hour, Ayah found Biddy, but after looking for Blanche, for over two hours, calling and calling they gave up and went home, thinking she would also give up and make her own way home. But that was not the case, by 6 o'clock, the family started to get worried. Alfred sent his six servants out to look for her. Four hours later they came back, shaking their heads; they could not find her, even after searching half the paddy fields.

It was now growing dark and starting to rain heavily, the Monsoon rains had started, then a terrible storm broke with thunder and lightning; there was nothing they could do until first light. Mama and Papa were praying and unable to sleep, they were beside themselves with worry. As soon as it was light, Alfred gathered up a search party, with the servants and neighbours they went looking for Blanche. It was just before noon that morning, Blanche was found curled up in a ball under a small bush.

She was shivering from being soaking wet and cold, it was still raining heavily. Thankfully, although she was wet through, she was still alive. God had answered their prayers. They took off her soaking wet clothes, wrapped a towel around her head, then wrapped her in a blanket. Alfred carried her home as fast as he could. One of the servants went to fetch a doctor. Blanche developed pneumonia, they thought she was going to die, Blanche pulled through, but it took quite a long time for her to recover.

After that terrible ordeal, no one could ever be sure, if she did! The heavy rain beating down on her head had made her ear very sensitive to touch, she suffered from slight ear problems for the rest of her life. While Blanche was slowly recovering, there was another terrible incident.

Late on a very hot summer evening, one of the young servants went out to the water pump to fetch water for the household. While he was waiting for the large buckets to fill, unseen at first, then he saw the Cobra snake before he had time to move, the Cobra struck; he was bitten on his foot, he was only wearing flip flops; the cobra had bitten him on his little toe.

He shouted, crying out for help. Alfred acted quickly, telling the servant to fetch the chopper immediately. Alfred chopped off the infected toe, letting it bleed away the poison, with the help of another servant, they marched him up and down the room, several times, giving him brandy to keep him going. One of the other servants had gone quickly for a Doctor; after four hours or so later, the Doctor arrived to give this young servant an antidote.

The Doctor later told Alfred that by acting so quickly, he had saved the man's life! The Doctor stitched up the area, around the missing toe. Alfred paid the Doctor, then arranged for the man to be taken to the nearest hospital. A week later, Alfred went to see him in the hospital ward, the area around his missing toe was slowly healing up and he was learning to walk with crutches around the ward. He thanked Alfred wholeheartedly for saving his life.

Soon the summer holidays would be over, time to go back to school. Blanche had made a reasonable recovery with the help of her nursing mother. She asked Blanche, "Darling, do you feel well enough to return to school?"

"Yes Mama, I feel so much better now. I think I am fit enough to go back to school." The girls were eager to see their friends Doreen and Irene again. Both their parents saw them off at the station, the only good news was that before leaving home, Nelly was now better, she had eaten something that had made her very sick. The girls travelled back to the Covent School with Doreen and Irene, telling them everything that had occurred over the holidays.

Both girls said How sorry they were. Doreen said, "Thank goodness everything has turned out for the best."

They arrived back at school for the start of the new term.

Both girls were now in different classes with different teachers. What a relief it was for Blanche, who was dreading returning to this school, but she was assured by Doreen that she would definitely be having another teacher and not to worry. Both the girls had nice new teachers, who were pleasant and school resumed as normal. They had been back at school for over three months when both girls were called to

Mother Superior's office by the Secretary, they were told to wait outside until they were called.

When Ivy saw Blanche, the girls were sick with worry because if you were sent to Mother Superior's office, it would mean that you have been very naughty. Blanche had been here before but never with her sister, so they were both shaking, wondering what they had done wrong; so after waiting for what seemed like hours to them, they were finally called in.

At first, they walked in very slowly but seeing the broad smile on Mother Superior's face, they quickened their pace and to their utter surprise, sitting opposite Mother Superior was their own beloved Mama. At first, they couldn't believe it, nor take in exactly what was happening. Mama just said, "I'm here to take you both home girls, you will not be returning to this school ever again."

Mother Superior then told the girls to hurry and pack up their belongings, then to go to the main hall to say farewell to all the teachers and your friends, even Mother Superior had tears in her eyes as she wished them all the very best. She said, "The nuns and herself would pray for them, don't forget them and let the school know how they were progressing."

The first place the girls went was to find Doreen and Irene, they were in the hall waiting; as they were special friends, they had been told to report there. All the teachers, who had taken their classes, even "Stern face" herself had come to wish them well and to say goodbye, even though she seemed to look sad. They said their farewells, most of the school came out to wish them goodbye. After collecting all their belongings, they left to catch the train, this time with their beloved Mama.

Chapter Eleven

On the final stage of their journey home to Bankipore, the girls asked Mama many questions. But Mama was very tired from the extensive travelling, all that she told them was that Papa was fine and not to fret, she had brought a large basket of fruit and drinks that would sustain them through their long journey home. Mama said, "Girls, when we get home, Papa will explain everything to you and it would be much better coming from him."

Everyone relaxed and they slept most of the journey, cuddled up tightly to Mama, who in turn did the same.

Indeed delighted to be returning home so soon, they both had difficulty accepting this unusual occurrence that they feared it was all a wonderful dream to be returning to their idyllic lifestyle and to see Jacky and Nelly again.

Nothing could have prepared the sisters for what now lay ahead. Very shortly all their lives would change forever. After this long tedious journey home, they were all exhausted but just seeing Papa on the porch with his arms outstretched to hug them, welcoming them home again. Then the dogs came bounding out, just to see their dogs again was a delight. After some light refreshments, they were all tired after their long journey. Papa had assured them that evening that he would give them a full explanation in the morning. They had a lovely warm bath before retiring to bed.

The next morning both girls awoke early, they were anxious to hear what Papa had to tell them. Even when they were all having breakfast, they noticed there was a certain air of excitement in the house; they could hardly wait for what Papa was going to reveal to them. Most Indian people seem to have a strange sense of inner perception and always seem to know just what is occurring before you do; of course, there were many rumours going around, but most of the servants preferred to listen to their "boss man" first. This event was going to be important to them, as it was to all, their futures also lay in the balance too.

After Breakfast, Papa made us all get comfortable, he said, "What I am about to say may take some time," just as we were all getting settled, the lounge door flew open and standing in the doorway was their sister Agnes.

We were so surprised to see her that we both rushed forward and gave her hugs even before we had time to speak to her. Papa commanded us to sit down, saying that there would be plenty of time for hugging later. "What I am about to say is very important to each and every one of us. I have some very upsetting news for you all."

The sisters quickly sat down and listened intently to what Papa had to say. "This sudden change of events will affect all our lives personally. It will be of the utmost importance to you all, we must not get too upset by what I am about to relate to you. This news comes from the high officials in the British Government. They have good reason to know that staying here puts all our lives in Great danger, even now as I am speaking to you.

I have decided that the best course of action is to leave this beautiful country and our home immediately. This is no longer a safe place to dwell. All the details and arrangements to leave have already been made. We will catch the two adjacent trains to the coast, there we will board a ship which will take us across the sea, via the Suez Canal to England. When we arrive in England, we will disembark from that ship and board another ship that will take us across the Pacific Ocean to Canada.

The voyage will take around six weeks. We shall be leaving the day after tomorrow, which should give us enough time to pack and dispose of all our household equipment. I have already informed relations and friends of our intentions. The British Army does not have enough troops to cope with this new uprising here, but they are sending troops, who will be giving us all the extra help we shall need to leave as quickly as possible."

Everyone was silent for a few moments, trying to take in what Papa had just told them. Then Biddy who was sitting with her mouth open wide said, "Papa, why are we going to Canada, are we going to live there?"

"Yes, we are going to live and settle in Ontario, where you will meet all my family of Knights. My stepbrother William Thomas, who I was very close to when I was growing up. William and his wife Mable are going to accommodate us. You will be meeting their family and my other siblings and their families, all living in Ontario. We have so many relatives living there. We will all live with Aunt Mable and Uncle William because he has the largest home until we can find a nice big house of our own. I am intending to join the police force there if they will have me."

They all cried in one voice, "To Canada!"

Mama just smiled at their surprised happy faces saying, "everything is going to be just fine, you must not worry about the very long sea voyage ahead. I am sure there will be lots to do on board the ship." The three girls went off to discuss everything papa had just told them.

Papa called his devoted servants and asked them all to sit down, he had something important to tell them; when he had finished speaking, they were not surprised, they all knew this was about to happen sometime, but not when!

All the next day, everyone except Blanche, was busy helping to pack the household goods. All their valuable goods would be packed very carefully by Evelyne. Blanche went out and played with their beloved dogs. The rest of their goods were to be sold off to dealers, who would be coming that afternoon. Which turned out to be quite profitable. That evening the family relaxed, spending time talking to Agnes about how she was liking her nursing career.

She said, "I am happy working as a nurse. It gives me a great feeling knowing I'm helping others to get well again. When we arrive in Canada, I'll try finding a nursing job in the local hospital."

The girls were then interrupted by Mama, "Come along, girls, it's time for you to start packing up your trunks and be quick about it."

"Yes, Mama," her three lovely daughters went off laughing. Papa had already told them it was only one trunk each, they must only take the basic essentials, the servants would come up and help them when they were ready. Blanche did a little then lay on her bed with a book, when Biddy saw her she said, "For goodness sake, Blanche, put down that book and help us pack, don't be so lazy."

Blanche replied, "Didn't Mama once say 'That that too many cooks spoil the broth'."

Biddy replied, "Mama also said 'Many hands make light work'."

Blanche said, "Well, anyway, I thought the servants were going to help us."

Agnes just rolled about laughing, knowing Blanche so well, "Don't worry Biddy, I'll help her pack." Biddy just rolled her eyes!

All their heavy luggage was to be taken to the station that evening, for shipment, also for security etcetera. When most of the packing was done, the three girls sat on the bed in their nighties; discussing their future, Agnes said, "I am looking forward to our long boat trip and starting a new nursing career in Canada."

Blanche said, "I don't really care what I do, I am just so happy not having to go back to that awfully freezing cold school and seeing that awful teacher Sister Helga again." She turned to her sisters and said, "WAPS, sorry I mean wasp, there you see, she did teach me something! My fingers still 'sting' when I think about that day."

Agnes and Biddy fell about laughing their heads off, then Blanche saw the funny side and joined in. Then Biddy turned to Blanche, "You do know that we will have to leave behind our precious dogs. What are we going to do, Papa is never going to let us take Jack and Nelly with us."

They both began to get upset. When Mama came in to kiss them goodnight, she said, "What are all these tears for?"

Biddy said, "Mama, why can't we take the dogs with us?"

"I am sorry sweetheart, but it is not allowed; they would have to go into quarantine, that would take weeks but I do have some good news, Jayed has offered to take the dogs and look after them; they will go to a very good home, where they will be looked after properly. Jayed will soon be in to say goodbye to you."

They got themselves ready for bed and waited, soon there was a knock on the bedroom door, Jayed's voice was clear, "Can I come in, girls?"

Biddy answered, "Yes, please do."

Jayed came to say her goodbyes; with a tear in her eye, she told the girls, "Don't worry about Jacky and Nelly, girls. Arthur and I will take great care of them. I will write to you as often as I can, I will keep you informed how the dogs are faring, I will also send pictures of them."

Blanche said, "Jayed, Jacky and Nelly will protect you from thieves and snakes coming into the house, as they have done for us. Will you kindly do something for us please, could you send this letter to our dear friends the ARMOURS, as they are still at the Covent school. It is just to tell them where we are going, that we will write to them when we get to Canada. I have addressed it already with a stamp to 'Miss Doreen Armour' % Mother Superior at St Joseph's Covent Private High School for Girls, Patna Bihar Bankipore, India."

"Yes, of course, I will post it tomorrow. Enjoy your boat trip, girls; look after yourselves, keep in touch." With tears in her eyes, she said, "Girls, I want you all to know that Arthur and I love you very much; we will miss you; we are so sorry to see you leave India; we hope your new life in Canada brings you all, much happiness."

She gave the girls a hug and a kiss, then sadly said, "Goodbye and God bless."

Leaving the room and gently closing the door behind her, they were never to see Jayed again. Mama put her head around the door, "Come on girls, lights out, tomorrow is a big day. Oh girls! I do have some more good news. Jayed is going to have a baby in six months' time."

"Oh! Mama! How lovely for them, Arthur will soon be a father."

Biddy chipped in saying, "I hope Jayed has a little girl."

Mama said, "Night Night, girls, it's a big day tomorrow."

"Goodnight, Mama," the girls answered in unison; she turned off the light and closed the door. The Daniels had also been busy, making their own plans to move to a safer location in the south of India and would be moving in a few days' time. That evening Mama and Papa did all the organising. Before Mr Daniels left, Alfred gave Arthur his stepbrother's name and address in Canada so they could keep in touch. Arthur then left to start their packing.

Jayed stayed the night, she was a great help, she managed to get everyone working. Agnes stayed up and helped and although it seemed an impossible task working together all night, by early the following morning, they were all ready and set to depart. Jayed left a few hours before dawn, taking the dogs with her. They all thought it was a good idea, as the girls would be less upset and the dogs wouldn't fret.

After an early breakfast, all the servants came in to say their goodbyes; they had been kind and had served the Knights family well. Alfred gave each of them a bonus of rupees to see them through the coming days. They all bowed their heads and thanked him. It was very moving, two stayed to lock up and the others left. Jayed had known the dogs as long as the girls had, she loved them too. The Daniels had been a large part of their lives in India, they were going to miss these lovely friends so much.

Arthur had always been a loyal friend to Alfred; he had done some fantastic gardening work for him. They would always remain the very best of friends. Alfred said to Evelyne, "I don't know how long we would have managed without the friendship and support of Arthur and Jayed."

Arthur had arranged to meet them at the station, he wanted to see them off on their ship. They were then ready to leave, they were just waiting for the removal van to pick up the furniture, carpets and other household items, which were all in very good condition. Everything of value had all been sold off. The removal van arrived, taking all the contents and household furniture. All had gone smoothly.

Chapter Twelve
Leaving India

The van arrived to take them, plus all their luggage to the station. When they arrived, it was absolutely crowded, but what a surprise to see most of these people were friends and neighbours that had come to see them off and to wish them all the very best.

The servant who had lost his toe came forward and said, "Mr Knight, I am now able to walk without crutches," and you will be forever in his thoughts. He wished him and his family all the very best in their new life in Canada. "Mr Knight, I will never forget you, thank you for saving my life," he gave Alfred a hug and slowly walked away.

When Mr Daniels appeared, they were all glad to see him. He helped them with their luggage. The train pulled into the station, they all got onto the train that would take them to the docks. When the train pulled out, they all blew kisses and waved through their tears, all they could see was a blur of colour. They were all so touched by the gesture, it was a lovely farewell these people had given them, one they would never ever forget!

The Knights did not remember much of the journey to the coast as they all fell asleep on the train. It was when they reached the docks that they became alert again. They couldn't believe just how crowded it was, also very noisy so that you had to shout to make yourself heard. Then Papa said, "We may have some time to wait as there are so many formalities to go through."

Mama and Papa both had to go off to fill in their "DECLARATION OF PASSENGER FORMS."

They were so thankful, they still had Mr Daniels with them. They were lucky enough to find three empty seats. Agnes was happy to sit on her suitcase while Arthur chatted to them saying, "Jayed and I will be moving down to Tamil Nadu in the south of India, but we hope to return back to BIHAR when it becomes a safe place for us to live there again."

Agnes looked up at Arthur and said, "Mama told us last night that you are going to be a father very soon, congratulations, give the new baby and Jayed a very big hug and kiss from us all."

Arthur smiled and said, "Thank you, girls, I will let you know when the baby arrives. Oh girls, I have something here for you to keep." He opened up his nap sack and gave them a lovely picture of their precious dogs Jacky and Nelly.

"Oh thank you so much, Mr Daniels, that's a wonderful picture of us playing with the dogs, we will have it framed and keep it forever."

Mama and Papa returned, Arthur had helped them in so many ways, carrying luggage and coming all this way to give his dearest friends a good send-off. He went off with Papa to organise some refreshments. They all wanted the Ladies restroom, Agnes and Mama went first, while the others took care of the luggage. They seemed to have been gone a fair while, they returned saying, "Sorry we had difficulty finding them." Then it was their turn.

The girls found that they were not very clean and awfully smelly. Blanche tied her hanky around her nose, but Biddy held her breath as long as she could. It was no surprise, the girls somehow got lost in the crowd; with so much pushing and shoving, it took for what seemed like an hour for them to find Mama, who had just started getting worried about the girls. Papa had managed to get them a tepid cup of tea and a biscuit, he told them that they would get a decent meal once they got on board; there was far too much going on, for any of them to feel hungry.

At long last, passengers were given permission to board and that was a feat in itself. Mr Daniels was allowed on board, he would have to leave immediately after the hooters blew for all visitors to leave the boat, there would also be sailors shouting, "All Visitors Ashore!" Arthur had almost missed the signal to go ashore, his heart must have been as heavy as ours. There were many farewells going on around us when Arthur "Papa's aide-de-camp" finally left, they all knew in their hearts that they would never see him again!

He then stopped and turned, "Call me Uncle Arthur in future."

The girls answered in unison, "Yes, Uncle Arthur."

He was more than worthy of the title! Arthur had to turn away quickly so that they could not see his tears! They all stood at the ship's rail, except Mama, who was feeling exhausted and tired from staying up the previous night. She asked a steward if he would kindly escort her to her cabin. They found it was difficult to see Arthur on the quay; papa spotted him first, it was crowded so they just waved, hoping he was still able to still see them. Papa pointed him out, as they were all sure he could see them, as they were all wearing black, most of the Indian people wore very bright colours.

They all felt very sad parting, leaving their dearest friends and Country. The family heard some months later that Arthur was upset for days, only seeing Jacky and Nelly at his home, reminded him so much of them. It somehow made him feel closer. We were sure the little dogs would have been hugged to death! Oh! What wonderful people these friends were, now they would be lost forever. They all had that same feeling that they would never see Auntie Jayed, Uncle Arthur or their new baby or their devoted dogs JACKY AND NELLY ever again.

As the Knights settled down into their comfortable cabins. They were choked up with so many emotions. They heard the sound of sweet music being played somewhere; as the ship slowly drew away from the wharf, neither of them had ever seen Papa "cry" before so they nudged each other and slowly moved away from him, so he could have some time to himself in his sorrow he had lost so much! Would the pain ever go away?

The ship was well away from the shore to continue on its long voyage, the three of them went up on deck to watch the thin rim of the coastline, slowly fading into the darkening sky. The next few days were spent sitting quietly in deck chairs, thinking about the future.

Would they be happy in this new country? Would they have to return to finish school? Were the Canadian people nice? Would they like the food? So many thoughts went through their minds. Agnes broke the silence, "Whatever happens, sisters, the important thing is we have each other, so we will make the most of it; let's just look forward to meeting our new family, now come on everyone cheer up and be happy!"

Chapter Thirteen

Mama made the girls aware of the dangers around the ship, she always kept a bottle of disinfectant around, keeping clean was the most important way to fight against germs. Mama just loved to sit in a deck chair and watch the ocean; it was so relaxing, watching the sea creatures, dolphins would often jump out of the sea, then down sending up a huge splash with just their tail fin slowly disappearing into the depths.

The ship must have been well out to sea when they saw the large notice board which said, "Bridge School For Beginners"; Meet the Captain who is now playing Bridge in one of the anterooms. The Captain met many passengers who had the same idea. Papa wanted to learn to play and would be joining the class another day.

The ship was now well into the "Bay of Bengal," heading towards the Indian Ocean. Papa also liked to play deck games on "A" deck where children were not allowed. He liked to keep himself fit, doing early morning walks around the ship's top deck. The motion of the ship made Biddy feel a little sick, so she ate very little until she got her sea legs.

One morning Papa decided to give the two youngest girls lessons. He felt he needed something constructive to do to keep the girls up with their school work, so he gave them some simple maths, to write a short story and read to him. This did not last long as he found there was so much going on around the ship. The girls were glad as they too were having so much fun on board.

Every afternoon after lunch, Alfred would go and play Bridge in the anteroom, where there were also Whist drives!

Alfred got himself involved in several of the ship's activities, he would meet up with people he slightly knew who played Bridge. There were plenty of things going on around the ship, something for everyone, who wanted to take part.

The three girls learned many things, all were amazed by just what they had missed. There were cookery demonstrations going on, where they were allowed to participate and allowed to take away whatever they had cooked. What fun!

They did enjoy cooking and eating the chocolate cookies they had made. They also loved to go to the "Play Acting Class," which was run by two professional retired actors. They would be put into fancy dress outfits to suit what parts they were to perform, then they would act out the scene from the script taken from a book or show, with older and younger passengers. There were keeping fit classes, swimming lessons and games in the pool.

Every evening, there would be a comedian, who would come on stage and tell jokes. Professional singers would take requests from the passengers. Stage dancers who would perform a variety of dances in traditional costumes. Some evenings, there would be dancing to a live band playing in the main hall. People would dress up for this event, wearing their evening gowns, dancing the night away. The Indian Ocean would have to be the world's most beautiful as the colour of the sea was a deep sapphire blue with so many dolphins swimming alongside the ship, not forgetting the colourful flying fish and sea birds flying overhead.

Papa had got himself so involved in the deck games; we only saw him at meal times, he would then be off to the top deck, where we were not allowed to go while the games were in progress. Mama would relax and read. We would often see her talking to people, making friends with ladies of her own age group! The ship stopped once, that was to take on a very special person, known locally as the "Guli Guli" man; he was some kind of magician, some of the people were saying that if the ship didn't stop and take this magician on board, it would bring bad luck to the ship!

This magician was a very good entertainer, who performed all kinds of magical tricks. The girls loved all this but when he brought out a live King cobra, the people were aghast; were any passengers brave enough to handle this snake if they dared. He had no participants, so he placed the cobra in a large basket with a lid, then covered it. Then he proceeded to open another taller basket, he then started playing his flute, out of the basket came a cobra which started to dance.

When he stopped playing, the snake slowly went back down into the basket, he placed the lid firmly back on. Their papa told them it was called "Snake Charming." This show lasted all afternoon. Someone started a collection for the magician, he kindly thanked the passengers. As he left the ship, he gave the ship his good spells! Leaving their ship for his own little wooden boat.

The special surprise came two days later when the ship was about to cross the Equator. Notices had been put up around the ship, but not many people bothered to look or read them. A message came over the loudspeaker from the Captain, he said, "Attention! Will all passengers assemble to the pool area in swimwear if possible or in something that would get wet. Father Neptune will be proceeding with this special event! Everyone who partakes in the crossing ceremony is asked to be at the pool at 2 o'clock."

Agnes said to Biddy and Blanche, "Are you two coming to the pool for this crossing event?"

Biddy said, "Oh yes, what fun that will be!"

Blanche shook her head and said, "No, I'm not going in the pool. I must not get water in my ear, but I will sit with mama and watch you."

"Come on then, Biddy, we must hurry and try and find something that we can get wet."

They rushed to mama's cabin, Mama gave them both two very long sashes which could be worn around their bodies. Ten minutes later, the girls join the queue around the pool area. What happened is that each person, in turn, must sit on a high stool with their back over the pool. Father Neptune would come towards you with a sea sponge which is covered in soapy froth, he then proceeds to wash your face, of course, everyone leans back and into the pool, they fall. Crew members were there to catch them, then give each one in turn a good dunking.

For this event, the pool area was packed with passengers, who did not want to take part. The younger children were very gently caught and then wrapped in a towel, then given back to their parents. This was great fun for old and young alike; the only people who did not partake were people that were disabled, had a fear of water or who just liked to sit and watch.

Their ship was making headway towards the Arabian Sea, heading for the Gulf of Aden, then on through the Red Sea. On reaching the Suez Canal, everyone on board would be allowed to leave the ship and have a day on land. After such a long time at sea, they saw the land, all that could be seen was desert, sand and more sand! There were a few Arabs walking alongside the canal with their donkeys and camels, they watched as the water would build up and their donkeys and themselves would be awash, they just smiled and waved to them, the camels being taller, seemed to miss it!

Papa said, "Building this canal was no mean feat. It was like it went on forever."

They had their meals as before, but there were very few in the dining room. They did think that the fish must have done well! It was still warm at night, the sky was beautiful with so many stars; one just felt if you only put out your hand, you could touch them! They all loved to spend time laying out on deck watching the stars, sometimes they would see an amazing shooting star!

The next morning, they were in The Great Bitter Lakes. The water here seemed so clear, but they didn't see any fish or anyone with small fishing boats, maybe because of the salt content of the water in these massive lakes. All the passengers were allowed to disembark, for the first time since leaving India, but only one day ashore. It would be great getting back their land legs. This stop was really meant for the crew to have a short break and catch up with a long-awaited rest.

All the passengers could not wait to get off the ship, go shopping or just walk on terra firma. Before leaving the ship, all the passengers were given warnings not to wear any jewellery or carry large amounts of cash. All valuables must

112

be taken to the purser's office for safekeeping. Arabs may come on board to sell the wares and many of the ship's crew would be on shore.

Papa took them for a long walk along the beach, many Arabs were selling all kinds of trinkets; they kept pestering them to buy their goods. Mama felt sorry for them and brought a bangle and some earrings. They passed by a food market stall and brought some light refreshments. They then took a slow walk back to their ship, where they could have a really good look at her. She was massive, they were amazed by how tall she was, painted black and white, with all different flags flying from her rigging.

Many of the passengers would be leaving this ship when they docked in Southampton for their destinations in England. When the ship finally docked, all the passengers on board had to disembark. All passengers changing ships for their passage to Canada had to follow the sign saying: PASSENGERS LEAVING FOR CANADA THIS WAY-->

The ship would be sailing on was called S.S. MONTCLARE. Their date of sailing was 15 September 1922, taking them on the next stage of their voyage, crossing the Pacific Ocean to Quebec in Canada, where their very long sea voyage would end. Alfred and Evelyne were given paperwork for their Declaration to Canada. It was a questionnaire which all passengers had to fill in!

Chapter Fourteen

For the most part of the voyage across the Pacific Ocean, the sea was calm but at times it would suddenly become rather rough, with huge waves that would rock the ship but because of our sea legs, we were now getting used to the sudden movement of ships. There were no views to wonder at, all they saw was sea and more sea for most of the sailing.

There were a few passing ships seen in the far distance or the odd birds flying high in the sky, that was the only interesting part of their journey. They did have a little fun playing games like Ping Pong and Table Tennis. In the afternoons to pass the time, Biddy would give Blanche singing lessons and teach her a few songs she had learnt while in the school choir, they would practice harmonising together.

Agnes would often be found studying her books on Nursing and asking her mama questions about the causes of different ailments of the body. But by now, they were all about "Shipped out"! All they were looking forward to was their arrival, which Papa said would be in a day or so. The next day they saw the land approach, passengers crowded onto the deck watching the land getting bigger and bigger.

All around us passengers were getting very excited, so were we. There was lots of hustle and bustle on board; as passengers were looking forward to going home, seeing their families and friends again. Some people, like ourselves, had made the long voyage to start a new life in Canada! There was great excitement everywhere on board. They all watched as the ship changed course and turned into its penultimate part of our voyage. They were almost at the end of their journey.

They were just waiting now for the ship to dock in Quebec, from where they stood they could just see the skyline of many buildings, as Quebec stands right on the coast. At long last, they were almost there; now only half a day before we finally arrived. They were all so thankful; after nearly a week, they could not wait to get off the ship and have a look around. It was a good job while sailing, that no one in the family mentioned the *Titanic* while they were on board; they had all heard that it had sunk when it struck an iceberg in 1912 on its maiden voyage to America. The girls would have been thinking about that and been very worried, that it could happen again!

The girls were a little apprehensive at meeting their relations for the first time, but happy to be starting a new life here in Canada! The very last part of the voyage was to sail down the St Lawrence river to Quebec, where they would disembark, then finally catch a train into Toronto, where they would meet up with aunts, uncles and cousins.

Finally, it docked and they left the ship for the last time. They caught glimpses of this beautiful old-fashioned city, they had heard so much about. Papa managed to secure a carriage that would take them, together with all their luggage, to a nearby hotel in downtown Quebec for one night; from there they would catch a train tomorrow afternoon for

Toronto, where their Aunty Mabel and Uncle William would be there to meet them.

Papa had to go and make arrangements and get train tickets for the last part of our journey and try and get through to William and arrange an estimated time of arrival at Toronto station. Mama and the girls went shopping. They could hardly believe that they would have difficulty, trying to understand these people as they spoke very differently to them! When they spoke, their voices sounded like they came from their nose, instead of their mouth. It was a drawling manner of speaking, "for use of better words."

Mama had to deal with the money, the girls could not understand the different currency; it was all too much for them, dollars and cents? It made no "sense" to them at all. Goodness knows, how were they going to cope. Only time will tell? Mama didn't buy much at first, but we girls did get a chance to have a good look around. Each one of them found the place enchanting, so very different from India.

Mama suddenly said, "We must look for something nice to take as a gift for Mabel and William."

Papa came back smiling, he'd managed to get through to his brother William and Mabel, he said, "They would be meeting them off the train at the station in Toronto. They will be waiting for us there, in the Hotel Reception, next to the Station."

That night after a scrumptious supper, they all slept very well, the beds were like sleeping on clouds, which they found out from the maid, were made from goose down feathers. After enjoying a rather large breakfast, all their tummies felt full. Papa said, "If you ladies would like to go for a walk or shopping one last time, then we should go now. Our train departs at 2 o'clock."

Papa and Mama found a very pretty Salt and Pepper cruet set, in a lovely blue and white Chinese "Weeping Willow Pattern." After having lunch, Papa gave them all a treat. It was a ride in a horse-drawn carriage all around the city, Quebec had such lovely shops and sea views; the girls noticed how people were dressed, so very different from the people in "India."

Biddy said, "Papa why do the people speak funnily here?"

"My dear, Biddy, it's the American accent, you will be speaking like them sooner than you think! So my dear "don't forget," we will also sound strange to them."

They arrived in Toronto on 21 September 1922. It was still early morning after they had eaten a good breakfast on the train! The train slowly pulled in and stopped at the Station. The family alighted to find the platform was crowded; they looked up and down the platform for the porters, who were thankfully bringing their luggage on a trolley, they followed behind them to the Station Hotel. When they entered the Hotel, Uncle William and Aunty Mabel were sitting in the Art Deco-style foyer, patiently awaiting our arrival.

This really was some welcome, they were overjoyed to see us, hugging and kissing, until they had to come up for air. Oh! What wonderful people these Canadians were; they were so blessed to have such lovely relations, the reception they gave them was amazing. People stopped to see what all the commotion was about and wanted to get in on the act and welcome them too. They all thought Papa had never looked so happy as seeing his brother William again, after so many years apart. They would certainly have such a lot of catching up to do.

William Thomas had two cars waiting outside the station. His car was a lovely Blue Model T Ford. The other car belonged to William and Mabel's eldest son Garnet, who had a large cab. He was waiting by his cab to greet them, what a handsome lad he was. With a wonderful smile and greeting, he started putting all their heavy luggage into his cab. They all got into the cars and relaxed. "Alleluia." They were nearly home!

Chapter Fifteen
Arrival in Canada

When they arrived in Orillia and saw the large white houses on West Street, they all looked like mansions to them. William pulled up by the main entrance, Mabel, Mama and Alfred stepped out. William unloaded their bags and went to park the car. Garnet dropped the girls off, he then unloaded their luggage and said, "I'll see you lovely cousins inside the house; after I have parked the cab, the servant will come out and take all the luggage inside."

He gave the girls a quick wink, then went off to park his large cab. The three girls followed behind Mama and Papa, Mabel mounted the white stone steps, they all followed. Mabel knocked on the front door with its large brass knocker; the door was opened by a black woman, she wore a silk scarf around her head, wearing a white apron. She said, "Good afternoon, madam," then they knew it was her maid, she welcomed us in and took our coats, she then called another black servant to bring in all their luggage.

Mabel led them into this huge hallway, where the broad staircase went up the middle of the house with many rooms to the left and right; she took them downstairs to a large bathroom to freshen up, she said, "When you are changed and ready, come back up; we will be in the large lounge on your right." She said, "The one with the green door." Then she said, "I will show you all around the house later."

The Knights went off to wash and change. When they were all freshened up, Mabel was waiting at the door, "Come this way." She took them into a very large lounge with a cocktail bar in one corner, in the other was a beautiful grand piano; suddenly, the room started to fill with a gathering of their Canadian relations who had come in from another room! Waiting to welcome them to Canada, William Thomas introduced them to his siblings.

He said, "Meet my brothers George Henry, Charles, Walter and sister Mary Ellen, they were all born in England, John was born here in Canada. They were accompanied by their families."

Then they were introduced to William and Mabel's sons and daughters, Garnet, James Edward, Pearl May, Rachel Ann, George Henry, William Charles, Morley Thomas. What a great gathering of relations. William and Mabel had put on this great party for them all, it was wild. The Canadians certainly knew how to party! The buffet food was scrumptious.

For the girls, meeting all these cousins and relations that they never knew was overwhelming, Agnes, Blanche and Biddy all had the most wonderful time, they had never enjoyed themselves so much. They all laughed at the jokes William told. Then he said, "Mabel and I are going to dance for you, could everyone clear the floor please."

The dance was a perfect waltz, Pearl played on the grand piano. Everyone clapped. They had always enjoyed ballroom dancing and had been to classes learning to dance while they were courting.

The food was the best the girls had ever eaten, followed by the lovely lemonade Mabel had specially made for them. The girls had never tasted anything so good as Maple Pecan Pie, it was absolutely delicious! During the evening Alfred said to Mabel, "You should hear Biddy sing, she has the sweetest singing voice. I know she would like to sing for all her relatives gathered here today, do you play the piano, Mabel?"

"Yes I tinker with the keys and play a little, but as you heard earlier, Pearl is the pianist in our family. Pearl can play anything by ear, but I did send her to have piano lessons when she was younger. I'll go and have a word with Pearl," who said, "Mama, I would be honoured to play and accompany Biddy and I would love to hear her sing."

Biddy and Pearl, went out into the hall to see if she knew the song Biddy wanted to sing, she said, "Yes, I love that song." She also told Pearl that she wanted to sing a duet with Blanche, Biddy started humming the tune, Pearl said, "Yes, that's a very old song, I do know it."

Biddy told Pearl that while on the ship, to pass the time, she had been giving Blanche singing lessons, helping her to improve her vocal cords; they would often practise singing together, sometimes it would be a duet and I would harmonise with Blanche. They went back to join the noisy party, Mabel stood on a stool and said, "Can I have everyone's attention, could you all be quiet for a moment? Biddy would like to sing for you, then Blanche will join her in a duet."

Pearl, Biddy and Blanche made their way to the Piano. Pearl took her seat, the whole room was silent, Biddy smiled and said, "I would like to sing *The Sweet Nightingale*." It was so lovely, her voice filled the room, everyone cheered and clapped, shouting Bravo! Biddy took a bow and smiled.

Mabel said, "Now, Biddy and Blanche would like to sing a duet, this song is especially dedicated to their dearest and closest friends, Arthur and Jayed Daniels, who are now looking after their pet dogs Jacky and Nelly, who they sadly had to leave behind. A very special mention goes out to their very dear friends, Doreen and Irene Armour. This song is called *My Little Old Log Cabin Down The Lane*, it goes something like this, *Take it away, girls*."

Pearl played the intro; Biddy stood beside Blanche and together they sang this very old song.

I am growing old and feeble now, I cannot work no more. I hope I'll soon be calling to my rest. My husband and my children, they have left this earth short and the spirits now are roaming with the bless.

Things have changed around the place. My friends, they all have gone. Nor will I hear them singing. I refrain now the only friend that's left me, is that good old dog of mine in my little old log cabin down the lane.

There was once a happy time, not very long ago. The neighbours use to gather around the door. They use to sing and dance at night and play the old Banjo. But there'll never play that Banjo anymore.

The Hinges all have rusted, the door has fallen in. The roof lets in the Sunshine and the Rain. Now the only one that's left me, is that good old dog of mine in my little old log cabin down the lane.

"EVERYBODY JOIN US AND SING."

(Now the only dogs we left behind, those good old dogs of ours) "IN THE LITTLE OLD LOG CABIN DOWN THE LANE. 'JACKY and NELLY'."

Everyone stood up and was clapping and clapping and said, "What a moving song that was!"

When the reunion party was over and the relatives started to leave, everyone was saying what a grand evening it had been, wonderful meeting everyone, especially meeting their long-lost cousins, the music and food. As they all slowly started to depart, hugs and kisses were given to each person, saying, "We must all keep in touch." They thanked William and Mabel for arranging this wonderful reunion. The second but last to leave was Pearl, who said she enjoyed playing the piano for them, she loved the songs they sang, "Biddy I would love to come over and play for you again if you will sing for me, deal?"

"Yes, it's a deal Pearl."

"Goodbye and thank you all for such a lovely party, one I shall never forget!"

Last to leave was Garnet, Mama and Alfred thanked Garnet for meeting them and bringing back all their heavy luggage. "It was a real pleasure; when you have settled in, I would like to take you all out and show you around Orillia."

What a kind, charming young man he was, he gave them a hug saying good night folks, see you soon, smiled and left.

Next Mabel showed them around their beautiful home, every room they saw, they said "Wow." The rooms were all large, their dining room was the biggest with a huge dining table with twenty-two chairs. There were two lounge rooms, adjoining the music room, where Biddy could sing to her heart's content. The next room was the library with so many books, it would take one a lifetime to read them.

All the rooms in this house were spacious, beautifully decorated; there were four reception rooms, a huge wide staircase, lovely pictures and paintings hung on the walls, with very fine furniture ideas! Upstairs there were six large bedrooms, plus two smaller single bedrooms with bathrooms. Two bathrooms, each having spacious airing cupboards. Downstairs were two generous size kitchens, between the kitchens were two storage cupboards; there was even a room for washing and drying clothes.

Two bathrooms with toilets, one at each end of the house. Mable took them down some steep steps, turning on a light as she went down into the basement, where they kept all the wines and soft drinks and non-perishable foods. If anyone had told them, they would never have believed it. In Canada, these were necessary because of the amount of staff, some of her family she had to feed at home. Also, the workmen that worked out on the prairies. They worked and lived on their land. The indoor servants and staff lived in the adjoining premises. The workmen had their own sleeping quarters, built well beyond the main House.

After they had been all around this amazing house, they all went outside, onto the lovely veranda. Soon everyone was feeling rather tired, saying goodnight to everyone, Mabel took them to where they would be sleeping. Mabel knew that William and Alfred had a lot to talk about.

Alfred and William, left on their own, said, "Alfred, I think it's time to tell you about father George and how he died. There was a leak in the roof and water was coming into the loft, so instead of getting the builders in, he thought he could tackle it himself. George managed to repair the roof, but as he was coming down the ladder, he missed his footing, slipped and fell, it was fatal, everyone was devastated.

Frances had a very tough time coming to terms with his sudden death. She felt she could not go on without him. Frances caught influenza and died on 12 January 1920. They are both buried in the Union Cemetery Ontario. I will take you to pay your respects when you have settled in."

William stopped talking. Alfred said nothing, he felt too emotional to speak. They silently watched the sun go down in the western sky.

The next day they got up late, unpacked their trunks and suitcases and just walked around the area. They sat in the perfect garden, looking at the beautiful plants and flowers, just relaxing. They needed to do that after their very long sea voyage. That evening when they were gathered together on the terrace, sitting on the garden swing chairs, Alfred and Evelyne gave them their gifts they had brought.

William and Mabel were overwhelmed by the lovely China cruet set and the four framed miniatures that Mama had made for them. They were all taken in India, one was of Mama and Papa, one of us three girls and one of the girls playing with their puppies, Jacky and Nelly. Mabel said, "They were beautiful," and thanked us. "I will get them up on the wall tomorrow," she gave them all a hug and kiss, saying she would keep them forever!

William and Mabel were very hard-working people, they owned the "Combined Harvesters International Corporation." Aunty Mabel was kept busy working most of the day in her office, but she always managed to find time for them, making them feel at home. They all felt that Mabel loved having them around, never neglecting them. She said, "We want you to treat our home like your own with no restrictions," she gave us a bedroom each, which was great!

Papa told the family that he would start looking for their own home; once they were settled here, I want you all to have a good look around this area until you find your bearings. When Alfred and William did manage to have some quiet time together, when all the young ones had gone to bed, they had lots to talk about! Alfred told William while in the army, how he learned to speak Hindi, at the same time learning to smoke a Hookah pipe, how it had started him smoking a pipe, William was intrigued and asked Alfred, "Do you still have your pipe?"

"Sadly No, while we were packing our trunks and suitcases, getting ready to move out of our house in India, I could not find it anywhere, we did a search and thought that one of the servants might have packed my pipe, but when we arrived here in Canada, it was missing. Whatever happened to my lovely wooden pipe, I really don't know. I felt gutted, as it was a lovely carved pipe given to me by my best friend Arthur Daniels, but Evelyne still has the lovely Dressing table set, mirror, brush and comb that Arthur and Jayed brought her."

They talked about their childhood and what fun they used to have together, reminiscing about all the pranks they got up to. "Didn't we get into serious trouble for scrumping apples, do you remember William how Frances locked me in the shed, a lesson for stealing."

"Oh yes, Alfred, I remember it well. I was given a good spanking, then being sent to bed without any supper."

"William, remember old Mr Grumpy, who got us into trouble, just by us kids having a bit of fun?"

"Yes that miserable old man, what a nasty man he was, surely he was a boy once, but maybe his parents were very strict with him and he never had any fun."

"Alfred, I also recall pushing you into the river, I had never seen you so cross with me, 'didn't you get punished' when you so kindly took the blame and got me off the 'hook', so to speak!"

"The worst time, Alfred, was when you fell from the tree."

William then wanted to see how the scar had healed, "Oh! there is still a rather long scar."

"Yes William, it did leave me with a noticeable scar, but I think it's healed quite well considering how bad it was."

"Alfred, I have a question for you, why did you always take the blame for me and our brothers and sister, for our bad demeanour?"

He looked at William and said, "Because you were all the family I had. I being the Eldest stepbrother, I felt it was my duty to take responsibility to protect you all, in any way I could. I loved you all as real blood siblings."

William with a tear in his eye said, "Now I understand, we all loved you too, Alfred. Alfred, when you left the family home in Worcester, that morning Father read us your letter, we were all in shock, we all loved you, each and every one of us. We were all so very sad, not knowing when we were going to see you again. We all missed you, Alfred, you will never know how much. When we eventually emigrated to Canada, life was good, we all liked living in Ontario Canada.

We all settled down here very quickly, we made it a happy loving home and we never looked back. But I would often think about you and hoped one day we would all see you again. Then Frances gave birth to our brother John."

They talked about why Alfred decided to join the Army, he talked about India, the awful uprising, about his war wound and how he met his lovely wife, Evelyne. They talked into the early hours, drank a toast to the old times and went off to bed.

It was quite a full house, they all got on splendidly, but little William Charles who they all called Willie, was the black sheep of the family; he would get up to all kinds of mischief and was always in trouble, he was naughty as well as cheeky, like in the book "Just William." Willie would climb up onto the roof of the house and hide there. Mabel and William were very soft with him and he got away with lots.

He taught his new cousins all kinds of things that they would never dream of doing in India, like climbing trees and swinging from a rope hanging from a tree. Indian girls didn't wear undies, so they were never allowed to play these kinds of tomboy games. Underwear was not worn in India, as it simply wasn't made with wearing sarees, these long dresses, they were not needed. Mama did not like her girls climbing trees anyway, as she was frightened they might fall and get hurt!

One evening, Evelyne was in her room thinking about the letter they had recently received from their friends the Daniels. It said, Dearest Alfred and Evelyne and family. We hope you are all well. Tell the girls that the dogs were still with them and were taken out every day for a long walk. Their daughter Jacqueline was now at school. They were very pleased to tell them that they now have a son called Robert Leonard, who looks just like his father. They had bought a new house in Dinapore Bihar India. It had a very large garden, ideal for the dogs to play in. We hope your new life in Canada is good and that you have settled down. We are both missing you all, please write soon, Lots of Love Jayed, Arthur and family (Jacky and Nelly) Enclosed is a picture of the dogs!

Evelyne wrote back telling them all that had been going on since they had arrived here in Canada. It was midnight when she finally got into her bed.

When Aunty Mabel found out that the girls did not wear undergarments, she took pity on the girls, she said, "Evelyne, why shouldn't the girls have just as much fun as the boys?"

Evelyne agreed with Mabel to go shopping at the first opportunity to buy some underwear and some warm clothing for the winter months ahead. Mabel took Mama out shopping, she showed Evelyne what she bought for her own daughters. "They wear pantaloons and breeches for the summer." So Mama bought several pairs of them, but she wasn't sure that the girls would wear them. If they were up to boys' games, maybe she should rethink as the clothes worn here were very different.

Mabel then gave her advice on what the ladies would most likely wear, for the harsh Canadian winters. There was another undergarment Mama had to buy that was bodices, these acted like a vest that kept their upper bodies together. Agnes and Biddy took to the new undergarment, except Blanche, Mama said, "No underwear then no climbing trees or playing with the boys."

She tested Blanche, every time she went out, Mama would check she was wearing her underwear, not wanting to be left out Blanche obeyed. They would soon be learning to ride horses; so with the cold winter approaching, they would be needing extra warm clothing to keep them warm. One

Saturday, Garnet had kept his word and came to take the family out for the day and show them around Orillia. They all loved the place and had a great day out.

He even treated them all to a lovely meal and said, "I want to see England and some of the world before I settle down. I have not yet met the girl of my dreams, but I do play the field," "as he put it," the girls fell about laughing. When they got back to the house, they were delighted to see Pearl.

"Well, hello everyone," she said, "I am here Biddy to hear you sing again and I will play for you. To seal our deal!"

Biddy sang and Pearl played. They all had a merry evening singing and getting to know one another. Their deal was done! Papa had been searching for many months, looking for a nice house for the family to live in. Papa by chance had a stroke of luck, distant relations of Mabel's had recently moved out to go and live in Boston to be closer to their family. Papa had found their dream home. It was a special home all beautifully decorated, they had left the Knights most of the furniture and fittings, how lucky were they.

Mama went to look at it and felt they had found the perfect home. The house was situated at the back of Aunty Mabel's, on the next street, just around the corner, which would please everyone.

In the Autumn of 1923, the Knights moved into their new home, everyone loved it; they had a big garden, how lucky they were to be so close to the lakes, where they would often sit and walk along the lakeside, watching the birds and swans. They loved this place, the people, the food, life here were what they all hoped for, it could not have been any better. They soon settled into a new lifestyle.

Agnes went off to the local Hospital to finish her Nurse's training course. Blanche went back to school to finish her last year of schooling. When Blanche left school, she went to work in the local Woollen Mills, where she made heaps of friends, liked the work and started to enjoy her independence. Biddy also went back to school, started typing classes, as she wanted to do office work, as well as her normal subjects. Papa brought her a typewriter and she practised every day after school.

Papa wanted to join the Police force, he did apply, but there were no local vacancies. He gave up that idea and ended up working part-time in their local shop, selling sweets, cigarettes and tobacco, which soon became a full-time job. Biddy kept up her singing and would sing at the Catholic Church services on Sundays. Her voice was getting stronger and better than ever!

Sometimes she would entertain the family, neighbours and friends and sing outside on the patio on an evening. Papa was so proud of her, to say that he spoiled her was an understatement. Biddy managed to wear the prettiest of dresses, which Mabel had made by the local dressmaker because finding her petite size was a problem. She always looked immaculate, which could turn heads.

Chapter Sixteen

As the years passed, Mama's health started to get worse, she started to develop other ailments which she tried to hide from them, but they all noticed that things were not right. They all soon became aware that the cold climate did not suit her at all, her legs seem to be giving her more pain. She started to become miserable, sitting in her armchair with her warm knitted shawl wrapped around her, often falling asleep during the day.

Papa was concerned, but she would say, "It's just intermittent dear, not to worry, this cold climate seems to be making the pain worse." Evelyne found that everyday jobs were a real effort and even with Biddy's help, everything she did was a struggle. Agnes was away most of the time working at the Hospital, Blanche would be out with her friends most evenings.

This went on for some time, until one day out of the blue, an official-looking letter arrived addressed to Alfred and William Knight. Alfred marched around to see William and showed him the envelope. William told him to open it, so he did, when they saw it was from a solicitor in London, they both sat down. Alfred began to read the letter. It was a letter informing Alfred and William Knight their grandfather

Thomas Knight and his wife Mary Knight, who had recently passed away, had left them both in their wills, to share their inheritance between themselves, which was to include their house and contents of their former home, also any savings in their bank accounts.

The house was in Yeovil Somerset and they should get in touch with the London solicitor, as soon as possible by letter or person whose names it applied to. They both decided to think about this and talk it over with their wives. Papa was in shock for two days, he was very upset about losing his lovely Grandma Mary. He thought about what he must do and decided to talk to Evelyne about his plan.

Papa talked it over with Mama, telling her about the letter and his intentions were to return to England and claim his inheritance and try to find the whereabouts of his dear mother. Evelyne was more than happy to go and live in England, where the climate would be more to her liking and she readily agreed. Alfred told her that he would very much like to start a business and open up a Cafe and Post Office.

He would run the Post Office with Biddy, while Mama and Blanche could run the Cafe, Alfred would employ two ladies to help them run their business. Evelyne said she would love to help run a small cafe shop with Blanche, she would also help with the cooking and washing up, it would give her some motivation to be active again.

Alfred went over to speak to William to tell him of his family's intentions. "Well, William, what have you decided to do with your share of the inheritance?"

"Alfred, I have talked it over with Mabel and she and I have agreed that when I receive my half of the inheritance, I shall pass my share over to brother Walter, as he needs the money, much more than we do. My business is doing well, I am comfortably well off, so I shall talk to him to see what he has to say!"

"That William, is a very kind gesture, to help brother Walter in his time of need. I think that is so very generous of you."

"So Alfred, what have you decided to do?"

"Well, William, I have talked it over with Evelyne, we shall take our daughters and return to England, partly to take Evelyne, she is unhappy here; the climate is not doing her health any good and giving her more pain in her leg; she wants to go and live in a warmer climate. Evelyne says she is quite happy to live in England. The climate here is much too cold for her, she has been suffering from aches and pains for some time, making her feel very depressed at the moment. I will take Evelyne and the family back to Yeovil Somerset where I was born.

I think the time is right for me to take my family and return home. I would also like to try and locate where my birth mother Amelia is living. I hope she is still alive. It would mean so much to me to see my mother again. With my share of the inheritance, I want to go into business and open up a Cafe and Post Office in Yeovil. I will try to find joint premises, where we will open a Cafe and Post Office next door to each other. Well, William, that is my intention.

My share of the inheritance will hopefully cover the cost of running these two small businesses, Evelyne and Blanche will run the cafe, Biddy and I will run the Post Office. I shall employ two ladies to help in the Cafe, One to help in the kitchen with the cooking and washing up and another lady to help Blanche to serve at the till and to wait on tables."

William was taken back, "Are you sure, that is what you're intending to do Alfred?"

"Quite sure, we will probably not be taking Agnes with us, but I shall give her the option. I think she will want to stay here. Agnes is courting, she told me that she has been dating a gentleman for some time now called Neil, who she met at a friend's party. I also think Agnes will want to stay here in Ontario to carry on her Nursing career. Agnes told me recently that she is about to be promoted to Head Sister."

Papa did not know exactly how much the entire amount would be, after splitting the money two ways, of course, there would be death duties and costs, but it was just the incentive he needed to get him motivated and start thinking about leaving Canada and moving back to England; it was also for Evelyne's sake, she needed to be away from this cold climate.

When Agnes was told, she was furious about the idea at first and said, No way would she be leaving Canada and moving to England, she loved it here and her job, she was just on the verge of being promoted to Head sister in charge. She was also courting a very nice gentleman. Papa said, "I thought you would not want to leave Canada, but I had to give you the choice, you can always visit us whenever you like, but never forget us, my darling, Agnes."

Blanche did not want to leave either, but when Papa said he would probably be opening up a Cafe, Blanche you would be in charge of running it with Mama, but only if you improved your attitude, cheered up and smiled more, "Blanche being in charge of running a café." Oh yes, she was up for that!

Alfred and William agreed to the arrangement, William said he would write to the London Office and ask for his inheritance to be sent by cheque, he had to include all the necessary information and paperwork needed. Also to fill in the forms, which came with the official letter. Alfred also wrote to them to say he was in the process of moving back to England; in the following month, he would visit the London Office, on his arrival back in England, to sign all the Official documentation.

Papa started to make all the arrangements to return to England. Their house was put up for sale, the contents were distributed to family and valuables were sold and anything remaining was given away. He made all the reservations for the voyage. They moved back to William's house until the day of sailing. Any other details William would manage later.

Agnes was willing to move in and live with Mabel and gladly pay them rent until she married, she was soon to become engaged to her boyfriend Neil. The evening before they were due to leave Canada, William and Mabel laid on a farewell dinner party. William and Mabel just invited Agnes and Neil for Dinner, so that Alfred and Evelyne could meet him before leaving Canada. Of course, Alfred, Evelyne and the girls were all anxious to meet him.

The meeting went off quite well, he was polite with a class of distinction about him, but Alfred and Evelyne, both felt the same, they did not feel they wanted to question him about his personal life; his handsome dark looks and piercing blue eyes made them feel a little uneasy. He was introduced to all the family and although he didn't talk much, he did tell the family that he worked for his father as a dealer in diamonds and that his father owned a Jewellery Shop. He gave everyone the impression that his family were extremely wealthy.

He seemed well brought up, with extremely good manners, very smartly dressed and well spoken. There was nothing to dislike about Neil Wilbur. The only thing that Mabel thought about him was that he was a little too reserved; she would have liked him to be a little more open about himself. From what little he said, they all agreed that he would be an ideal partner for Agnes. They all hoped and prayed that Neil would dearly love and care for Agnes, their beautiful daughter, that if she did love him and one day marry Neil, they hoped Agnes and Neil would be a very happy loving couple.

The days before their departure, they had already said their farewell to their many friends and relations and some of their relatives made the long road trip to wish them a safe voyage back to England. Pearl and Garnet came the day before to say their fond farewells, to wish them safe passage, back to England. Pearl said, "Don't be surprised to see me over there, I am hoping to travel and see the world before I settle down!"

William and Mabel helped them pack all their belongings, not many words were spoken as they were all choked up with emotions. It would be a sad goodbye, to this lovely family that they had all grown so fond of. For in their hearts they knew, they may never see them again.

.

Chapter Seventeen
Return to England

On the day of departure, many relatives came to see them off, they would keep in touch, they did have Agnes to keep the families together. The date of departure was 24 May 1925. The crossing would take the ship five days. They were sailing on the "Canadian Pacific Ship" named "MELITA." Departing from Quebec, this was a very emotional day for all their cousins and families, who came to see them off.

Garnet drove them and William to the docks in his large cab. They had come to see them off on their ship. They boarded the ship and they sailed away, many relations had turned up to wave them goodbye. They all waved back, would they ever see these lovely relations again, it was heart-rending as they sailed away from the shore.

The voyage back across the Pacific was wonderful, the sea was calm and the sun shone every day, giving them all a lovely tan colour. Mama, Papa and the girls enjoyed this trip immensely. Mama told the girls, they both have grown into very pretty young ladies, your superiors will address you as such. That made the girls feel like adults, becoming aware of their shapely figures.

Mama let them put her lipstick on, they wanted to buy some of their own. The first thing the girls would do, when they arrived in England, was to buy themselves lipstick. They even started brushing their long hair with a hundred strokes each night, which Mama thought was quite unnecessary.

Now the girls were thinking about maybe meeting their Grandmother Amelia if she was still alive. To see Yeovil where their Papa was born, this was all very exciting, especially running a Cafe and Post Office. Their ship pulled into Southampton docks on 29 May 1925, then they caught the train to Yeovil. Alfred booked them in for a week, staying at the Old Coaching Inn. They all spent a goodnight's sleep there, followed the next morning with a hearty full cooked breakfast.

Directly after breakfast, Papa left to catch the train up to London to claim his inheritance. Everything went smoothly and to his surprise. Once the house was sold, his half of the total amount would be paid directly into his bank account. Alfred went straight to Barclays Bank and opened an account in his name. He returned back to the solicitors and gave them his bank details. Then caught the train home, a very happy man.

The next day he went to look for rented accommodation, just until his grandmother's house was sold. He found a two-bedroom flat which was not very clean, but together they would clean it up, it would do until the house was sold. In the meantime, he would look for two vacant shops together.

After two months, they were lucky enough to find what was perfect, an old-fashioned Sweet Shop with a two-bedroom flat above, next door was an adjoining old Stationary Shop; they were exactly the same in size with two bedrooms upstairs, including a small bathroom a tiny kitchen and a sitting room with dining table and chairs. They would turn the old run-down sweet shop into a Cafe, the shop next door would become The Post Office. Both the shops were in a very run-down state, they had been neglected for a very long time, waiting for someone to buy these premises, to renovate them.

Alfred thought they would be bringing two good businesses back to the Town. The two adjoining shops were situated on the High Street on West Coker Road. Lady Luck was certainly on their side. The owner of these two properties was Mrs J. Mitchell, who they had found out through their neighbours that dear Judy Mitchell was suffering from terminal cancer and became very ill, she was admitted to Hospital where she sadly passed away nearly two years ago.

Judy Mitchell had been married, her husband and eldest son were both killed in a tragic car accident three years ago, when their front tyre burst, the car left the road and hit a tree, they were killed instantly. Judy and her sister Jill were running the two shops at that time. Judy never quite got over the loss of her family. Her younger sister was her only comfort. Jill had been living in Devon when she heard the devastating news that her Brother-in-law and Nephew had been killed. She came back to give Judy comfort; with her support, Jill helped Judy to run the two shops.

She sold her house in Devon and moved back to live with Judy. When Judy died, Jill had already met someone, who she intended to marry. She put the two properties in the hands of the Agents, leaving both properties empty. After she married, she and her husband moved back to Devon. These two properties had been up for Sale for well over a year. It was going to take a lot of hard work to bring these properties up to what was required.

Alfred got in touch with the local builders to transform the two old buildings. When all the work was completed, it was a total transformation, all bright and welcoming, with new fixing and fitting, new tables and chairs, beautiful red and white tablecloths. Evelyne put tiny vases on the table for flowers, giving the Cafe a fresh look. They moved in and all pitched in to do some work upstairs. To paint and update the bedrooms with new beds, wardrobes and dressing tables. Everyone was happy and could not wait to start working. Before they opened the shops, Alfred employed two ladies to work for them in the Cafeteria.

Alfred gave the jobs to Matilda Walker who was 41, she was a very good cook; she had spent six years working as a cook in a West End London Restaurant, until the untimely death of her husband. She then moved back to Yeovil to live with her unmarried daughter Rose Walker. Matilda liked to be called Tilly. The other lady was Jean Gill who was 22. Tilly was a happy soul, she was always smiling and laughing, everyone liked her. Tilly would give Mama a rest and make her sit down during the day, whenever Evelyne looked tired.

Jean Gill was a real fun girl, she would crack jokes and make you laugh, somehow she always seemed to make you feel good about yourself; she also had the knack of making the customers smile, their regular customers liked her warm and friendly personality and would keep coming back.

Jean became very close to Blanche, they became good colleagues and friends. Papa and Biddy ran the Post Office, they also sold newspapers and magazines. They all worked well together, both businesses doing very well. This arrangement worked well for over two years.

On Papa's Sunday off, he would often take the air; while on his walk around the area, he would look for a house, where they could live all together. One bright sunny day, he was walking down "Back Kingston Road" when he saw a sign which said HOUSE FOR SALE, apply at Yeovil Estate Agents. He believed it could be his old family home, he recalled that in the small box room where he slept in his cot, he vaguely remembered there was a loose floorboard, where his Mama kept her savings.

He wondered if it was still hidden there! Could this be the same house where he was born? As all the properties along this road all looked identical. He made some inquiries at the estate agents in town. The manager there was very obliging, he was given the keys to view the property to let the agent know if he wanted to make an offer on this property, he wrote down Alfred Knight's personal details. He said, "Mr Knight I would like the House keys returned to this office by 5 o'clock."

Alfred walked quickly back to the house to view the property. The downstairs was in very good condition, he made his way upstairs to the little box room, to have a look to see if there were any loose floorboards, after lifting the carpet and underlay, sure enough, the old floorboard was still loose, he lifted it up, to his amazement the small wooden box was still there. He knew for certain now, that it was the very home where he was born!

He picked up the small wooden box and opened it, but his heart sunk to find it empty, but he thought the lid felt heavy, taking a closer look inside the lid, was a hidden compartment, under the concealed lid was a beautiful gold locket and chain. He gently opened it, inside were two miniature pictures, a baby on one side and a picture of a beautiful-looking lady on the other. Alfred stared at the pictures for some time, not quite believing who he was looking at.

He turned the locket over, to find his name inscribed in the tiniest of words Alfred Frederick John Knight. 1866. He knew then it was a picture of himself as a baby boy and a picture of his beautiful mother. He stared at the pictures for another few minutes, he was in total shock to find this little treasure. He placed the locket back in the box and put the small box into his jacket's inside pocket, where it would be safe, intending to show his wife when he returned home.

He replaced the underlay and carpet, took another good look around the house, locked up, then left to return to the agent's office. On returning, he put in an offer, which was accepted. Alfred felt more than happy that he would actually be living in this very house, where he was born. It would bring back all the treasured memories, he had kept locked away since he was a very young child.

When he returned home, he could hardly control his excitement, Evelyne took one look at him and said, "Alfred where have you been? I have been anxious, you have been gone all morning and half the afternoon, our Sunday dinner has gone cold, I will have to pop it into the oven and warm it up."

"Well, darling, while you do that, I have some very interesting news for you. Evelyne, you will never guess what, I have just bought a cottage, it's in very good condition. Would you believe that it is the very same cottage where I was born?"

"No Alfred, don't be silly, how can that be possible!"

"Well, you just take a look at this," he took the small wooden box out of his jacket pocket and opened it up; there inside was the gold locket and chain. Alfred put the locket into her hand, as she opened it, the look on her face was mystified.

"Who is this baby and who is this fine-looking lady?"

"Evelyne it's me, yes, it really is me, as a baby and that is my mother."

She looked at Alfred in disbelief, "Really."

"Evelyne darling, just look on the back of the locket," she turned it over and saw the inscription.

"Oh my word, this is unreal, however, did you find it?"

"Darling, let's eat and I will tell you all about how I came to find this little gold treasure. The cottage has been kept in very good condition. It's quite a small cottage and only has two bedrooms, so when you and I are ready to move out of this flat above the Cafe, I will put our flat up for rent. I will let Blanche and Biddy carry on living at the flat above the Post Office, where they have made it their own.

We will be able to move into my parent's old home within two weeks. Of course, we will have to furnish most of the house, but the previous owners have left the carpets and curtains, plus a very nice extending square dining table and six chairs."

"Oh Alfred that's very good news; you my darling, have had a very successful day. I am amazed that you found that the floorboard was still loose, after all these years, what a wonderful surprise."

There was another surprise waiting for Alfred. While Alfred was out on his long Sunday walk, Evelyne was busy getting their Sunday lunch prepared when there was a knock on the front door. Evelyne thought who could be knocking on my door on a Sunday morning? Evelyne went to answer the door, there stood a little old lady, who said, "Good morning, madam, I am a close neighbour, who lives down the road, are you Mrs Knight?"

"Why yes, can I help you."

"Well, Mrs Knight, this letter arrived at my house yesterday. I have been to a few houses this morning and I hope this letter belongs to you; it has my house number, but the wrong name; as you can see."

Evelyne took the envelope in her hand and looked at it. "Yes this is our letter, it is from our daughter who lives in Canada, it is her hand writing. Thank you so very much for taking the trouble and bringing the letter to me."

"That's quite alright, glad to be of service to my neighbours, good day Mrs Knight," Evelyne thanked the lady again and closed the door. Evelyne opened the letter, it read—

Chapter Eighteen

My Dear Mama and Papa,

I am writing to let you know that I am now Mrs Agnes Macmillian Wilbur. Neil and I were married on 4 July 1926 at Our Lady of Hope Catholic Church in Sudbury Ontario. Mabel and William were my witnesses. It was a small Wedding ceremony. Neil has bought a beautiful house overlooking the stunning views of Lake Ontario. We are both very happy to be married and living in our lovely new home. Agnes wrote down her new address. We both send our love to all the family, hoping you are all well. Tell Blanche and Biddy to write to us, sending all our love to you both.

Agnes and Neil xxxx

After Alfred had related his accounts of his morning's events, Evelyne was still in utter surprise. She then took Agnes's letter out of her pocket and said, "Alfred, I have another surprise for you," she handed him the envelope; this letter was delivered by hand this morning by a kindly neighbour, it went to her house by mistake, it has her door number, but with our name on it with a Canadian stamp.

Alfred read the front of the envelope, this looks like Agnes's writing, "Read the letter, dear."

After reading it, he looked at Evelyne and said, "Darling how many more surprises can we take in one day?"

"I think my dear many questions need to be answered, why on earth did Agnes not give us some idea in advance that she was getting married, even though we knew it was going to happen at some time?"

They hoped and prayed that Agnes would be happy with Neil, for the rest of her life. Evelyne was very religious, the children were all brought up to say their prayers every night, she would make sure that her daughters attended church every Sunday for Mass. Her thoughts returned to her daughter and Neil, she wondered if Neil Wilbur was of the Catholic Faith, she really had no idea. Thinking back to their last evening in Canada, there were so many questions that they should have asked Neil when they had the chance.

Agnes being very religious, suddenly crossed Evelyne's mind that Neil might have changed his religion so that Agnes would marry him. Agnes was now 26 years old and they hoped that one day she would give them grandchildren. Apart from what little Neil had told them that his family were in the Diamond trade, little more was said at the Farewell Dinner, they really did not know anything more about his background, they only ever got to meet him once; thinking back to that last evening, most of the conversation was spent talking about Alfred, Evelyne, Blanche and Biddy returning to England to open a cafe and post office.

The evening was cut short because Neil suddenly said they had to leave early as he had to drop Agnes back at the Hospital and that he had a very long drive home. They themselves also needed an early night, as they would all be leaving early in the morning for their long voyage back to England. Evelyne remembered that on that last evening, just as they were retiring to bed, Mabel said to Alfred and Evelyne, "I thought Neil was the perfect gentleman, but he was a very quiet one," they had both agreed. Sadly, would this be the last time they would ever see this loving family again?

This letter from Agnes had come as such a sudden surprise, from their daughter, announcing her marriage to Neil. Evelyne wrote back to Agnes and Neil the very next day.

Dear Agnes and Neil, Papa and I were very surprised to hear that you got married without our knowledge. We would like to wish you both health and happiness. Please send us some pictures of your wedding day.

Agnes darling, it would have been nice to have had an advanced message from you, as your announcement came as quite a surprise to us all. We send our love and wish you both a very long and happy marriage together. Take care of one and other, Lots of love and hugs, Mama and Papa xx P.S.

Papa wanted to know if any of our other relations were invited and if you had any Bridesmaids? Also if you are still working at the Hospital as Head Sister or are you a lady of leisure now? Blanche and Biddy send their love, I have asked them to write to you. xx.

Evelyne posted the letter to Agnes and Neil in Canada that morning. That evening while Alfred and Eveline were sitting talking, she suddenly turned to Alfred and said, "Oh Alfred, I have just had an awful thought, maybe Agnes and Neil did write and tell us about their coming wedding date. I wonder if their letter could have also gone to the wrong address like this one had?"

"Evelyne my darling, we may never know."

Alfred then said, "What little we know of Neil Wilbur, he is now our son-in-law, he gave us both the impression that his family were wealthy. I expect our daughter will now be mixing with the 'well-to-do'."

"Yes Alfred, that could well be true."

The Knights would soon find out!

Chapter Nineteen

It was towards the end of the second year that Biddy and Papa had run the Post Office together. Biddy spent many days thinking about moving on. She was getting tired of sitting behind her counter all day. Biddy wanted to find a more rewarding job, it was time for her to move on. So she made up her mind to tell Papa after Dinner that evening.

After a lot of arguing with her papa, she told him she wanted to spread her wings. "Papa, I am going to apply for a copy typist job at Lysants Aircraft Factory, WESTLANDS SEAPLANES. I will find myself a flat to rent, to be near the Aircraft Factory."

Papa was very disappointed, but he said, "Biddy, I will not stand in your way, but I will need to replace you at the post office? So before you leave, there are three things I would like you to do for me. Firstly, would you sit in while I interview any new applicants. Secondly, I would like your feedback as to who would be the best suited for the job. Lastly my dear, I would like you to kindly train them up before leaving home."

"Of course, Papa, I would gladly do those things for you."

Alfred put a sign outside of the Post Office which read "POST OFFICE PERSON WANTED APPLY WITHIN."

In the following week, they had three people who applied for the job, Alfred interviewed all three, while Biddy sat with him, listening and taking notes. The first to apply was a lady, Anne Grey, who was aged 45, who had worked in a large house as a maid for over fifteen years, who had recently been dismissed because the house had been sold to new owners, where she would not be needed anymore.

Alfred asked her a few questions about herself. Was she in good health? Would she mind sitting at the counter most of the day? There would be a half-hour coffee break in the morning and one hour for lunch. There would also be a tea break in the afternoon for half an hour. All breaks could be spent in his cafe next door. They talked about the hours of work and wages. He told Anne Grey that he would let her know by mail if she had been successful within the next few weeks, as he had more people yet to interview.

The second was a young lad who had just left school, with no qualifications. The boy's name was Jack Thompson, aged sixteen. The questions Alfred asked him were a little different, "Why have you applied for this job, Jack Thompson?"

He answered, "Well sir, when I reach the age of nineteen, I want to join the Army and become a soldier."

Alfred was reminded of the time when he himself wanted to join the Army. Jack went on to say he needed a job until he was old enough to enlist in an Army Career, in the meantime he wanted to learn a skill and to get some job experience behind him, in selling and dealing with customers, talking and meeting other people. Alfred discussed the working conditions, wages and hours. "Thank you, Jack, for applying for this job; we will let you know by post within two weeks if you have been successful. Thank you for your time, Jack Thompson."

"Thank you, Mr Knight."

The third applicant was a young lady, her name was Frances Lane, age 18 who was bright and pleasant to talk to. She had worked in a bank for three years until her kind manager left. He had been replaced by her new manager, who she could not get on with; he was always grumbling and moaning about everything from the weather to the mountain of work, to pains in his back. As soon as she had found another suitable job, she would hand in her notice.

Alfred discussed what the Post Office work entailed, the hours of work and pay, she said, "I live in Wincanton, Mr Knight. I am learning to drive," her mother would drive her to work until she passed her driving test, "this job sounds just what I am looking for, Mr Knight."

"Well, Frances, we will let you know in writing within two weeks if you have been successful." Frances shook hands and thanked him for the interview.

After all three applicants had been interviewed, before leaving they were asked to give their Names and Addresses. They were all told they would hear in writing Mr Knight's decision within the next two weeks. Biddy and Papa spent the rest of the afternoon discussing each of these three applicants. It was a hard choice and after a lot of deliberation, they both agreed that the lady from the bank, Frances Lane, would be the most suitable.

So Biddy typed out a letter offering Frances Lane the Post Office Job. She also typed out letters for Anne Grey and Jack Thompson:

I am very sorry to inform you that you have been unsuccessful this time. But thank you for your time.

Alfred signed the letters Yours faithfully A.F.J. KNIGHT.

Biddy gave Frances a week's training, which was more than they could have asked for. Frances was the ideal Post Office person, dealing with all the postage stamps for British and overseas mail, all types of parcels, postal orders, telegrams, etc. She had a very friendly customer manner. Alfred was now feeling better about Biddy leaving home.

Biddy applied to Lysants Aircraft Factory as a Copy Typist, she was given an interview and was offered the Job. She had long ago passed her touch typing exam with distinction. Biddy started work at the Local Aircraft Factory the following week. Within that week, Biddy started looking for a one-bedroom flat. Biddy did find herself a one-bedroom flat overlooking the main road, it was rather noisy and small, she would look for something more permanent, away from the busy main road, when she knew for sure that she would like her new typing job.

She was given a typing and filing job working in the offices, with an older woman called Joan Duncan. She was pleasant enough, with a strong Scottish accent, but Biddy found her a little bossy. She showed Biddy what she had to do, it was mainly typing letters, using the filing system and ordering Aircraft parts. Biddy liked her new job, plus the pay was very good too.

On her first week, while at lunch in the canteen, she was introduced to her boss's secretary, Angela Barclay. After a week or so they became very good friends, having lunch together and sometimes meeting up with other colleagues after work. She asked Angela if she knew where she could find lodgings, as the flat where she was living was so noisy, with traffic passing by, often waking her up in the night and was far too small. Angela told Biddy that she rented a large two-bedroom flat, she said, "Biddy, if you are willing to share the rent money and any expenses, you are more than welcome to move in with me. I will take you to view my flat tomorrow after work."

Angela took Biddy to have a look round, instantly Biddy agreed, she loved the flat. It was lovely and cosy with plenty of space, away from the noisy traffic. Biddy moved in the following weekend. Biddy was happy living in the flat, she gave Angela half towards the rent, Biddy also offered to pay half towards fuel and food bills. They shared the chores, they were both happy living together, they had a lot in common and became like sisters.

Angela was two years older than Biddy. Angela told Biddy she had a steady boyfriend, his name was Paul Sommerfield. His father Jack was American, his mother Jane was English. They met in Florida U.S.A. while Jane was on holiday with her parents. She was sixteen when she met Jack, he was eighteen, they were staying in the same Hotel.

They saw each other every day spending time together, he even took her on a boat down the EVERGLADES, it was love at first sight. When Jane had to return home with her parents, Jack was living in California with his parents. She would write to Jack, he would return her mail. He wanted to marry her, so he gave up his job and came to England to marry Jane. Paul was their only child, when he was fourteen, this almost breaks my heart to tell you, Paul's Mother was killed in a traffic accident after another car was speeding down the highway went out of control and crashed into hers, both the other driver and his two passengers were all killed.

His Father looked after him until he was sixteen, then Paul started work at Westlands Seaplanes, as an apprentice Engineer, he was happy and settled in. His father, Jack, was so lost without Jane and he told Paul he was thinking of going back to live in California where he had a close family. When his father told him, he wanted to return to America to live, he asked Paul if he wanted to go with him, Paul said, "No father, I am happy to stay here and live in England."

His father Jack returned to America, leaving Paul the House and contents. Angela said, "Paul became an Engineer here at the Aircraft Factory where I met him. Paul and I have been dating for about six months, I love him and he loves me. When we get married, we are going to live in America. So we can be near his father and his stepmother Pamela, who Jack remarried two years later."

Angela could drive and had her own car, she would drive them to and from work. One morning while driving to work, she said to Blanche, "I think it would be a good idea for us to have an evening in the flat together, maybe after work on a Friday. I could cook us a lovely meal, then we could curl up in our cosy flat with a bottle of wine. What do you say?"

"I say it's a brilliant idea, an evening with you Angela, sounds great!"

Angela was also a very good cook. On their first evening together, Angela told Biddy that her parents lived in North Wales and she didn't get to see them, as often as she would have liked. I also have an older brother David, who joined the Merchant Navy, she hadn't seen much of him since leaving school.

"Now that's enough about me Biddy, now tell me all about your childhood growing up in India."

The girls would spend all evening chatting and getting to know each other. They would chat about the past, present and future. Biddy would often sing, Angela loved to hear her sing while accompanying her on her guitar she had learnt to play from her late uncle who had once played in a folk group. Angela was pleased when Biddy told her she was also a Roman Catholic, so every Sunday morning, they would go to Church together. Mama, Papa and Blanche, would meet up with them there. They liked Angela and often invited them around for Sunday lunch.

Biddy made many friends at the factory, Male and Female. One morning she was very busy in the office, covering for Joan Duncan, as she was away for a week's holiday in Scotland. Biddy had twice the workload when there was a knock on her office door and a young man, opened the door, he said, "Sorry to interrupt you. I'm Frank Swaffield, I was sent by my manager to ask you if you could type out these orders, they are important, he would like them ready by this afternoon. I will collect them at about 4 o'clock, if that's OK with you miss, sorry I'm fairly new here, I do not know everybody's name yet."

"Oh that will be fine, Frank. I will have them typed out ready for collection this afternoon, by the way, my name is Ivy, but friends call me Biddy."

"Well, Biddy, I would like to be your friend, so until I see you later bye for now," he smiled at her as he closed the door. Later that afternoon, Frank returned, "Hi Biddy, have you managed to get all that typing done?"

"Yes just about," as she handed him the letters, he said, "Have you worked here very long, Biddy."

Biddy smiled at him and said, "No, I joined the company about six weeks ago, before working here, I spent two years working for my father at the Yeovil Post Office; I wanted a change, so here I am. My colleague Joan Duncan has taken a week's holiday, so I am working all alone this week."

"Well, Biddy, I am training to be a manager with the company, I really like it here; do you live locally, Biddy?"

"Yes I share a flat with Angela Barclay, we live about two miles away, but my parents live in Yeovil."

"Yes I have met Angela, she is my boss's secretary, well, that's a coincidence my parents also live in Yeovil. Biddy, would you like to go out on a date with me sometime?"

She looked at him and smiled, "Yes Frank, I would like that."

"How about going to the Cinema next Saturday, they are showing a film called *Man's Castle*, it stars Spencer Tracy and Loretta Young."

"Sounds great, Frank!"

"Next Saturday then, shall we meet, say about 7 o'clock outside the Cinema."

"Yes Frank, that's fine."

"Gosh, I'd better get back to the office or I'll be getting fired," he said, they both laughed, as he left with a nod and a smile.

Frank Swaffield and Biddy started dating. His parents were neighbours and lived across the street from the Knights, they all became friends. Biddy had been dating Frank for over eight months. They had a lot of fun together. He would often take her to the pictures, to see the latest films. It was seeing all these classic movies that got her thinking that one day she would love to become an actress. Biddy was slowly falling in love with Frank and he returned her love.

Biddy never told her parents about her love for Frank at the time, because of religious differences. She knew her parents would never accept her marrying Frank, as he was Church of England, she knew it was forbidden by the Catholic Church for couples getting married, they had to be of the same faith or they could, of course, change their Religion. Biddy did not want to upset Mama and Papa, also she did not want to lose Frank, who she was in love with. He had already asked her to marry him.

One evening while Angela and Biddy were having their Friday night together, Angela said, "Biddy, I have something I must discuss with you. Paul has asked me to marry him, I have said yes. I will be moving out of this flat shortly, would you like to carry on renting this flat. I will leave you all the furniture, as when I am married we will be living in Paul's own home, would you be happy to carry on living here, Biddy?"

"Oh Angela, that is such good news, I would love to carry on living here. I have had a big increase in wages and I will be just able to pay the rent and live here. As you know Frank has asked me to marry him and we are now secretly engaged; as you are my best friend, I will tell you that I am worried, Frank is not of the Catholic faith and if my parents find out, I know that my father will never agree to me marrying Frank, so I don't know what to do?"

Angela thought for a moment and said, "Biddy if Frank loves you enough, he will change his religion when the time comes, then you could both live in this flat together until you can afford to buy your own house."

"Thank you so much, Angela, you are an Angel, Frank has already said that he's going to ask my father very soon for my hand in Marriage. But I might deter him for the time being."

Biddy told Frank that he should postpone asking her father for her hand, as she knew what her father would say. She tried to explain to Frank that her father would say that they were both still very young, that they should wait a year or two, save their money to buy their own house. We have plenty of time Frank, please don't look so unhappy darling, we are engaged. Frank had bought Biddy a beautiful diamond ring, she only wore it when she was with Frank. They both started saving and opened a joint Bank Account. One day they would own their own property.

One day while Blanche was busy in the Cafe serving lunches, a rough-looking man came in and sat at a table, Blanche went over to serve him, he started chatting saying, "Hello my lovely, what have you got to offer me today?"

He winked at Blanche, being a little shy with strange men, she smiled and said, "Would you like to see our menu, sir?"

"Are you on the menu, my lovely lady?"

Blanche laughed and feeling a little embarrassed, said, "I will fetch the menu for you, sir," and walked away. She went out to the kitchen and said to Jean, "There is a rough-looking young gentleman in the Cafe who is being very cheeky, would you serve him for me."

"Yes that's OK, I know how to deal with this kind of man," when Jean went out with the menu, the man was gone!

A week later Jean was sick and did not come to work, so Blanche had to wait on tables on her own, as it was also Mama's day off. Tilly was alone in the Kitchen, they hoped it wouldn't be too busy. About ten that morning. Blanche was helping in the Kitchen, the cheeky man came in and sat waiting at a table. As Blanche came through into the Cafe, she saw the rough-looking man who had been cheeky to her, seated at the same table, waiting to be served.

Blanche had no option but to serve him, she approached the table and said, "Good morning, sir, would you like to order breakfast?"

"Yes please, I would like to order the full English Breakfast, with Toast Jam and Tea, thank you."

Blanche wrote down what he was having and went into the Kitchen, relieved! When the food was ready, she went to his table to serve his breakfast, he said, "I wish to apologise to you, my dear. I am so very sorry, I was so rude to you the other day, please forgive me, er, what's your name my dear," he smiled gently saying, "I would very much like to take you out, would you come out with me sometime? I will come back next Friday and ask you again, if the answer is no, I shall be very disappointed, but will you please give me an answer, one way or the other. I will return next week for your decision my dear?"

When Blanche came to clear his table, he walked up to the counter to pay his bill. She said, "I do not often give my name to strangers sir, but I will think about what you said, if you must know my name, it's Blanche. I will give you my answer next Friday. May I ask your name, sir?"

"William Hancock, but you can call me Billy. I work on the railways in Yeovil and I live locally, until next Friday, I bid you good day, Blanche."

She watched him as he left the cafe.

Mama was very good at keeping in touch, she would often write to Mabel and William Thomas, keeping them up to date, she also sent mail to India to their dear friends Jayed and Arthur Daniels, who they would never forget! The last time they heard from the Daniels was to say that both dogs were well, their daughter Jacqueline was now doing well at school and Robert will soon be starting the infants class. The dogs are getting old now, but still as adorable as ever, they still love being taken out for their daily walks. Hope all were well and send love. Arthur Jayed and family. Xxx.

The Knights received a very long letter from their Eldest Son Alfie.

Dear Mama and Papa, I have managed to trace you through Mabel and William Thomas, as we have been sending our mail to them. After leaving India two years ago, I have now settled in Le Havre France, where I have met a lovely lady called Louise Beaulieu, we have been courting for the last year, she attends classes learning to sew, Louise is intending to work in design couture, as that is where her interests lay.

We are now engaged and starting to make plans to get married next year. Mama and Papa, Louise would love to meet you and my family and visit England. We would very much like to come for a visit. She is French and speaks very little English, so maybe you can teach her a few English words, while she is there. I have not seen any of my dear family since you all left India, such a long time ago. It will be great to see you all again.

I am sure we will have so much catching up to do and lots to talk about. If it is convenient to visit you and stay for a weekend, please let us know, so we can arrange a date to come over after we hear back from you. This is our new address in France. Looking forward to hearing from you soon. Lots of love Alfie and Louise xxx.

Evelyne and Alfred were over the moon when they read Alfie's letter, they had not received any mail from Alfie since they arrived back in England. Alfie's mail, although far and few between, was still sending his mail to Canada.

Evelyne started writing that very day, saying they would love them to come for a weekend and suggested that they come the last weekend in August. They were so longing to see their son and to meet Louise, his fiancé.

Let us know what time you will arrive on Saturday? I assume you will catch the ferry across the channel, then catch the train to Yeovil, where you can pick up a Cab to us. Looking forward so much to seeing you both, lots of love Mama and Papa xxx.

Blanche had been having trouble sleeping, thinking about whether or not she should go on a date with Billy. If she accepted at least, it would be a night out, she had nothing to lose, so she decided she would accept and go out with him. That's if he ever came back to the Cafe again? She would give him her answer on Friday. She spoke to Jean about this proposed date with Billy.

"Jean, I have never been out with a man before, I am a little nervous."

Jean smiled, "That's quite normal on a first date, Blanche, if you need some advice, after work on Tuesday we can go up to the Old Coaching Inn, there we can have a nice little chat, I will try and give you an idea of what is expected of a girl, on her first date."

So after work on Tuesday, they walked down to the public House, Jean ordered two pints of Ale and placed the Ale's on the table, she sat down, Blanche pulled a face and said, "Jean I have never drunk alcohol," but Jean told her, "You should try it, Blanche, you may even like the taste of it, I find it helps one relax a bit."

Jean honestly did not know quite where to start, because talking about sex was a very delicate subject, as she was not sure if Blanche even knew the facts of life. After a few sips of Ale, Blanche said, "it's not bad, I quite like the taste of Ale."

Jean thought that it might give herself some "Dutch courage" to talk, but she did not want to make Blanche drunk, so she said, "Blanche, you must sip the Ale and make it last as long as you can. The first thing I want to say to you is 'Do not' let this man Billy touch you. Holding hands is fine, but be very careful, as men sometimes only take girls out for their own pleasure, do you know what I mean?"

Blanche frowned and said, "No not really."

"Did your mother ever talk to you about sex education?"

"No Jean, mother would never talk about things like that, but my sister Agnes, who is a nurse, did once tell Biddy and me that when we reach the age of about 13 or onwards, every woman would get her monthly periods and what to do about it. She said it was called ovulation when eggs are formed in the ovaries of a woman. Only after a woman gets married, she can start having a sexual relationship with her husband. I think Mama must have told her to tell us, so we didn't start getting pregnant before marriage."

"Blanche, as your friend, I am going to tell you everything that you should know, going to a Catholic Convent School, where nuns were teaching, didn't help then?"

Blanche slowly shook her head. By the time, they had finished their Ale, Blanche was well informed, as to how she should behave on her first date. She now felt much more confident, she thanked Jean and gave her a hug, "You're the best friend a girl could have. I will take all your good advice, thank you so much for your guidance Jean, I don't feel nervous anymore."

"I hope your date goes well, Blanche and remember what I said, good luck!"

They left the pub happy and went home. Blanche felt good, she had drunk her first Ale. Now she could look forward to her first date with confidence. She could not wait now, to see Billy again.

Chapter Twenty

The Knights were about to receive very bad news from Canada.

My Dear Evelyne and Alfred, I have some very disturbing news about dear Agnes. This will come as a huge shock to you all. I regret to tell you that Agnes and Neil's marriage has turned out to be a total failure. We feel that it is our duty as a family to tell you what has happened and gone devastatingly wrong. We understand that in their short marriage together, Agnes could not carry out her marriage duty, as far as we can gather from Neil, that their marriage was never properly consummated.

He also said that Agnes found that being intimate was not only painful but also sinful. Agnes could not let him love her, as a husband should, with his beloved wife. Neil wrote me a heartfelt letter, telling me that this has been going on for nearly a year until he could no longer take her rejection when wanting to make love. He told me that he would visit me at the weekend to explain everything.

After Neil came to see me, he almost broke down, he said that although he dearly loved Agnes, she did not respond and return the passion he desired from his wife. Telling me that he was becoming a totally frustrated husband. He said he would often find her on her knees constantly praying for forgiveness. If he tried to show her his love, with kindly tenderness or hold her, even console her, he even tried pleading many times, for her to talk to him about her problems, but she would not, she would slowly walk away and say, "I love you Neil, but just leave me be!"

She would then go and have a very hot shower as if to wash away her sins.

Telling me that as her husband, he could not stand being rejected in this way, Mabel, it is becoming too much for me to endure, although in my heart I still love Agnes, but the situation was now becoming unbearable, so the only kind thing he could think of to do was to allow her to go into a Convent to live with the nuns.

He knew the nuns would take good care of Agnes, she would have her own room, where she could pray with or without the nuns. He had to pay the Reverend Mother for her upkeep. Agnes seemed quite happy and content living in the Covent. Neil would visit her once a week, she told Neil that she may take her vows and become a nun herself. Neil then said, *please would you write to Alfred and Evelyne on my behalf and explain everything. I would be very grateful to you. Thank you for seeing me today. He said he would write and keep me up to date. When he left me, we were both feeling so very unset.*

We will be praying for Agnes, I will keep you up to date with Agnes's progress. We will be thinking of you all, sending all our love.

Mabel and William. Xxx

They did hear from Mabel again within the following months. She mentioned that Agnes had settled into the Covent and Neil went to see her regularly every weekend, he said that he was finding Agnes so much happier and relaxed in his company. She told Neil she liked living in the Convent, the nuns took very good care of her, they were all so kind. Agnes spent the next year or so with the nuns. Then things started to change for the worse.

One afternoon Sister Kay told Agnes, Reverend Mother, wanted to see her in her office. Reverend Mother told her kindly to take a seat, she went on, I have to inform you, Agnes Wilbur, that your husband Neil Wilbur is filing for divorce, on the grounds of irretrievable breakdown of marriage in December 1927. Agnes fell apart and went totally to pieces, none of the nuns could console her. Neil was granted a divorce absolute on the grounds of irretrievable breakdown of marriage, in June of 1928.

After Neil Wilbur was granted his divorce, he remarried in July 1928. In 1930, Mr Wilbur and his wife moved away from the area. Mable only ever heard from Neil once after that date. He just told her that he was now divorced from Agnes, that he had remarried and was going to move to Palm Springs California in America. No one ever heard from Neil again. I am so very sorry, but I now have to tell you the saddest news of all.

After Agnes had been told by the Reverend Mother that Neil had grounds for divorce, that she would soon be divorced. Agnes slowly started acting very strangely. One morning after the usual early morning prayers, Agnes had disappeared, none of the sisters had seen her. By lunchtime, Agnes still did not make an appearance. Sister Kay, who had befriended her, Agnes liked Kay; they got on so well together, Kay started to worry about her when she did not turn up for her lunch as they always sat together at meal times and went looking for her, as she just felt something was wrong.

Sister Kay went up to Agnes's room and knocked on her door, calling her name, but there was no answer, she tried the door, but it was locked from the inside. Sister Kay put her ear to the door, she could faintly hear the sound of a shower running. Sister Kay ran to the office and told Reverend Mother, who gave her the duplicate key; on returning, she found Agnes in the shower, running very hot water over her body. Sister Kay had to pull her out, Agnes was red all over.

Things started to get even worse, Agnes would stay on her knees for long periods of time. Although the nuns prayed and tried very hard to help her, the nuns could not manage or be responsible for her very strange unreasonable behaviour. She was at one point refusing to eat her meals. The nuns could not cope when they found her wandering around the convent very late at night, it was time for Mother Superior to have Agnes taken out of the convent and have her put into a care home.

I have to tell you that sweet darling Agnes, is now in a Mental Institution in Whitby cottage Hospital, Ontario Canada. We are both so very sorry, our hearts go out to you all. Poor Agnes, how can this happen to such a kind, generous and loving soul. Maybe to cheer her up, you could all write to her, hopefully, she may even write back. I enclose her forwarding Address. We love you all and miss you. Love to everyone. Mabel William and family. Xxx.

That day Alfred and Evelyne were both heartbroken, for their lovely daughter Agnes, who was always the kindest and caring person, they both fell into a deep depression. They would have to break this sad news to Blanche and Biddy, but they needed a little time to take it all in. They knew that their daughters would both be terribly distressed by this very sad news. But life goes on good or bad.

Evelyne wrote back to Mabel and William:

Dear Mabel and William, We are so sad and shocked to hear, all this about our darling Agnes, saying how distressed they both were, we are very grateful to you; we do understand it could not have been at all easy, having to write about this. We feel sure that God will bless her and make her well again. We will all pray for her. When we see the girls, we will relate this tragic news to them...All our love Alfred and Evelyne. We will all write to Agnes xxxx.

The next letter Evelyne wrote was to their daughter Agnes, but the words were hard to write.

Dear darling Agnes, We are all heartbroken for you, we are so sorry your life has turned out so wretched, remember we all love you dearly, we are praying for you. Be strong, have faith and God will take care of you and make you well again. Time my darling is a good healer. We all hope you soon feel better, please write to us soon, my darling.

We look forward to hearing from you. All our love, Mama, Papa, Blanche and Biddy. xxxxx.

Chapter Twenty-One

Back at the Cafe, the week had gone so quickly and it was Friday afternoon already. Blanche was nervously waiting for Billy to come into the Cafe, which now had a small shopping area, which sold sweets, chocolates, cigarettes and bottled drinks. By late afternoon, Blanche turned to Jean, "I don't think he is coming, we might just as well close the shop for the day."

Blanche was just about to close up when Billy arrived, looking a lot better than he did the last time they had seen him, at least he had a clean shirt on. He walked in, doffed his cap and wished Blanche and Jean a good afternoon, Blanche said, "Billy can I get you a cup of tea, we were just about to close the cafe for the day."

"No that will not be necessary, I am not stopping, I just came in to see what your answer would be, "Is it a Yes or No, Blanche"? Oh I see you are now selling cigarettes, I would like to purchase some if it is not too late."

Jean glanced at Blanche, Jean looked at him, "Yes sir, I will get them for you," off she went to get the cigarettes. Blanche looked at Billy and said, "If my answer is yes Billy, where were you thinking of taking me on this date?"

"Well, I have a free day tomorrow, we could meet outside the cafe at 6 o'clock. We could then get a cab into Wincanton to a nice old Pub called 'Uncle Tom's Cabin's'. The landlord who runs the pub there is so nice and friendly, I visit there often, we could have a lovely meal, where the food is excellent, enjoy a nice long drink and get to know each other a little better."

Blanche answered, "Fine Billy, that sounds nice, yes I would like to go out with you tomorrow evening."

"Excellent I look forward to our date then, Blanche."

Jean casually came over and handed him the cigarettes. "No charge, Billy. They are on the House."

He doffed his cap, "Thank you, kind ladies," saying his goodbyes he walked out the door, looking very pleased with himself. Blanche locked up the Cafe.

As the ladies said good night, Jean said, "Don't forget what I told you Blanche."

"No Jean, I won't."

"I'll see you on Monday, Blanche, It's my weekend off, have a nice time tomorrow evening." Jean walked off home, waving goodbye.

Blanche stood waiting at the Cafe door, precisely at 6 o'clock. Billy came up the road towards her, greeting her, then he took her arm, they walked on down the High street, Blanche making small talk about the lovely weather they were having and that business at the shop was doing well. Billy was most interested in how much money they made each week, but Blanche said, "Well, I have no idea exactly how much the cafe makes, only that father takes care of that side of his two businesses, the cafe and the Post office."

They walked on to the Taxi park, Billy ordered a cab, as it was too far to walk to Wincanton. When they arrived at this very old thatched Pub "Uncle Tom's Cabin," Blanche just loved the wide oak beams, the huge open fireplace, she was in awe of this quaint *olde worlde pub*. After finding a little cosy corner, they sat opposite each other, he said, "What would you like to drink, my dear."

Blanche started to stammer, er, "I'll have 'a' a pint of Ale please."

"Would you like to look at the menu and choose what you would like to eat?"

Blanche picked up the menu, took a quick look, "Oh I don't know, maybe the Steak and Kidney Pie would be nice."

"Right then two pies it is, good choice."

Then the Landlord appeared, "Hello Billy my good fellow, how are you?"

"I'm good, thanks," Billy introduced Blanche, she smiled up at him, as he said, "Hello how are you, I think I know you, haven't I seen you working in the cafe in Yeovil High street, I do believe."

"Yes, you are correct, I run the café."

"I'm very pleased to make your acquaintance, Blanche, I have eaten in your cafe, the food was very good, now what drinks can I get you?"

"We will have two pints of your best Ale and two Steak and Kidney Pies, please landlord."

"I will put your order into the kitchen, I'll bring your drinks to the table, no need to come to the Bar."

He soon returned with two pints of Ale. "The waitress will bring your meals shortly, do have a nice evening." They thanked him and he returned to the Bar, as the place was now starting to get rather busy. Billy told her that Uncle Tom's Cabin went back to 1891 and was reputed to be.

Haunted by a little girl. There have been many strange happenings in the Cellar. Late at night noises could often be heard, things moving about or missing, but when investigated, the cellar door is unlocked by the owner, no one is in there!

"Oh, how intriguing," she replied.

Billy told her that he was born in London Near St Pancras in 1901. His father was once a Jeweller Repairer. "My father sold the business and moved the family to Plymouth, where they now reside. My mother's name is Rose Ellen, father's name is William James, he now works on the docks as an H.M. Dockyard Ship-fitter, I have two brothers, who still live at home."

He went on to tell Blanche that he worked on the Railways as a Locomotive Fireman. "I have worked on the railways since 1916 when I turned fifteen. I am always black and covered in coal dust. I have been doing this job for the last six years. I live in a flat in Overcombe, Templecombe. I have not been home to see my parents for quite a long time."

Blanche then started to talk about her father, serving for his country in the British Army, being posted out to India, then being wounded by a gunshot to his shoulder. It was while he was in hospital that he met my mother Evelyne. She was his nurse and tended his wound until he was able to return to his Army Barracks. While nursing him they got to know each quite well, they kept in touch by letter.

She talked about their very long voyage from India via England to Canada. "My eldest brother, Alfie, joined the Navy and stayed in India, when he retired from the Forces, he moved to France, where he met his girlfriend Louise. When we arrived in Canada, we met all my father's family, we lived with his stepbrother William and his wife Mabel. Father soon found a house of our own. We lived there for three years, with my two sisters Agnes and Ivy in Ontario before returning to England. My sister Agnes stayed in Ontario and married her husband Neil there."

Blanche glanced round, at the big grandfather clock standing in the corner of the pub behind her, before they knew it, the time was 10 o'clock. Blanche said, "Billy, I would like to go home now, as it was getting late and her Mama and Papa would be starting to worry about her."

Billy went back to the bar and spoke to the landlord, "The food was excellent, they both enjoyed their meal. Please landlord, could you order a cab, to take us back to Yeovil."

"Of course, we can Billy, I'll get my assistant barman to do it for you."

"I would like to settle my bill now," Billy paid the bill, leaving a very nice tip. The landlord thanked him and hoped to see them both again soon. They left the pub saying, "Goodnight thanking the Landlord."

The cab was waiting outside. When they arrived back at Blanche's house Billy walked her to her front door. "Will you go out with me Sunday in one week's time, as I shall be working away this Sunday, we could go for a picnic Blanche, if the weather is good?"

"Yes I would like that, I will make up a basket of sandwiches and cake, we'll walk to the park and feed the ducks, what time shall we make it?"

"Shall I call, at say 2 o'clock, Blanche?"

"Yes I must go in now, Papa will get worried, I'll see you in two weeks' time, thank you for a lovely evening, good night, Billy."

"Goodnight Blanche I look forward to our next date," Billy slowly walked away as they parted.

Blanche very quietly opened the front door, then quietly tip-toed up the stairs when her father's harsh voice said "WHAT TIME DO YOU CALL THIS, YOUNG LADY?", stopping abruptly, she turned to face her Papa, "Your Mama and I were starting to get worried about you."

"Oh, I am sorry Papa, to tell you the truth, I have been out on my first date, with a boy named Billy."

"Oh, is that so, well the next time I see Billy, he is going to get a piece of my mind, what sort of gentleman brings his new lady friend home so late? I my dear will be having words with him, Goodnight Blanche."

Blanche went to her room and got into bed, when there was a tap on the door, Mama put her head in and said, "Don't take too much notice of your father, Blanche, he is just trying to be overprotective, father and I have both had a very bad few days, my darling."

Mama walked over to the bed and sat on the edge. Blanche looked at her Mama, then saw the sadness in her eyes, "Mama, please tell me what has happened." With her head looking down, she slowly told Blanche all about Agnes, Blanche burst into tears, "Oh no Mama no!" They cuddled each other, then Blanche, still sobbing, said, "No wonder Papa was so cross with me!"

"I didn't want to tell you about all this very bad news, Blanche, but I knew you would find out sooner or later; we all know that Agnes is strong, she will recover; before we sleep tonight, we will say a prayer for dear Agnes, also remember that time is a good healer, I feel sure, God is on her side. Blanche darling, don't worry about what Papa said, I will talk to him, everything will be fine, you'll see."

"Mama, when are you going to tell Biddy about Agnes?"

"Well, I think the best time will be, Sunday after Mass, together we can break the news to her, you at my side will make it a little easier."

"I love you so much, Mama."

"My darling, Blanche, I dearly love you too sweetheart," Mama was tearful as she said Goodnight Blanche with a hug and a kiss.

Blanche said, "Goodnight Mama."

At breakfast the next morning, Papa was very quiet and Mama was trying to make idle conversation, Blanche looked up at her Mama across the table and Mama winked. Nothing more was said and Blanche helped mama with preparing the Sunday roast lunch. Before they all left for Church. Biddy did not turn up for church that morning, Angela was on her own. She told Evelyne that she was in bed with a chesty cough, so she thought it best to stay at home.

On Monday morning, when Blanche and Mama arrived at the cafe, Jean was already there. She had a few moments with Blanche alone, before opening time, "Blanche, how did your date go Saturday night?"

"Oh it went very well," we seem to have a lot of things to talk about, there was no kissing or anything like that, it was purely platonic. He played the perfect gentleman. "We have a date for next Sunday weather permitting, we are going to have a picnic lunch in the park."

"Well, good for you. Well, Blanche, I have something very important to tell you, please don't be offended by what I am about to say. I've told your Mother and Tilly not to tell you, as I wanted to tell you myself. I am leaving my Job here, I have already handed in my notice. I had to give your father a week's notice so that my last wage packet could be made up with my final pay and notification of leaving the Cafe at the end of the week.

I know now I should have told you, Blanche, that I have a boyfriend called Peter, who works in the Police Force. He is five years older than me. I never mentioned him before, as I did not want you to be envious of me. His family are moving away, down to Cornwall, he is their only son. We have been dating for about six months, I love him and he loves me. Last night he asked me to marry him and I said 'Yes' so together we will be leaving Yeovil next week. We are going to live with his parents until we find a house of our own."

Blanche was speechless, this news was quite a blow, she would be losing a very dear friend and working companion. Once Blanche had taken in the news, she said, "Jean, I will miss you, I am pleased that you have a boyfriend and will be getting married, I wish you all the happiness in the world. I want you to know Jean, this has come as a complete surprise. I really had no idea that you had a boyfriend, you sure kept that a well-hidden secret."

Blanche looked at Jean with a smile and they both laughed. "Jean, please keep in touch and send me your address, I hope you will still come up for a visit sometime."

"Yes, I will write to you Blanche. I wish you all the very best with your new boyfriend Billy, let me know if your relationship with him becomes serious." It would be a sad parting for them both.

The following Sunday, Biddy and Angela walked towards the Church and met Blanche, Mama and Papa. Mama said to Biddy, "How are you feeling now, darling?"

"Yes I am better now, Mama, my cough has all gone."

"That's good to hear. Now Biddy darling, can you meet us alone after Mass? We have something very important to tell you, wait for us outside the church."

Biddy gets the feeling that something is very wrong and becomes rather worried. In Church Angela was sitting waiting, she turned to Biddy as she sat down next to her in the pew and whispered, "I think something is wrong with Mama and Papa, they want to speak to me alone after Mass, I'll see you later back at the flat."

Angela nodded, "that's fine, Biddy, don't worry."

After Church, Mama and Papa and Blanche were waiting outside for Biddy, she looked at them and said, "What have you to tell me Mama, you all look very worried about whatever is wrong?"

"We have some disturbing news to tell you about Agnes; come, we will find that quiet corner of the churchyard where there's a seat, we can sit and talk."

Mama told Biddy about the letter she had received from Aunty Mabel, Blanche held Biddy's hand, Mama explained everything that was in Mabel's letter, Biddy was in total shock, she turned to her Mama with tears in her eyes and said, "Mama if only, she had come back to England with us, this never would have happened. I am totally so deeply sorry for our dear sister Agnes. Why did this have to happen? It's so upsetting, I am so sorry for her Mama, Agnes does not deserve this." With tears in her eyes, she said, "I will write to her, I will try my very best to cheer her up."

"If you can come over to the house now my love, I will give you her address. If you want to stay for lunch, we have a roast dinner prepared at home."

"That will be lovely, Mama, we can sit and have a nice long talk, it has been a while now since I have been back home. I want to hear all about what you have been doing, Blanche."

When they arrived back at the house, Blanche suddenly remembered she had a date with Billy at 2 o'clock. "Oh Mama, I am so sorry, but I totally forgot to tell you, I have a date with Billy at 2 o'clock. Mama, could you keep my roast dinner in the oven for me? I will warm it up when I return home. I promised Billy I would make up a packed lunch, as we are going on a picnic this afternoon. So I will quickly make up some sandwiches now."

Papa tutted and Mama said, "Go ahead dear, there's plenty of bread and cheese, oh and there's some fruit cake in the cupboard I made yesterday. We will have our dinner now; don't worry dear, I will save some for you."

The rest of the family sat down to a perfect Roast Beef and Yorkshire pudding, followed by mama's homemade Apple pie and custard.

Blanche tells Biddy all about her new boyfriend. "His name is Billy, I have only been out with him once, he is not your usual kind of fellow, but he seems very nice and I am attracted to him."

"I was wondering when you might start courting."

Biddy tells them how happy she is at work, that she is dating Frank Swaffield, she said, "Mama, I am having the time of my life, I have made lots of new friends, my social life is great, I must go now as I also have a date tonight. Thank you Mama for the lovely Dinner. I will write to Agnes."

Mama gave Biddy Agnes's address in Canada, she gives them all a hug and kiss and leaves saying, "See you all next Sunday at Church." Not long after Biddy left the house, Billy was knocking at the door. Blanche picked up the picnic basket and shouted, "Goodbye see you later, Mama, for my roast dinner," and she was gone.

Chapter Twenty-Two

Blanche felt so happy, now she had a boyfriend of her own. she was becoming very fond of Billy. She would make the most of going out with him and was starting to enjoy herself. Blanche told Mama later that day, that she had another date with Billy on the following Sunday, "Mama Billy will be calling at the house for me at 5 o'clock, he is taking me to the pictures in Yeovil to see a film. I am so looking forward to it, but I might be home late. Do you think papa will be angry with me if I am late back home again, Mama?"

All Mama said was, "You're a pretty girl, Blanche, Papa worries about you, he thinks that some men may take advantage of you. But you're old enough now to start dating and to mix with nice gentlemen, maybe one day you will meet the perfect man and get married, have lots of children, but you should play the field a little, to see what kind of man would suit you and if you're the kind of girl, that would suit him.

Be careful with men Blanche, never get intimate, kissing is as far as it goes, my love, but have fun, go ahead and have a good time. You're young, you have your whole life ahead of you, all I want is for you to be happy my love, by the way, Blanche, when he comes to call on Sunday, I would like to meet Billy."

Blanche put on her prettiest summer dress and Mama dressed her long hair in plaits with lovely silk yellow ribbons tied up around her head. At 5 o'clock, there was a knock on the front door, Blanche went to open it. He stood there smiling, with two small bunches of flowers, "Hello Billy, I am all ready."

Mama appeared and Blanche introduced them, "I am very pleased to meet you Billy," they shook hands.

Billy gave Mama her flowers, "These are for you, Mrs Knight."

"Thank you, Billy, they are lovely and these are for you Blanche."

"These smell lovely, Billy, I will just go and put these flowers in water."

Mama smiled and said, "Blanche tells me, Billy, that you are taking her to the cinema. What film are you going to see?"

"We are going to the cinema to see the 1927 film called *The Final Extra* starring Marguerite de la Motte and Grant Withers."

As they were leaving, Mama said, "Billy, you take really good care of our daughter, have a lovely evening and enjoy the film."

"Mrs Knight, I will bring your daughter back home hopefully before 9:30, as soon as we can get a cabby home after the film ends. Tomorrow I am moving to my new flat on West Coker Road. I have a friend with a large van, who is going to help me move." Blanche and Billy said, "Cheerio" to Mama, she watched them, as Billy took Blanche's hand as they happily walked down the street, towards the Hire Cabby Service Station.

The next morning a letter arrived from France, from their son Alfie, saying he would be arriving with Louise, his fiancé, the following weekend. They would only be staying with them one night, as he was teaching Louise English, they may find it very hard to understand her language. Papa was so happy when Mama showed him the letter. They must get organised and make up the beds, "Alfred, I want to make their rooms look lovely, ready for their arrival." They would certainly have lots to talk about!

Blanche had a lovely evening at the cinema, Billy brought her an ice cream and after they arrived back, Billy made another date, they would go for another picnic in the park, the following weekend. Blanche was slowly falling in love, as time went by, they started seeing each other every weekend. Their afternoons were spent walking around the lake, feeding the ducks and relaxing in the sun, talking about their past and the future. And going to the pictures to see the latest films.

It was becoming apparent that Billy was a rough and rambling boy, she didn't think her Papa would ever approve of him! It was something about his rough and ready appearance that appealed to her. They kept the dates going. One day soon, she would introduce him to her Papa!

Alfie and Louise arrived and they all got on well. Louise was extremely polite and gracious, but Mama and Papa could not interact much with conversation, so Alfie had to act as interpreter for her. They told Mama and Papa that they had fixed their wedding date and they would be getting married in Le Havre, France on the 30 April next year. They all enjoyed the Roast Chicken dinner and Apple Pie dessert. They then relaxed with a bottle of French Wine that Alfie had brought them.

Alfie started telling his Mama, Papa and Blanche, all about his life in France. He told them that he had opened up a perfume Shop, he said the business was doing very well. Alfred and Evelyne both so enjoyed their company. In the evening, Alfie got out his violin and played for them. After such a busy day, the ladies said they were retiring to bed, Louise said, "BONNE NUIT" while Evelyne just said, "Goodnight all"; Alfie replied "Sweet dreams."

They knew the men had lots to talk about and talked they did, well into the night. They talked about everything that had happened since they had left India. How Alfie stayed in India with the British Navy, until he was 21 years of age. How he had met Louise in France, through his French Navy friend Pierre, Louise was his cousin, who also lived very near. After leaving the Navy, he went to live near his best friend, whose mother was a French teacher.

Alfie wanted to speak fluent French and he was invited to have lessons at their house once a week. He would often take his violin and play for them. Alfred talked about how they had to endure the very long voyage from India via England then on to Canada. He talked about their short few years living in Canada and how they returned to England, as Mother could not endure the cold winter climate there.

Alfie went on to say, "I was very sorry to hear, papa, about the passing of my grandfather George and your stepmother Frances. I regret that I never got to meet them. Papa I must try at some time, to travel over to Canada and meet my long-lost cousins."

Alfred spent a great deal of time talking to Alfie, about Agnes's troubles, Alfie was lost for words, over his sister's troubled marriage to Neil. Alfie could not quite believe that

Agnes was now living in a Catholic Institution in Canada, he then whispered in a very sad voice, "How could this all happen to my lovely kind sweet Sister, Papa?"

Alfred then went on to discuss Blanche's new boyfriend, what I have seen of him I am not keen at all, I have not actually met him yet, but I think he looks a rough rake, not the kind of gentleman I want for my daughter. Then Alfie said, "Father, you must meet him first before you make an assumption about him, you must understand that it's Blanche's choice, let her decide, she may well soon tire of him."

"Oh I do hope so Alfie," he replied. After another glass of wine and a short pause, Alfie said, "Papa I am truly so sorry for Agnes, life on this earth can be hell for the unlucky ones. Maybe Agnes has so much faith, that God will bless her and make her well again."

Alfred just nodded, "I hope to God you are right Alfie!"

Alfred told him how well his business was doing, we have a new lady who replaced Biddy, at the Post Office, she practically runs the office on her own. "Our cafe is also doing very well financially. Biddy is sharing a flat with her work colleague, she loves her job typing in the offices at the Aircraft Factory. She seems very happy."

"Well, that's good to know, Papa." Then Alfred started to yawn, they both knew it was time for bed. "Alfie, just to let you know, Biddy will be in to see you both tomorrow, after Mass."

Alfie and Louise got married in Paris and had a lovely wedding. The service was in a Catholic Church with a French priest taking it. As the service was in French, it was quite hard to understand what was being said. Louise looked amazing, she had four bridesmaids, two were her younger sisters and the other two were close friends. When Alfie asked Pierre to be his best man, he was honoured to do so.

The reception was a grand affair, it was held in a nearby hotel. Only Alfred and Evelyne attended the wedding, but they came back with some lovely pictures. Biddy could not get the time off work, Blanche did not want to go without Billy, as he was working away. He was not really interested in that side of the Knights family anyway. The happy couple spent their honeymoon in the south of France. Alfie and Louise Knight were soon to become parents, they had two children, Evelyn and Philip.

After spending at least three years in the institution, Agnes was now on the mend and she was given her own cottage at the Ontario Hospital, Whitby, where she slowly got better and better, making some close friends. Blanche and Biddy would write to her regularly and Agnes would write back. Biddy went to visit her on several occasions, always returning with the good news about her health and wellbeing.

Biddy and Frank had now been together for over a year. Angela had moved out of the flat months ago. Biddy now had a place to herself, where she could entertain her friends. It was somewhere to go after her evenings out. Frank and Biddy became very close, Biddy was very much in love, but she was saving herself, for when they got married, they were still saving hard. They would sometimes spend all evening talking about their future lives together. Then by the end of the evening, Frank would drive home. By the end of the year, they would have enough money to put down on a house. Then they would get married and have a big Wedding.

After Blanche and Billy's long courtship, Billy one evening, after a few drinks, said to Blanche, "I love you, Blanche, will you do me the honour and marry me and become my wife. I will talk to your father soon and ask him for your hand in marriage."

She said, "I love you too, Billy."

"Yes, I will marry you; now I think it's about time you met my father."

Chapter Twenty-Three

The next evening, Blanche saw Billy, she told him that her Mama had invited him over the following Sunday for dinner at 1 o'clock, so he could meet her Papa for the first time. When Papa met Billy, he was shocked at the sight of him, he was not even wearing a tie or cravat. After a quick formal shake of hands, Alfred did not like the look of him and thought he was not the right man to be courting his daughter. But he then thought about what Alfie had said, that Blanche may soon tire of him, then she would meet a man of some standing and good manners.

Billy turned on the charm with Evelyne and told her it was the best roast beef dinner he had ever had. She thanked him, they all enjoyed a glass or two of wine Mama and Blanche went into the kitchen to wash up and clean away, to give the men some time to talk. Alfred questioned Billy about his job and prospects for the future.

"Have you got a savings account and would you have enough money to live on, if you became unemployed Billy?"

"No sir, I live from week to week, pay my rent and bills; for the time being, I will just carry on with my job working on the railways. Mr Knight, I am a British Rail fireman and I have been working on the railways since leaving school at 15, where I failed my leaving exams, with no qualifications. I am now looking for a new trade or profession, where I don't have to go home hot and sweaty covered in coal dust every day. Maybe I could learn to be a Train Driver or Signalman. At present, I am working as a railway stoker."

Maybe Billy was thinking and hoping that when Alfred retired, he would leave him his shop/cafe business or even perhaps after he was married to his daughter.

Alfred did not get on well with Billy, there was tension between them. After they had another glass of wine, Billy then took the initiative and Boldly asked Alfred for his daughter's hand in marriage. Alfred was adamant and said positively, "No Billy, you are not worthy of my daughter's hand in marriage."

Billy then lost his temper, he said something detrimental and stormed out of the house, slamming the front door behind him. He was so full of mental hurt and anger, he made his way to the local pub. There he drank several pints of Ale. He then stormed down to the Cafe, by this time he was very drunk, he staggered around to the back of the Cafe, threw a brick breaking the window, got inside and did some damage to the interior of the Cafe.

He staggered back towards Blanche's home, stopping when he saw Blanche running down the road towards him, he was in a very bad way. He broke down on his knees, telling her what he had done and why, he then told her what her father had said to him. He begged her forgiveness, he said, "I have been drinking, I was trying to drown out the hurt and anger I felt for your father. I wanted to take my vengeance out on him."

Blanche told him, "Billy, you must now come back to the house and confess," which he did not want to do, but she begged him saying, "Billy if you truly love me, you must do this one thing for me."

"I do love you, Blanche, so I will confess to your father what I have done tonight."

Her father was in shock and because Billy and Blanche were in tears, Billy said Mr Knight I have done a dreadful thing tonight, after he had admitted what he had done, he said he would pay for any damage to the Cafe, that he was truly sorry as he was drunk and angry. He pleaded and said, "Mr Knight, please do not call the police."

Alfred told him to go home and he would speak to him another day. Alfred then began to feel guilty about the whole incident, he would try to make some changes. He would sleep on it! Early the next morning Alfred went down to the Cafe to see what damage Billy had done. It was not as bad as he had thought, one broken window, two broken chairs and a few smashed ashtrays over the floor. He closed the shop for a few days, he ordered two new chairs and a new window pane, by the end of the week all was good, he then reopened the shop for business.

Against Alfred's word, because they loved each other so much, they decided that they would go ahead and make their own Wedding arrangements between themselves. Blanche told her Mama about their intentions, who then told Blanche that she wanted to meet up with Billy in "Uncle Tom's Cabin" in Wincanton at 7 o'clock on Saturday evening. It was important that she speak with him.

When Evelyne and Blanche arrived at the Pub, Billy was in there anxiously waiting. Billy got up and greeted Evelyne and said, "It's lovely to see you, Mrs Knight, what would you like to drink," he ordered three soft drinks at the bar and they sat down to talk.

Evelyne said, "Look, Billy, I don't object to you marrying Blanche, but there is one thing that might change Alfred's mind and give you both his blessing, it would also make me happy."

"What is that, Mrs Knight?"

"Billy you are of the wrong religion, I believe you are Church of England, now if you were to change your religion to Roman Catholic and marry in the Catholic Church, he would not object to you marrying our daughter."

"Firstly Mrs Knight, I would like to say how very sorry I am for what damage I did to the Cafe. I was so angry and unhappy that I lost my temper and I took it out on Alfred's Cafe. How much do I owe Alfred for the repairs?"

"Do not worry about that, it has all been taken care of, Mr Knight said he was sorry too, he told me he was out of line, the way he spoke to you. Let's forget all about this, put it behind us and move on."

"Thank you so much, Mrs Knight, you are very kind, please thank Mr Knight, I am so glad you have both forgiven me."

Billy looked at Blanche and said, "Mrs Knight I would gladly become a Roman Catholic and practice your religious beliefs if you and Mr Knight agree to give us your blessings."

Evelyne stood up and said to Billy, "I will do my best, I shall speak to my husband tonight, I shall give you his answer tomorrow." Blanche and Mama said Good night to Billy. Blanche with Mama caught a cab home in silence. When they arrived home, Alfred was hungry and waiting for his supper,

"Where have you been, my dear, I didn't know you were going out?"

"Alfred, first I will just get the supper ready, I will discuss an important matter with you later."

After they have eaten and cleared away, Blanche says, "Mama, if you want me, I am going up to my room to finish reading my book *Daughter of a soldier*."

"OK darling, I'll bring you up a nightcap later."

Blanche lays on the bed picks up her book then puts it back down, she lays back and starts thinking about her future life with Billy.

Alfred sat in his favourite chair, Evelyne settled herself down beside him. "Alfred dear, I need to speak with you."

"If it's about Blanche and Billy, well out with it dear, let's hear what you have to say."

"Well, I went to speak with Billy tonight, Billy wanted to pay for the damage he caused to the café. I told him what you said. He was so truly sorry and wanted to thank you, he is so very grateful that you have forgiven him."

"I have asked Billy to change his religion, of course, I assumed he was from the Church of England. I asked him if he would change his faith to become a Roman Catholic."

"That's if he has any faith at all, Evelyne."

"Now, Alfred, there is no need for your sarcastic remark, is there? Billy dearly loves Blanche and Blanche loves Billy, they are intent on getting married. Blanche says she is old enough to make up her own mind and she will marry, with or without your consent. So Alfred please tell me, if Billy agrees to change his religion, will you give them your blessing?"

He was silent for a few minutes, then he said, "It seems to me, Blanche, I don't have a choice, if she is intent on marrying him anyway, then I will with reluctance give them my blessing, 'Matter Closed'."

"Now go and tell Blanche they have our blessing and to go ahead and make plans for the wedding day, at the local Catholic Church, but only when he changes his religion."

Mama took Blanche a mug of hot chocolate and told her the good news. That night everyone had a good night's sleep. When he saw Blanche the following morning at breakfast, he said, "Blanche, if you are serious about marrying William James Hancock, then Mama and I will give you our blessings, you may go ahead and get married, but remember this Blanche, if you take your Holy Vows, by the Catholic faith, you must follow them. So remember this (for better or worse), you make your bed, you must lie on it."

When Biddy next came for a visit to see the family, Blanche told her the news, "Biddy, Billy has asked me to marry him, I have said yes." She showed Biddy her engagement ring. "Billy and I have planned to get Married next March. That will give us all plenty of time to organise the Wedding, to write and send out all the invitations, Billy will soon be converting to the Roman Catholic Faith. When Billy became a Catholic, Mama and Blanche started to make arrangements for the wedding, they booked the Catholic Church and the place for the wedding reception, which would be held in "Horse and Coaches Hotel."

Billy wanted to hold the reception in the Cafe, Blanche said, "Don't be silly, Billy, it would be far too small to seat all our guests."

Biddy was so happy for her, "Blanche, I will help you in any way I can." She gave her a huge hug and said "Biddy, would it be at all possible for you to bring Agnes over from

Canada to England for my Wedding. I would dearly love you both to be my Bridesmaids. It would make me the happiest bride ever, to see Agnes again. How wonderful it would be to have both my sisters attend me on my Wedding day! Biddy, do you think there is any possibility that Agnes could be here for my wedding? Would you be prepared to fly out to Canada and bring her back to England for my special day and see her off, on her return flight back to Canada?"

"Yes Blanche, I think that could be arranged, but I would have to write to Agnes first, to see if she is fit and able to make the long journey here Blanche."

"Oh Biddy, could you do that for me, darling."

"No problem Blanche, I will write to Agnes tomorrow. The good news is, the last letter I received from Agnes was to say, she was now living in a tiny cottage on the Hospital grounds, where she could run a semi-independent life. Saying that she was very happy as there were many cottages, she had already made lots of friends. One special friend called Susan Whynot lives in the cottage next door. They spend a lot of time together, Shopping and playing tennis, board games, Cards and weekly quiz nights. I will write and ask Agnes if she would like to be your Maid of Honour at your Wedding. On Saturday, 10 March 1928. If Agnes agrees to come, I will book the flights."

"Oh Biddy, I love you dearly, how can I ever thank you enough."

They give each other a big hug. A week later, Biddy received a letter from Agnes.

My dearest Biddy, I would be honoured to be a Maid of Honour at Blanche and William's Wedding. It will be wonderful to see Mama and Papa and dearest Blanche after all this time and you again, my little sister Biddy. Biddy if you would kindly meet me at London Heathrow Airport, a week before Blanche's Wedding day, I will book the flights from Canada, I will let you know the times of arrival and dates. Biddy, I am well now and I am quite happy and able to travel to England alone if, of course, I get permission from my own hospital doctor. It would save you all the trouble of the long flights both ways. I will write and confirm the outcome, love Agnes xx.

Two weeks later, Biddy received the letter she had been waiting for, Agnes would be flying into London Heathrow Airport on 4 March at 11:55 a.m. She wrote:

I cannot tell you how excited I am, I got the full permission I needed from my doctor to fly to England. I do not have to worry about travelling to the Airport.

My best friend Susan's father, Mr Whynot helped me to obtain a passport, he is a police officer in the Toronto police force. He is married with two other daughters, Susan is the eldest. He is a very nice gentleman. He told me he would be quite happy to drive me with Susan to Toronto Airport, to see me off. They would both meet me on my return flight and drive me back to the Cottage Hospital. I am so looking forward to meeting you, Biddy, at Heathrow Airport. If there are any problems please let me know. All my love hugs and kisses to everyone, your loving sister Agnes xxx.

In the following month, all the arrangements had been made, all the Invitations had been sent out. Blanche received the wonderful news that when Agnes arrived in London, she would be staying with Biddy at her London flat in Curzon

Street. Biddy was having both their bridesmaid dresses made, she had also ordered the Wedding cake to be made by a local baker she knew. The cake would be sent to "The Horse and Coaches Hotel" Yeovil, the day before the Wedding.

While Agnes was staying with Biddy in her flat, she took her to see the sights of London. They visited the Tower of London, St Paul's Cathedral, Buckingham Palace and Biddy took Agnes on a boat trip down the Thames. They went and did some shopping in Oxford Street and enjoyed a trip on an open-air bus. They dined in the finest restaurants. She took her to the RITZ for afternoon Tea. Agnes was so happy to be reunited with her younger sister again. They had so much reminiscing to do.

Chapter Twenty-Four

It would not be long until the wedding day when Biddy would drive them down to Yeovil. Two sisters wearing beautiful bridesmaid outfits. Agnes was so looking forward to being her sister Blanche's maid of honour. Soon the big day arrived. On 10 March 1928, Evelyne was so proud to see her beautiful daughter walk down the aisle on the arm of her father Alfred John Knight to give his daughter away. Their best man was her brother Alfie Knight.

William James Dicker Hancock married Blanche Emily Constance Millicent Knight, as they took their vows at the altar, in the Holy Ghost, Catholic Church Yeovil, Somerset. Her sisters Agnes and Biddy looked lovely in their cream lace dresses, Agnes was maid of honour, Blanche was the happiest she has ever been. Her best friend Jean and her husband Peter Lewis were there, they had travelled up from Cornwall. Tilly and her daughter Rose were also invited. Angela and her husband Paul Sommerfield just managed to make the wedding. They had booked their flights and would be flying off to live in America in a week's time. They did not stop long at the reception, but they gave the bride and groom a lovely wedding present of His and Hers towels and a beautiful China teaset and wished them both a very happy life together.

Alfie and his wife Louise came with their two young children Evelyn and Philip. They had travelled over on the early morning ferry from Le Havre. Billy's parents, his mother Rose Ellen and father William James and his brother Sidney travelled up from Plymouth. Their close friends and neighbours Mr and Mrs Swaffield also attended the wedding. The wedding was everything Blanche could wish for. She was over the moon to see her sister Agnes again after all this time. She did spend what time she could with her, but she had so many other guests to talk to. They did manage to get some time together after the amazing reception when most of the guests had gone home.

It was the happiest day of Blanche's life, everyone she had ever loved or respected, all her best friends were there to see her, to wish her and her husband a long and healthy happy life together. The food was excellent. Lots of champagne was drunk, pictures were taken, the weather was good and the sun came out. While the close family were outside, the last pictures of the bride and groom had been taken. Alfred noticed that Blanche's face looked slightly swollen, he didn't mention it, he just thought she must have knocked herself while getting ready. When he got home that night, he asked, "Evelyne, did you notice that Blanche's face was very slightly swollen?"

She said, "No Alfred, I did not notice, I thought our daughter looked beautiful. Anyway darling, she was wearing her wedding hat."

Alfred said no more, it was very late and they went to bed. Biddy drove Agnes back to Heathrow Airport to see her off to Canada the following day. It was a sad parting, Agnes promised she would keep in touch.

For the first six months of marriage, things were good, but when Billy started drinking again, he would sometimes come home drunk and disorderly. Blanche would get cross with him. They would go off to bed arguing, then he would say sorry to Blanche and they would make it up. When Blanche found out she thought she may be pregnant, she never told Billy, as she wanted to be sure. Billy came home drunk one Friday night after visiting the Pub, he had been paid and he would often spend a great deal of his weekly wages, on booze and cigarettes.

Blanche never said anything about being pregnant, until he started to abuse her, she cried out, "Don't hit me, Billy, please don't hit me, I think I am pregnant."

That night Blanche had a miscarriage. Billy comforted her saying, "You should have told me earlier, Blanche, I am so truly sorry, I will stop drinking and this will never happen again." She loved him so much that she soon forgave him.

"Blanche darling, please don't tell your mama and papa about the miscarriage. It will only upset them, we will try again for another baby and everything will be fine, I promise you that, my darling Blanche."

Blanche was still not over the loss of her first unborn child. One week later Biddy was visiting Blanche, she noticed that Blanche was looking a bit pale, so she asked her if she was feeling unwell. She broke down and confided in her sister, telling her that she had recently miscarried, she never told Biddy that she had been abused by Billy. All Biddy said was, "Blanche, I have heard many mothers miscarry their first pregnancy, take heart, next time will be fine, I'm sure."

"Please do not tell Mama and Papa."

Biddy gave her a huge hug. "Don't worry, cheer up Blanche, I will not tell anyone trust me, I will be back to see you very soon goodbye Blanche."

Biddy had her own troubles. She was slowly falling out of love with Frank, she carried on going out with him, she just could not break his heart, He was so loving and kind to her. So she continued their relationship.

By the end of March 1929, Blanche was pregnant again. On 29 December 1929, Blanche gave birth to a healthy girl, who they named Eveline Rose, she was a very bonny baby. They were still living in Billy's rented accommodation in Overcombe Templecombe. After a year, the flat was becoming just too small for them and baby Eveline, so in 1930 they moved to Wincanton, five miles up the road, to a shared house, then moved to Tunbridge Wells Kent from 1933–1934. They moved again to Morning Street in Lewes, East Sussex. They moved yet again to Grange Road in Lewes.

After four years or so, Alfred decided it was time to sell the post office and cafe shop, move out of the cottage and buy a house. They moved to Station Road Andover, where he opened a small sweet shop. Tilly was offered the job if she was willing to serve behind the counter, but she declined the offer, as she wanted to take early retirement. So Alfred served behind the counter on his own. He employed a housekeeper called Eithel Williams, as Evelyne was finding it hard to manage now. They lived there for about a year, then sold the house and sweet shop. They then moved to a very nice house in Cell Barnes Lane Andover. Alfred would never dream of passing the business over to his son-in-law Billy Hancock. He never approved of him and could never trust him.

The next five years passed very quickly and Eveline would soon be starting school. Eveline spent a lot of her early years with her beloved grandma and grandpa, Alfred would often take her out for walks, to feed the ducks at the nearby pond. In summer, he would buy her ice creams. He looked after her well as he knew she was not getting the love and attention from her parents and felt she was not being treated well by her father. Grandpa was lovely to her, he started to keep bees for a while, Eveline was at her happiest when she was with them, away from her parents. He would read to her and grandma would let her watch her make cakes, she would let Eveline cover them with coloured icing. Eveline and grandpa would sit outside and enjoy her iced fairy cakes and drink grandma's homemade lemonade.

One day Biddy found she was pregnant, she never told anyone, although she was still secretly engaged to Frank, they had put their years' savings into one bank account, so they could put down a deposit, to buy their own home. But being pregnant was not what Biddy had planned or wanted. She knew she did not love Frank anymore and wanted her freedom and her independence, she could never marry Frank. He was not a Roman Catholic and her parents would never have agreed to her marriage anyway, especially as she had sinned being pregnant before marriage.

This situation needed a lot of consideration, Biddy asked herself the question: Could she marry Frank even for the sake of her unborn child? The answer was clear in her mind, No, she did not love Frank anymore, she could never marry him now. But what was she going to do in her situation being pregnant? What would her only options be? Biddy would have to give this very serious thought. A sudden idea crossed her mind, Biddy could go and talk to Blanche and ask her to bring up her baby when it was born. No, surely that would be too much to ask of any married sister. Biddy would give this serious matter a lot more thought.

This of course would be a solution to Blanche and William's worrying problems. She would find them a house with more space, which would have a garden, Eveline would have a baby brother or sister and a garden to play in. The house would have three bedrooms, they would all have a decent living space. It was no life for Blanche or Eveline living in such a very small shared house with only the two bedrooms, without a garden. She would give this idea of hers a whole lot more thought, as she still had time on her side.

In the meantime, Biddy would visit her brother Alfie in France, she would tell him she wanted to visit and spend a holiday with them, she told them she would like to learn to speak French. Biddy wrote to Alfie and Louise, asking them if she could stay to have a short holiday with them. They wrote back and said they would be delighted to have her stay, for as long as she wanted. They had lots of room and yes they could teach her French. Biddy told the rest of the family that she was taking a holiday to France, she was going to visit brother Alfie and sister-in-law Louise in Le Havre. She would be away for some time, as she wanted to learn to speak French. Within a week, she was on her way, on board a ferry boat to Le Havre. Alfie was there to meet her, then he drove her to his beautiful home.

While Biddy was in France, she started to get lessons in French from Louise. One morning the first signs of the morning sickness had started, Biddy just told Louise that she had this problem with her tummy since being on the long sea voyage, from India to Canada, but she said "not to worry it didn't last long." It soon stopped and nothing more was said.

Alfie was kept busy running his perfume Business and Louise made and sold her designer clothes. They employed a nanny to look after the children, Louise had an extra-large room, where she made and designed clothing. They were both kept very busy, during the day.

One hot sunny weekend, Louise suggested they go down to the beach for some swimming and sunbathing. Louise gave her a lovely designer swimming costume to wear, it was yellow with gold trimmings and suited her. She thanked Louise and wore it on the beach. Louise noticed that Biddy was getting a flat stomach, then it clicked that she must be pregnant. That evening when they were alone, Louise casually asked her if she was pregnant, Biddy looked at her in dismay. "Please do not tell my brother or anyone about this, Louise, yes I am in the family way."

"Who is the father of your child, is it Frank your boyfriend, that I heard you were going out with."

"Louise, to tell you the truth, I was secretly engaged to my boyfriend Frank for over a year, but I recently wrote to him, breaking off our engagement. We were so young, he was only eighteen and I was only seventeen. We were only teenagers, he was the only boyfriend I have ever had. I thought that I really did love Frank then, But I realise now I do not love Frank anymore. I will go and see him in person when I return home and give him back his engagement ring. I want to become a singer and dancer and try my luck at becoming an actress. I am going up to London to join the Chorus of a West End Nightclub. I want to make a new life for myself. I will never divulge or disclose to anyone, who the Father of my child is. I honestly do not know where to turn. Please help me, give me your advice, Louise."

"Biddy, I think you should go back to England and think about the baby's future. The baby needs a father and mother. It is your life, you must do what is best for your unborn child. You say you do not love this man called Frank, I expect Frank is still in love with you, Biddy, you loved him enough once to become engaged to Frank, so you could maybe reconsider, I am sure he would marry you even though you are pregnant."

"No never, I do not love Frank anymore, I could never spend the rest of my life with him, even if I was not in the family way. I have been giving my situation a lot of thought lately, I would dearly like your advice on what I have in mind, this information is for your ears only. Louise, this is only between you and me, this is what I had in mind, I will tell you only if you swear on the Holy Bible and promise faithfully that you will not disclose this information to anyone, not even Alfie! I will tell you my deepest thoughts."

Louise found a small Bible, with her hand on the Bible, she promised and swore not to tell anyone. Then Biddy slowly told her what she was preparing to do. "I will go and see Blanche and Billy, explain my situation and ask them if they would be prepared to adopt my unborn child."

Louise was lost for words and sat silently thinking, "Well, Biddy dear, the way I see this difficult situation is, you have two options: To ask Blanche and Billy, if they will take your baby when it is born and bring it up as their own or your other option is, to have the baby adopted and the baby be taken to an orphanage. I do realise that it is a very hard decision for you to make Biddy darling. Well, that's my advice, I just wish you all the luck in the world and I will pray that whatever you decide to do, everything will turn out for the best, for you and your unborn baby, Biddy."

"Thank you so much for your advice, I will seriously think about what you have said Louise." She gave Louise a hug and after a few more days, Biddy left France and returned to England.

Biddy gave herself time to think about what she was going to do. Once she had made up her mind, she got in her car and drove to see Blanche and Billy. When Blanche opened the door, it was a real surprise to see Biddy, looking tanned and rather bigger, "Hello Biddy darling, did you have a good holiday in France, with Alfie and Louise?"

Blanche gave her sister a big hug. "How have things been with you and Billy, Papa told me how he likes a drink or two, has he stopped drinking now?"

"Yes, things have been good between us, he has stopped drinking and we are both getting on really well and both happy at last."

"My, Biddy, you have put on a little weight since I last saw you, the food must have been so good in France."

Biddy gave Blanche a worried look. "Yes the food was great, I had a very good holiday, a nice rest, learned a little French, the weather was perfect, warm and sunny."

"That's good, you needed a holiday after working long hours at the Aircraft Factory."

"Blanche, I must have a very serious talk with you and Billy, is he at home? This is of the utmost importance."

Frowning, Blanche said, "Yes Biddy, he is lying down having an afternoon rest, I will go and wake him up." When they were all sitting together, Biddy told them all about her unwanted pregnancy, she told them straight that she did not want to keep this unborn child. After hearing about her sister's pregnancy, it came as quite a shock to Blanche.

Biddy went on, "If Mama and Papa found out, I had got myself in this condition, out of wedlock, she would never forgive me, I am sure Mama would say, 'I brought you all up to be good Catholics and you have let me down.' After committing a sin like this, she would probably never speak to me again! Even so, I will never marry the father of this unborn child. I do not love him, I have no more to say about the father, except I will never ever disclose to anyone the father's name to my unborn child."

Blanche felt so sorry for her sister and said, "Yes Biddy, I think you could be right, Mama would probably never forgive you."

Then Biddy told them what she had planned. "There is no need for Mama and Papa to ever know about this."

After hearing what Biddy had to say, they both fell silent for a few moments, Blanche looked at Biddy, "Are you absolutely positive you want Billy and me to have your baby, to bring up your child as our own?"

"Oh Blanche, I have never been more positive in my life, I only want what's best for my unborn child."

Blanche said, "I thought you were engaged to Frank Swaffield, is he the father of your baby?"

"Oh Blanche I finished with Frank a long while ago, I found out I did not love him after all, I was so young when Frank and I were secretly engaged. I wrote to Frank months ago, breaking off our engagement. I shall be going to see him after the birth, to give him back his engagement ring, as I have not yet had an answer from him."

"Biddy, did Frank know about your pregnancy?"

"No, I swear to you now, he knew nothing about my pregnancy. If you will both go along with my plan, I will give you all the financial support and guidance you need. I will find you a house with a garden, so you can move out of this shared two-bedroomed home. It will be a weekly rent but do not get into any arrears, your rent will be very little, which you will be able to afford. What do you think, Billy, would you and Blanche be prepared to bring up and support my child?"

Billy looked her in the eye, "What is this plan of yours, Biddy?"

She then explained to them what was on her mind. "When the time comes to give birth, I will book into Southlands the Workhouse Hospital in 2 Upper Shoreham Road, Kingston-by-Sea. After giving birth, at the hospital, under your name Mrs Blanche Hancock as mother, giving your name Mr William Hancock as the father. I will find a nearby flat for you to live in after I am discharged from the hospital, I will drive to the flat, I have seen one up for rent, it's Flat 1a Albion Street Lewis, I will make the necessary arrangements. I will come straight to the flat with the new-born baby. I will give my new-born baby to you, dearest Blanche, for you both to nurture and love, to bring up the baby as your own child for as long as you are both husband and wife.

"Billy, I will expect you to totally support the child, with lots of love and affection. I promise I will support you both, in any way I can. I hope this unborn child brings you joy and happiness as a family. It could be a brother or sister for Eveline. I will give you both time to think about this very serious situation. I will return in a week's time, to see what your answer will be."

"Yes Biddy, Blanche and I will need time to think about this and to discuss this delicate, serious situation. We will give this a lot of thought, we will have a definite answer for you next week, Biddy." Biddy left, leaving everyone in deep thought. What would their answer be?

After a worried week, Biddy returned to find out what their answer would be.

Together they were both in total agreement, Billy then told Biddy, "We have given this matter a lot of thought, we have both made our final decision; Blanche and I are both willing to bring this new-born as our own child, it will be lovely for Eveline to have a baby brother or sister. We will go along with your plan and we are looking forward to holding our new baby."

"Oh, thank you both so very much, you have taken a great burden off my shoulders, I will always be eternally grateful to you both. If you don't object, I would like the child to be christened in the Catholic Church, I want to attend the christening. Now, I would like you both to keep this our secret and that nobody else in the family will ever know."

"Biddy darling, you have our word."

Biddy went ahead and bought herself a house in Sussex; she wanted to live nearby in case there were any unforeseen circumstances. She would just wait until after the christening. In the meantime, she found a flat, not far from Southlands Hospital, where the Hancocks could live until after the birth, in Albion Street Lewes, which was not far away from the hospital where Biddy would give birth.

Chapter Twenty-Five

Biddy was admitted on 4 March and gave birth to a healthy boy on 26 March 1936, at Southlands Workhouse Hospital, 2 Upper Shoreham Road, Shoreham-By-Sea, West Sussex. Biddy was discharged on 9 April 1936. Everything had gone according to plan. After the birth, Biddy drove to 1a Albion Street with her newly born baby boy. Biddy was now driving her own Bugatti car. Biddy gave Blanche her new-born baby boy, she gave Blanche all the necessary things she would need for baby Michael. He was a beautiful baby with bright blue eyes. Blanche loved him from the moment he was in her arms. It would be at least three months after the birth that the Hancocks finally had his birth registered as William, on 26 June 1936. They later changed his name to Michael Simon.

Biddy enjoyed her lovely house in Brighton with views overlooking the sea. After Michael's christening, Biddy would sell up and move to London, Biddy was now free to enjoy her life as a singer and dancer. Michael's christening took place at the Catholic Church in Lewes, then they went back to the flat, where Blanche and William took the oath. They both swore on the Holy Bible, that Michael's birth was never to be discussed with anyone and never to be known, who his real parents were, so help them. When the formalities were over, Eveline was called and came into the room and looked at her Mama, her baby brother in her arms, Eveline said, "Aunty, that's my new baby brother?"

"Yes Eveline, he is beautiful and he has been christened Michael, but I think your Mama will let you call him Mickey," and they all laughed.

"Oh Mama, he is so lovely, can I hold him?"

"Yes sweetheart you can, if you sit with me we can hold Michael together, as he is very delicate, you can give him a very gentle kiss on his forehead, then he must go into his crib." They had a little celebration of champagne, a small christening cake and a buffet.

Before Biddy left, she said, "I will keep in close contact, just to make sure everything goes well. I must be notified if there are any problems or anything else, to let me know." She gave Blanche her address in London. She had already put her house in Sussex up for Sale with the local estate agents. She said her farewell giving Eveline and Michael a kiss, she gave her sister a big hug, shook hands with Billy, thanking him and departed. Biddy drove away in her Bugatti car, back to her flat in the West End of London.

Biddy came to see them two weeks later and said she had now found them a house to rent in Lewes with a garden. "You will be able to move in on Monday 22nd July, I have paid the first week's rent, from 22nd July, your next rent payment will be Monday 29th. The rent book will be sent to you with a letter of conditions. The landlady, Mrs A Falconer, will call the house to collect the weekly rent on a Monday morning. It is important that you do not get in arrears with the rent payments. Is that all clear? I hope you like the house, well folks, I will be on my way. I will be in touch."

She gave them all a hug, they thanked her for her kindness, she drove off with a wave. They liked the house with the lovely garden. They were all very happy for about six months, but trouble was on the way. Billy would go away for weeks at a time, without a word and life was becoming very tough for Blanche, Billy would often be sent to other locations with his job on the railways, which was understandable. But not leaving Blanche with enough money to pay the rent was unthinkable.

They were soon in arrears with their weekly rent. How was Blanche going to pay the rent arrears with no money? Failing and refusing to pay their weekly rent. They would be in big trouble, Blanche was left to deal with this problem herself, it made her feel nervous, how could her husband do this to her and their children.

An important letter arrived for Mr and Mrs W. Hancock, Blanche opened to find it was a summons, Mr W. Hancock would have to appear at Lewes County Court on Monday 5 December 1936 before his Honour Judge Austin Jones. The landlady, Mrs Ann Falconer, widow, of 106 Malling Street, made a claim for possession of a house in Malling Street, occupied by Mr and Mrs W. J. Hancock. The solicitor's letter explained, if the defendant was unable to attend court, they must write to Mr J.M. Hillman, explaining the reason in detail. Blanche wrote to the solicitor, saying that Mr W. Hancock was unable to attend court, owing to working away. Mrs B. Hancock was also unable to attend the court, being infirm, she was looking after her new-born baby and her young daughter. That her husband Mr W. Hancock was working away, she was unable to contact him, leaving her with no money, in which to pay the rent arrears.

On behalf of Mrs B. Hancock's solicitor, Mr Hillman had put in an affidavit to that effect. Mrs Falconer, the plaintiff objected to the affidavit, saying there was nothing wrong with the applicant. Mr Hillman said, "The defendant was nearly six weeks in arrears with their rent since October 6th, but they were not claiming for that. The plaintiff said it was a decontrolled house and that they had refused to pay the rent arrears."

"Your Honour, that is only since the plaintiff gave them notice to quit."

The plaintiff said, "She has a guilty conscience and that is why she does not come here."

"I shall make an order that Mrs Hancock's evidence is taken before the Registrar." The learned Registrar took down all the evidence. Later the application again came on. "If there are any additional costs, they will have to pay them because you have made it necessary." His Honour, addressing the Plaintiff saying: "Why have you given us all this unnecessary trouble? I shall make an order for possession of the premises in fourteen days. You, Mrs Hancock, are lucky in being let off the rent arrears. I will allow you to pay the costs at 5 shillings, which must be paid over the next month. There will be extra costs, as I warned you. That is the absolute finish." Blanche's kindly neighbour looked after her children that morning, while she had to make an appearance in court.

When Billy arrived back home a few days later. Blanche was in an awful state, "Oh Billy," with tears in her eyes, she cried, "where have you been all this time?"

"Oh I am so sorry, Blanche, I lost my job, I was caught drinking while working and they sacked me, I started looking for another job. But Blanche I did send you cash through the post, did you not receive it?"

"No Billy I did not." She told him they had been summoned to court, for failing to pay the rent arrears. "I sent a letter to Mr Hillman, the solicitor whose name I had to contact if I could not attend court. I explained to Mr Hillman that I was unable to attend court, due to having a baby and young daughter at home. I was not feeling well enough at this time, to be cross-examined in court. I told him that I had only refused to pay the rent, as I had no funds to pay the arrears with. I said that Mr Hancock has been away working on the railways. I have not seen him for quite some time. Mr Hillman sent me a reply to my letter to say, I did not have to attend court at this time. He would attend court, on my behalf, with an affidavit, and will inform me of the outcome at the court hearing. You will at some time have to go and see the Registrar and give your evidence. The outcome was, Billy, we have been evicted, we have two weeks to move out. We have been let off the outstanding rent arrears, but we have to pay the court fees, at 5 shillings over the next month. Plus extra costs. We have no option now but to find somewhere else to live. William paid off the court fees."

Then they moved to priory road in Tonbridge. Here Mr Hancock ended up in Court this time, for a man assaulting him in the street. He gave evidence that the man grabbed hold of him, he tried to fight him off. William Groombridge pleaded not guilty. He said he saw Mr Hancock walking down the street and went to talk to him about an incident that happened in the Pub the night before, he told the court that Mr Hancock was drunk and disorderly and pushed him over as he left the Pub, he said he saw him walking down the street and wanted an apology, then a fight broke out. Mr Hancock tried to take him to the police station for assaulting him. Mr Groombridge managed to get away. In court, Mr Groombridge said, "He did not touch Mr Hancock, but only wanted an apology," with no witnesses the case was dismissed.

There were two more court appearances involving the Hancocks, fighting and falling out with their neighbours on shared properties. It was never really serious. They just moved on to yet another property.

Blanche did write to her parents when they moved on, so they knew where to contact them. Making excuses for Billy, saying he was always moving around with his labouring jobs. Poor Eveline attended many different schools. As soon as she settled in one school, she was taken out and moved to another. Would her parents ever settle in one place, she felt so unhappy at home. She would play with her baby brother and push him around in his pram. He was a very good baby and never cried much.

At night, Evelyne would hear her parents, when they were together, they would often be arguing and shouting at each other. Once she heard her Mama cry out, but she was too frightened to go to her. So she would hide her head under the pillow, Mama often had bruises on her face or arms, she would make excuses and say she slipped over, that she needed some new shoes when she could afford them!

Frank had received Biddy's letter, but never answered it. Having not heard from him. Biddy decided to drive down to see Frank personally, to make sure he had received her official letter ending their relationship. She would return the engagement ring and draw out their joint savings from the bank and give him back his share. He was not at all pleased to see her, he only asked her why had she broken off their long engagement. "I explained all this in my letter, Frank, I do not love you anymore. I have met someone else who I am now dating; I have come here in person to break off our engagement and return the ring. Also, while I am here, I will go to the bank and draw out our joint savings and split it between us. If you have been wondering where I have been these last six months, I have been on holiday to France to stay with my brother and sister-in-law, I needed to get away for a holiday and have a nice long rest."

"I have now decided to make a new life for myself in London. I want to become a singer and dancer, I would like to give acting a try and become an actress. I am looking to have total freedom, with no commitments. So I am returning your ring, ending our relationship." She went to hand him back the ring.

"I do not want the diamond ring back, Biddy. Sell it or keep it in memory of me, I have no use for it anymore."

Putting the ring into her handbag, she said, "I will now go off to the bank and draw out the savings, I will return your half, with a statement, if you are not in when I return, I will post it through the letterbox. Goodbye Frank." Biddy returned with his share of the savings, she did knock, but he did not answer the door, so she dropped it through his letterbox and drove back to London. Frank was heartbroken, but he was a handsome lad, he would someday find another lady, settle down and be very happy. The Swaffields remained very good friends. They kept in touch with the Knights, even after they moved away.

It was to become apparent that Biddy had been dating a very wealthy man, who maybe had bought her that lovely house in Brighton-by-sea; this unknown boyfriend also bought her a very posh Bugatti car. How long their relationship lasted, no one knew, it was only in later years that a picture was found of her with her wealthy boyfriend, standing in front of this beautiful house with his arms around her, beside them was her fabulous car. Perhaps she may have lost the picture while she stayed in France or did she disclose this secret to Louise while she was staying there. Maybe it was Louise alone, who thought that this man could well be the father of her unborn child. Was the house in his name, did he buy the car for Biddy as a present? This was to become (Magpie Seven) for a secret never to be told. Biddy may well have told Blanche in the strictest of confidence. She surely would have known that Biddy was not that rich. She knew that she would never have had enough money to buy a house overlooking the sea and that very expensive Bugatti car, expensive clothes and Jewellery. It did seem strange as to why Biddy would buy a house in Lewis.

Chapter Twenty-Six

Michael was christened in the Catholic Church, Biddy had to wait until 26 June 1936 before Blanche and Billy had Michael christened. After all the legal documentation was signed. Biddy very soon sold her beautiful house and left for London, where she shared a flat with her close girlfriend. She joined the London stage singing and dancing in the chorus. Biddy was doing what she enjoyed most, living the good life and mixing with her posh friends, plus earning a very good salary.

One day Blanche had a lovely surprise. There was a loud knock on the front door, she opened the door and Mama and Papa stood there, they had come for a visit. Blanche was delighted to see them. Eveline heard them and came rushing in from the garden, with her arms opened wide, grandpa picked her up and hugged her, then she gave her grandma a big kiss and hug. She was so happy to see her grandparents. Billy was not there, as usual, he was working away. They greeted each other with cuddles and kisses.

Blanche said, "Mama and Papa, I have a big surprise for you both." She took them into the tiny bedroom and there lying on his cot was baby Michael fast asleep.

"Who is this beautiful baby, Blanche?"

"Well, Mama, did you not receive my letter?"

"No Blanche."

"Mama, meet your new grandson, this is baby Michael, he is nearly five months old." Blanche told them that Billy had become an alcoholic, but he was trying so hard to control his alcoholism. Papa had a job keeping his mouth tightly closed.

"We both wanted a brother for Eveline, so we decided to adopt a child from the local orphanage, so when we saw Michael, we legally adopted him. They said he was a new-born, that his mother had abandoned him after birth. You will be pleased to know Mama, that Michael has already been christened in the Roman Catholic Church."

They felt a little hurt, but they just said, "Blanche, we would have liked to have been notified and attended Michael's christening. This has come as a complete surprise to us, to know we have another grandchild."

"Mama, I did write and tell you and Papa about the adoption of baby Michael, but I did not get any reply from you."

"Oh, Blanche, I am so sorry the reason why we didn't receive your letter, was because we very recently moved to another new house in Whynot Lane Andover, which is a much nicer area, your letter most probably went to our old address in Cell Barnes Lane. It is my fault, my love, I should have written and told you, darling, please forgive us, dear."

"Blanche, just before Papa and I moved to our new house, we had a letter from Alfie and Louise. They said how much they enjoyed having Biddy stay with them and hoped she had a nice time and enjoyed the rest. Biddy told them that she was intending to go and join the London Chorus. Biddy sang for us while she was here. We both think she has such a very sweet singing voice, she sang that old song called 'Perfect Day' and 'Barbara Allen'. She told them that her friend and flatmate Angela had taught her many folk songs. Alfie said it brought back memories of when we all lived in India. We had many entertaining evenings. I even played the violin for her. We were both sorry to see Biddy leave France. We hope you are both keeping well, sending you lots of love, to all the family Alfie and Louise."

"That's nice, Mama, I am so glad Biddy had a good time with Uncle Alfie and Aunty Louise."

Mama was looking down at Michael in his cot, he had just woken up. "He is such a beautiful baby, Blanche, with those pale blue eyes, tight blond curly hair." Both grandparents loved him from the moment they saw him. Alfred told Blanche that they had plans to one day move to London, to be nearer Biddy, as they would be able to see her more often, they also wanted to see her performing on the stage singing and dancing. "It would save her the long journey down to Somerset and back just to see us. She has recently moved into a much larger flat she is sharing with a close friend in Soho. Biddy has told us that she is so very happy working in the nightclubs. Singing and dancing in the chorus, she would also like to try acting and become an actress."

Mama and Papa spent the next few days with Blanche. They all went out on Friday for a walk down to the lakes. Where Eveline fed the swans, Michael lay in his pram, good as gold. They watched the ducks, then found a nice friendly pub where they sat outside, enjoying a very fine ploughman's lunch. Papa even had a pint of Ale. Then they made their way home. That evening Papa played cards with Eveline showing her a few card tricks, then he read her a bedtime story.

Blanche let Mama put Michael to bed, they all retired for the night. The next day was Saturday, being Market day, the sun was shining, it looked like it was going to be a lovely day. So they made their way to the market, Alfred bought his granddaughter a book of fairy tales, looking around the market, on the toy stall he saw a teddy bear and bought it for his grandson.

Blanche bought some fresh grapes, strawberries, raspberries, blackberries and cherries, to make a lovely fruit salad dessert for Sunday lunch, giving Mama and Papa some fruit to take home with them. They found a very nice restaurant by the river. They sat outside enjoying the lovely warm summer sunshine. Papa ordered cheese and ham sandwiches, with a pot of tea and slices of chocolate cake. Mama and Papa were leaving for home today, they would be catching the late afternoon train back to Yeovil. When it was time to leave, they said their sad goodbyes.

Eveline said, "Thank you so much for my book and Mickey's cuddly teddy bear." She laughed as she said, "Grandma and Grandpa, I think he loves Teddy already!"

"Thank you, dear Blanche, for the fruit, we will have a lovely fruit salad with clotted cream when we get home." Before they departed, Alfred gave them their new address. On the train home, Alfred told Evelyne about the strange dream he'd had last night at Blanche's.

He said, "It was a vivid dream. I was walking through a graveyard and saw a headstone which was inscribed with the name 'William White BORN 1846 DIED 1914'. It was the grave of 'Amelia's brother'. I then woke up. It might have been a premonition, but I do think it's time to try and find out where my mother is, whether she has died or is still living somewhere! Tomorrow Evelyne, I am going to visit all the local churches in Yeovil, to see if I can find any records of her death. She may be buried in one of the local churchyards, where I can pay my respects."

"But Alfred, my love, you must be optimistic and think she is still alive and well. Why don't you take your locket with you, it might bring you good luck?"

"Yes, I will take it with me, my dear. I am sure if I do find my mother, she would love to see the locket again." When they arrived home, feeling rather tired, they had their supper followed by fruit salad and clotted cream. Then they retired to bed. It just might be a long day tomorrow!

Early on Sunday morning Alfred was up dressed and had his breakfast. "Darling, don't make me any lunch today, it may take me some time, it could be a long day."

"That's fine, Alfred, we can have our main meal when you come home. I hope you find out where your mother is, good luck my love. Oh, have you remembered to take the gold locket with you, my dear?"

"Yes, it is safe in one of your little ring boxes, I have placed it inside my jacket pocket." One large kiss and he was off. Alfred went out in search of all the local churches, to try and find out if his mother was buried in any of these cemeteries.

He started his search at St John the Baptist's church, he talked to the clergyman, with no luck, then he tried the oldest church in Yeovil, the St John's Protestant Church; he talked to the Vicar, but still no luck. He tried another church, St Michael All Angels, he spoke to the Reverend, who suggested that he try the Catholic Church of the Holy Ghost. He took a very long walk to this Church. He knocked on the vestry door and said, "I am Mr Knight and I wondered if you could help me, Father?"

"I am Father Henry, do come in, I am relatively new to this parish, How may I be of help to you, Mr Knight?"

After talking to the Father for some time, he explained he was looking for his mother Amelia Knight who he had not seen since he was three years old. He asked the Father if he knew Amelia Knight or any of the Knight family attending this Catholic Church, maybe still living in Yeovil or buried in the churchyard. Father Henry said, "I have only been the priest here for two months, I do not know the congregation by name yet Mr Knight. I am sorry I cannot help you, I'll bid you a good day, may God bless you, I will pray for you, that one day you will find your mother."

"Thank you, Father Henry, for your time."

As Alfred passed the Church door, he thought he would enter the Church just to have a quick look inside, when he saw a lady sitting down praying in the first pew, nearest the altar, her veiled head bent forward in prayer. He looked up at the large crucifix hanging over the altar, something spiritual made him kneel down in the nearest pew and pray, he closed his eyes and said the Lord's prayer and made the sign of the cross.

The lady was slowly struggling to get up, he watched as she used her walking cane, very slowly limping down the aisle towards him. The lady looked very old but vaguely familiar. He thought he recognised her, as she approached his pew, he said, "Excuse me Madam, but I think I might know you, please could you tell me your name?"

"Why sir, I don't know you at all, so if you don't mind I need to make my way home."

"I beg your pardon, madam, but may I just tell you my name?" The lady faltered and looked at him. "My name is Alfred Fredrick John Knight, born in 1866 to Amelia Knight, my father is George Knight, do these names mean anything to you, madam?"

The woman went as white as a sheet, he thought she was going to faint, he took her arm and said, "Please madam, would you like to sit down for a moment?"

She said, "This is surely no dream, my prayers have finally been answered, I can hardly believe you are my long-lost son Alfred, who has returned to me, after all these years. Yes, Alfred, I am your mother, Amelia Knight."

Alfred embraced her saying, "Oh Mother, I thought I would never ever see you again, shall we go out into the sunshine and talk?"

"Yes Son, that would be good." They found a bench beside the Church next to the Park, they sat down and had a very long conversation. Amelia started by telling Alfred where she was now living, I live with my distant relative, Rose White and her husband Edwin Jennings, at 67 Reckleford Hill Yeovil, Rose was a cousin on my Father's side of the family, she was a nurse when Rose married Edwin she gave up nursing. "They both help to take really good care of me. I have lived with them since 1911. After your father took you away from me, I went back to live with my mother and father, Ann and John White, your Grandparents. Alfred, I never got over losing you, my son. I suffered a nervous breakdown in health, my parents could not help me, they had no alternative, but to put me into an Institution, for my own safety, where I would be cared for and receive the best possible treatment. While I was living at the Institution, both your grandparents passed away. When I came out of the Institution, I went to live with my brother William and his wife. Do you remember your father, George, working with William in the Leather Trade?"

"No Mother, I was far too young."

"Well, it didn't work out very well, as his wife and I did not get along well together, so I left. I had heard that my sister Hannah had divorced her husband for adultery the year before. She was living alone, so I went to live with Hannah. We got on really well and everything was fine until she met a gentleman who she had fallen in love with. She wanted to get married again, so she asked me kindly if I would leave, as they wanted the house to themselves, which is understandable. I then ended up living where I am now, with Mr and Mrs Jennings. They are wonderful folks, I am happy living with them. They both take really good care of me, Rose cooks my meals, bathes me and helps me to get dressed every day."

"I like to try to be independent, while I can still walk a little. I do love to get out on my own, at least once a week to attend Mass on Sundays. I attend this Catholic Church when I am able. My brother William carried on in the Leather business until after our father John died, he then sold the business, not long after I left them, they all moved away. The Jennings later bought the Leather business and are still dealing in the Leather Trade. Alfred my son, I can now leave this life happy, knowing I have seen you, my precious son, again."

"Mother, I have something to show you." He reached inside his jacket pocket and took out the little box and said, "Hold out your hand, Mother," and he placed the locket into her withered hand.

She stared at the gold locket for a moment and said, "Will you open it for me?"

When she looked closely at the tiny pictures of Alfred as a baby and herself, she started to cry, he put his arms around her and said, "Mother, do you remember hiding this locket in a little wooden box in my bedroom, next to my cot, under a loose floorboard, when I was just a baby of about three? I just vaguely remember you putting something there, I think you put the locket there for safe keeping. It was a very good hiding place Mother, no one breaking into our house would have found it, that's for sure."

Amelia just smiled and said, "Do you know what Alfred, when I sold the house and moved back with my mother and father, I forgot all about the beautiful gold locket."

"Mother, I feel bad about telling you all about this, but I think you should know what happened to me, after my father George took me away from you, he took me to Wales with his friend, he called her Fanny. When we arrived in Wales, he told me that Frances Taylor was going to be my new Mama. Then we moved to Worcester where father married Frances, she legally adopted me. Frances soon gave birth to a baby boy called William Thomas. I would often ask my papa, why did you take me away from my Mama?" He would answer me and say, "Alfred, your birth mother was far too ill to look after you, but that you will see your birth mother again someday and your grandparents too."

Amelia looked at Alfred with tears in her eyes. Alfred gave her a hug and said, "Mother, I do have some good news for you. It should make you happy when I tell you I had a stroke of good luck. My dear wife Evelyne and I have managed to buy that same property where I was born. It was up for sale, while I was looking to buy a house for my family. I walked along the street and I saw the long row of cottages, they all looked exactly the same, one of them had a FOR SALE sign outside. I just could not remember which cottage we lived in, as they all looked identical! I went into town and managed to pick up the keys from the local estate agent.

"I was anxious to have a good look inside, to see if it was the same house, where I was born, as you may remember mother, all the cottages along that road look the same. Mother, when I stepped inside, it looked just the same as I remembered it! When I went to look upstairs, the first room I entered was the little box room, where I slept in my cot. I pulled back the carpet and underlay, to my utter surprise, it was still there, in the little wooden box, where you had left it, still hidden under that loose floorboard. Then I knew for sure, Mother, it was the same house where I was born."

"Alfred, George bought me the gold locket as a wedding gift. When you were born, I had our pictures put inside it. Keep it always, Alfred, in memory of me."

He felt so sorry for her, never having the chance to bring him up. Alfred went on telling her how he met his lovely wife Evelyne in India, after being shot in the shoulder, she was his nurse and tendered his wound. She lovingly brought me back to health again, when I was sent back to the hospital after I caught malaria. How the family had to endure the very long voyage from India via England to Canada. But they all did. Amelia said, "Alfred, will you meet me here, next Sunday at the same time, after Church?"

"Yes Mother, that will be lovely. Now Mother, I must get you home, they will be worried about you, I will walk you to your home." Slowly they walked up Yeovil High Street, onto

Reckleford Hill. As they walked along, he told his mother he had a married son called Alfie, living in France, with his wife Louise. "I also have three daughters, Agnes who lives in Canada. Blanche and Biddy live in England." Alfred said, "My wife Evelyne and I will soon be moving up to London, to live near our youngest daughter Biddy. Blanche is married to Billy and they have two children. Eveline and Michael."

"Alfred my son, I would love to meet them all. I look forward to meeting my daughter-in-law, Evelyne."

"Oh dearest Mother, there is so much more to tell you, about me and my family, but when we meet after Church next Sunday, perhaps you would like to come back to your old house, where we now live for Sunday dinner."

"Oh Alfred, that would be lovely, I will look forward to next Sunday." They slowly walked to where his mother lived.

Alfred gave his mother a big hug, he was almost in tears, as he said, "Goodbye Mother, Evelyne and I will be waiting for you, outside the Church, on the bench at 12 o'clock next Sunday. I am sure Rose and Edwin will be delighted to know after all these years, at last, you have found your son Alfred. Tell Rose you will be late home next Sunday, I will see you home safely." He kissed his mother and slowly walked away.

When he arrived home, Evelyne was waiting for him, "Hello darling welcome home, It's been a long day without you, sweetheart." His wife had their supper ready, she had been patiently waiting for him to come home.

He said, "Hello darling" with a smile on his face, "You'll never guess what has happened today."

"Please tell me, darling, don't keep me in suspense any longer."

"Let's sit down and have this delicious-looking meal you have prepared, I am famished and I will tell you all about the most fascinating day I have ever had! Well, Evelyne my mother is still alive, would you believe that! I met up with her today in the Catholic Church." He went on to tell her every detail of the day's events.

All Evelyne could say was, "It's truly unbelievable, I told you the locket may bring you good luck and it did! You must have been so very happy to see your mother again, after so many years, honestly Alfred, it's a miracle! We must celebrate." She went to the cabinet and took out a bottle of wine, she filled two glasses and they had a wonderful evening. Evelyne could not wait to meet her mother-in-law, what an amazing day it had been! they emptied the bottle of wine, they both slept very well that night.

The following Sunday they went and sat on the park bench, where Alfred had sat with his mother the Sunday before. Alfred and Evelyne attended another Catholic Church. They had booked a cab to this church and went and sat on the bench, where they sat anxiously waiting. When at last the Church doors opened, they watched as the congregation started coming out, some stopping to speak with Father Henry. Some shaking hands, the last few greeted the priest as they passed. When the last person of the congregation came out through the Church door, there was no sign of Amelia. Because of her disability, they knew it would take her much longer. They waited and waited, but still, Amelia did not appear.

So Alfred said, "Wait here darling, I will go and see if my mother is still inside the Church praying." Alfred entered the Church to find it was completely empty.

Alfred knocked on the vestry door, the kind Priest opened the door and said, "Hello Mr Knight can I help you." They talked for a while, Alfred told him that he was here today to meet up with his mother who he had found in this Church praying after their conversation last Sunday afternoon. "After leaving the vestry, I went into the Church and said a prayer when I saw a lady in the front pew praying when she made her way towards me, I thought I recognised this lady and although she did not recognise me at first until I spoke to her and told her who I was, I cannot tell you Father what a joy it was to see my dear mother again after all these years. She was overjoyed to see me again, it was quite a shock for her as she could not believe it was her only son Alfred."

"Father, it was a miracle, I had not seen my mother since I was three years old, when my parents separated, my father left and took me with him. He later remarried. This was quite a surprise to Father Henry. My mother and I sat outside and had a long conversation. Amelia told me that she has gone back to her maiden name of Amelia White. My mother and I arranged to meet here today after Mass. Father, my wife and I are here today to meet her, but she has not made an appearance and I am worried about her. She told me that she attends this Church when she is able. She lives at 67 Reckleford Hill."

"Mr Knight, I am very sorry, it grieves me to tell you that Amelia White, if that is her maiden name, who lived with Mr and Mrs Edwin Jennings at 67 Reckleford Hill, Yeovil, sadly passed away last Monday after a sudden heart attack, her funeral took place here yesterday afternoon. It was a very quiet funeral where only a few relatives were present. If only I had taken a few details from you, Mr Knight, when you were here last Sunday, I would have contacted you. Mr Knight, if you would kindly follow me, I will show you where Amelia White was laid to rest, where you can pay your respects."

Alfred was so sad, he could hardly hold back the tears. He told Father Henry that his wife was waiting outside. When Evelyne saw Alfred with the priest, she could see how sad he looked, she guessed the worst. She slowly followed behind them, through the graveyard, where they found flowers around a freshly dug grave. Alfred thanked the priest, they both paid their respects. Alfred, with sadness and a heavy heart, slowly walked home with his wife in silence.

Chapter Twenty-Seven

Dear Biddy,

I desperately need your help, Billy has been drinking heavily and coming home drunk. We have recently been summoned to court, for not paying the rent arrears, even refusing to pay, Billy had not been leaving me enough money to pay the weekly rent. We have been evicted many times. Sometimes I don't see Billy for weeks, he says he has to keep changing jobs. It is not good for Eveline, as she has attended at least four different schools, she is becoming a handful at home, is it any wonder?

Billy has been spending most of his wages on drinks at the pub, as he often comes home intoxicated. Now it looks like we shall soon be moving again. I am so worried, I do not know what to do or where to turn. I am a little worried as from yesterday afternoon, Eveline started to get sick. I am finding it difficult to cope, Michael has started waking up at the night. I am not sleeping well either. Every time we are evicted, we just have to pack up and move on. I have to keep sending Mama and Papa our new address. Telling them that Billy keeps changing jobs.

This is our address at present. Please come soon, all my love Blanche. X.

Biddy arrived the day she received her letter, Blanche broke down and cried, she was thin, there was hardly any food in the cupboard, the small rented house was in a very untidy state. Eveline was sick and throwing up. Biddy told Blanche, "Not to worry, darling, I am here now and I will take care of everything, Blanche I am going to find you somewhere else to live, this place is too small. I shall go and see the estate agent and find something bigger with a garden. Then I will take Eveline and book her in to see my doctor in London."

Michael seemed quite happy playing in his cot, with his toys and teddy bear. Biddy gave Blanche money to pay the outstanding rent and to fill the cupboard with food. She said, "I am going to take Eveline now, when I return, you will be moving to another house, as soon as I can possibly find a suitable home for you and the Children."

Biddy then went to the local estate agent and found a three-bedroom house to rent. It was in West Peacehaven Nr. Brighton. She arranged for the rent to be paid monthly. She paid three months' rent in advance. They said, "Mrs Knight, the house will need some inside repainting and will be ready for you to move in within three weeks, we will send the details to your present address." She gave them Blanche's address, then drove down to London and booked her in with her doctor. Eveline needed her tonsils out, she was transferred to the Royal Hospital, where her operation would take place. she would have to spend a few weeks in recovery.

Blanche nor Billy came to see her in hospital, only Biddy and her friend. Biddy even had to sign the papers, for Eveline to have the operation. Biddy made up her mind to visit her Mama and Papa in Andover. She told her mama Blanche needed her help, she was in a bad way. "I drove down to

London this morning, to take Eveline to the London Royal Hospital because she had to have her tonsils out. She will have to stay in Hospital for a few weeks to recover. Michael's fine mama, but when I saw Blanche, she was in tears and very depressed. She needs you now mama, more than ever. When I saw her this morning, she was saying she hadn't seen Billy for over a month, leaving her with no money to buy food or pay the weekly rent. Mama, I have already arranged for Blanche to move to another house far away from Billy, who has been getting drunk and disorderly again. Mama, can you come and stay with Blanche for a little while?"

"Yes, of course, I will, whatever time it takes, to see Blanche happy again."

"Mama, I will come and collect you after Blanche moves into her new home, in three weeks' time." Biddy kissed her parents and drove back to see Blanche.

Biddy was quite aware that Blanche was being abused by Billy and had been for a long time. But what could she do? She made up her mind to move Blanche as far away from Billy as she could. She knew that Blanche would never leave Billy, as she married him for better or worse. Moving Blanche where Billy could not find her, was the only answer. If only!

Three weeks later, Biddy was back to help Blanche pack up and move into her new home, the removal men came, they both cleaned up and moved out. Biddy drove Blanche and Michael to their new house in Peacehaven. Biddy opened up this semi-detached three-bedroom house and the removal men brought in the furniture, which wasn't much, one double bed and two singles, a baby's cot. Two wardrobes, dining table and four chairs, a three-piece suit and a sideboard, four lamps, curtains and carpets. Biddy helped her bring in all the other things, pictures, bedding, linen and all their clothing, that were packed in her car. Together they made up the beds, hung up the curtains and laid the rugs around the house. Someone had left two old bedside cabinets, which were very useful. The kitchen already had lots of drawer space. It was indeed a very fine house.

Biddy drove up to London to pick up Eveline, but they would not let her leave as she had caught some infection, it was not serious, but they wanted to keep her in for observation. Then she drove on to Yeovil, where she picked up her Mama on her way back. She placed her suitcase in the boot and drove to West Peacehaven, which was a lot of driving for Biddy in one day. But she loved driving her car!

When Blanche saw her Mama, she was so happy and gave her a big hug, made them both comfortable and gave them tea and a piece of cake. Blanche had cooked a roast beef dinner which they would have later. She gave Mama a tour around her new house, then Mama said, "You, Blanche, should be very grateful to your sister, she has done you proud, this is a very nice comfortable home." Mama heard the baby cry, Michael had just woken up, it must be time for his feed.

Mama and grandma walked into the small bedroom and there standing in his cot was Michael, he stopped crying when he saw his mama with grandma, mama picked him up. After being fed, he smiled at everyone, then grandma took him in her arms, rocked and sang to him, then he slowly fell asleep. Blanche gently carried him into his bedroom, cleaned him up, put him in his nightie, laid him down with his teddy, kissed him goodnight, turning off his little light, Michael was still waking up for his nightly feed.

While Blanche was upstairs, Biddy spoke to mama about some solution to Blanche's situation. Mama said to Biddy, "I think it would be a good idea to take Eveline back to Andover with me when she is released from the Hospital."

Biddy thought that a brilliant idea. "She can spend time with her grandpa who adores her, just until Blanche feels better, that will give her more time to spend with Michael."

When Blanche came into the room, she told them that dinner was ready; while they were enjoying their meal, Blanche said, "I am missing Eveline so much, I hope she will be feeling better and coming home soon."

Mama said to Blanche, "I think it would be a good idea darling if Eveline spends some time with grandpa and me when she comes out of hospital until she has fully recovered and got her strength back. It would also give you time for yourself and to spend more leisure time with Michael. Would that be OK with you Blanche?"

"Yes, if that is what Eveline wants, I think that will be fine, it may do her good to spend some time with her grandparents, grandpa adores her. Except that, I do think she should return home, to start her new Catholic school, when the new term starts."

The next day Biddy said that she was taking them all out to dinner. She told Blanche that she would do her hair, even though she didn't like the water near her ears and complained the whole time, Mama and Biddy knew why! Biddy curled her long dark hair, it looked really smart. She put on her prettiest dress and Biddy put some lipstick on her, then they all went out, dressed up to the nines for dinner.

When they got back, they all agreed that the steak was excellent and they had all enjoyed their meal. They thanked

Biddy for treating them. Michael was so good, he never cried once. Later that evening Blanche packed Eveline's clothes and some of her favourite books.

The next morning Biddy drove mama to the London Hospital, to pick up Eveline. She was so happy to see her grandma and at last, she would be going home. On the way back to Somerset, grandma told Eveline that she would be staying with her and grandpa for a while until she was back to full health again. She smiled, "Oh Grandma, I am so happy to be seeing my dear Grandpa" who she loved so much. "I am missing mama a lot though, will I see her soon?"

"Yes my love, when you are feeling stronger again." Eveline decided she must be a very good girl and be on her best behaviour, even though she knew she will not be sent to bed or scolded for being naughty. She wished that her grandparents lived next door, so she could see them every day.

When they arrived at Whynot Lane Andover. Alfred was overjoyed to see his wife, he gave her a hug and kiss, "I am so pleased you are back darling, it's been very lonely here without you." Then seeing Eveline he was delighted, Biddy explained to Papa why she had brought Eveline with her.

"Papa, you will be pleased to hear, Eveline will be staying here with you for a few weeks or so."

Grandpa picked her up and gave her a big hug and kiss saying, "Are you all better now, my precious girl?"

"Yes Grandpa, I am all better now," she replied.

"Well, Alfred, here I am, back home now with your favourite granddaughter." He took her into the sitting room and sat her on his lap.

He loved her dearly even though she kept him on his toes, she was a very lively child. "Granddad, shall we go for a walk? Granddad, shall we play cards or we could play draughts, will you tell me a story?"

"My darling Eveline, let us get you settled in first, have a drink and some supper. There will be plenty of time to do all those things. But first I must speak with grandma and your aunty." Grandpa gave Eveline a book to read. It was "Hansel and Gretel." She could not read very well yet, but she could look at the pictures and grandpa would read the book to her later.

Mama said to Biddy, "Oh Biddy what a lovely looking baby Michael is, he is so good too, I am so proud of Blanche and Billy, giving Michael a home and a brother for Eveline."

Biddy quickly changed the subject and said, "Blanche seems a whole lot happier now she is in her new home, new baby son, glory be, she is finally away from Billy. Now I think she will be fine, I shall see she is OK, Mama. I will make sure she never gets behind with her rent."

Evelyne said to Alfred and Biddy, "I think the best way we can help Blanche is if we can get Eveline into our school in Wincanton, at the beginning of the new term. It would take the pressure off Blanche, just until Michael is a little bit older."

Alfred said to Biddy, "I did hear from our very friendly neighbour, the Nightingales, that their daughters go to the local school, they say it's very good, their two daughters are a bit older than Eveline, I'm sure their girls would not mind taking Eveline to school and look out for her. I will have a word with Mrs Nightingale tomorrow."

"That is a very good idea Papa, I will stay here tonight and leave in the morning, Goodnight everyone." The next morning Biddy got ready to leave for Whitehorse Street,

London, where she was now living in her own flat, above a hairdresser shop. She said, "I will call back and see you all in a few weeks' time, to see if everything is alright." Saying her sweet farewells to everyone, she drove off in her Bugatti car, back to London. Time was passing by and we were now well into the nineteen thirties, Biddy was still singing and dancing on the West End stage, she was enjoying life to the full, mixing with rich and famous film stars, hoping to join them one day and become a film star.

Alfred went to talk to the friendly neighbour, Mrs Nightingale. "Hello Alfred," she said, "do come in."

Alfred explained to Mrs Nightingale that his granddaughter would be staying here, with her grandparents for a while. "Eveline's mother is suffering from depression. Eveline has just come out of the hospital after having her tonsils out. My wife and my daughter Biddy, have just spent a week with her mother Blanche, there has been an improvement and when we left, she was starting to feel so much better. Evelyne and Biddy talked it over and agreed that she may cope better when her son is not waking her up at night. Her husband works away, Blanche is often on her own for weeks on end. So we will be looking after her for a while, after her operation, she caught an infection and had to stay in hospital. She is well now but needs to get her strength back."

"We will take her out every day for fresh air and daily walks. We all feel that it will do them both good, For Eveline to fully regain her strength, before attending school, also for Blanche to have a well-needed rest. But Eveline does need to go back to school when the new term starts. Do you think the school your daughters attend would take Eveline when the new term begins? Until Blanche is more able to cope."

"We would be so grateful if you could ask the Head Teacher on our behalf if there's a place in the school to take Eveline. If she does get a place in the school, it would make our lives so much easier, also do you think that your daughters would mind, kindly taking Evelyne to school and bringing her home with them?"

Mrs Nightingale showed sympathy, "I understand her mother's stress," she said, "Yes Mr Knight, that will be fine. I will make an appointment with the Headmistress, who is very nice, to see if Eveline can start at the beginning of the new term. I am sure my daughters will take Eveline to school and bring her home."

"Thank you so much, Mrs Nightingale."

"It will be my pleasure, good day, Mr Knight, I will let you know the outcome."

Alfred went back to Evelyne, telling her what Mrs Nightingale said. "Well, that's great, Alfred, let's hope they can find Eveline a place."

Grandpa found Eveline finishing her breakfast, "Oh Granddad, what are we going to do today?"

"Well, after you have helped Grandma with the washing up, we are going for a walk down to the river. We must take some stale bread, so we can feed the ducks. Grandma will not be coming with us, as she has a bad leg. When we come back, I will teach you to play a good card game, called 'Casino'. It is easy to learn and will help you with your adding up. Then we will have our lunch. After lunch, we will have a nap, then I will read you a story called 'Little Red Riding Hood'. Then I would like you to draw me a picture of Red Riding Hood walking in the woods and meeting the big bad wolf, you can then colour your picture in, I have some crayons in the drawer."

"Then while I have a little rest, Grandma wants to show you how to knit. We will have our supper. If you are a good girl, I'll read you a bedtime story." The day went by very quickly, soon it was time for bed. Grandma got Evelyne ready and tucked her in, Grandpa picked up the book and read her "Goldilocks and the three Bears." Even before he had finished reading the story, she was sound asleep. Evelyne turned off her light and everyone had a good night's sleep.

"Today, Eveline, Grandma is going to teach you to make gingerbread men's biscuits. Then we will go for a walk in the woods and pick some wildflowers for Grandma. We will have our lunch, after lunch, we will play casino to see how much you have learned, let's see if you can beat me. The winner gets a gingerbread biscuit. Then I will show you a few card tricks. We will have a little rest, then Grandma is going to give you another lesson on knitting. By then it will be bedtime and I will read you a story, called 'Jack and the Beanstalk'."

A week later, Mrs Nightingale knocked on their door, saying, "I have just popped around to tell you the good news. I have spoken to the Headmistress and yes, they have a place and will take Eveline into their school on the first day of the new term, her teacher will be Mrs Cotterell, she is very nice."

"Thank you so much, Mrs Nightingale, that's great news, will you come in for a cup of tea and cake?"

"No thank you, the girls and I are just going out to visit my sister, I will speak to you again soon."

"Thank you again." Evelyne closed the door feeling very happy. Eveline was so happy and content to be living with her Grandparents and so looking forward to starting a new school.

The Nightingale family were such nice neighbours, their daughters Daisy and Vivian were to become Eveline's best friends. Eveline would have been content to spend the rest of her childhood living with her grandparents. But unfortunately, that would never happen.

Chapter Twenty-Eight

One evening Blanche was putting Michael to bed, she was now happy and content. She gently placed Michael's teddy bear in his cot beside him, he looked so adorable, she kissed him and covered him up. Blanche was now feeling so much better, she had started to put on a bit more weight. Blanche started getting ready for bed, while she was brushing her long dark hair, she suddenly heard a loud knock on the front door. Rather startled, she could not think who could be knocking at her door at this late hour. She peeped out between the curtains to see, to her utter surprise, Billy was standing at the door. He glanced up and saw the curtain move, he banged again, she was helpless and went down and opened the door.

"Hello Billy," she said, surprised.

He said sarcastically, "Are you going to invite me in or am I going to stand on the doorstep all night?"

"Oh yes come in, it was just a shock to see you tonight."

"If you're shocked, Blanche, well I sure am, what is the meaning of this, why have you moved to this house and left the flat? I think as my wife, you have a lot of explaining to do."

"Billy, I will tell you the whole truth, I had a letter from the bailiffs that they were coming to take away the furniture if the rent for the flat wasn't paid by the end of the week, Baby Michael has been crying a lot, while Evelyne started constantly being sick. Billy, I had no idea where you were, so I wrote to Biddy asking her to help me. She came, only to find me in dire straits. There was precious little food in the cupboards. I was very thin, there was no money to pay the rent."

"Biddy immediately went to the Houses for Rent Office and found this house with a little garden in a cheaper area. She paid three months' rent in advance on this property. She told me to pack up everything I could, as she was moving me to this House, where there would be move space. Biddy then left, taking Eveline to see her own doctor, as we were very worried about her. After an examination, the Doctor said it was her tonsils, she needed to go into the Hospital immediately to have them removed."

"Eveline was taken to the hospital, where she would spend two weeks recovering. This London hospital was where she would have the best medical care. After the operation, Eveline caught an infection and they kept her in for another week. I would have liked to have gone to see her for a visit, but I had no money for the return fare. Biddy went to see her and also signed her operation papers, on our behalf. Why are you so cruel to me, Billy? I thought you loved me, don't treat me like this, if you really care about your wife and children."

The only thing that Blanche could think of was her father's words: "You made your bed, now you must lie on it, for better or worse."

"How did you manage to find out where I was living, Billy?"

"Well, Blanche, it wasn't easy when I returned to the flat and found the place deserted, I knocked on the neighbour's door, all they said was that you had moved out, but had no idea where." So I caught the train to Yeovil and went to see Evelyne and Alfred. When I knocked on the door at Station Road, the door opened to a woman I did not know, she said, "Can I help you, sir?" Well, yes, I am looking for the Knights who live here. "Well, sir, they moved out, we live here now, sorry I cannot be of more help to you." Then I caught a cab to Wincanton to Uncle Tom's Cabin, to see if I could find out if they might know where Evelyne and Alfred Knight had moved to. Well, when I spoke to the Landlord, he said, "Yes, they sold the small shop in Station Rd and moved to 26 Cell Barnes Lane Andover."

"I did not stop for a drink as you might have expected, but caught another cab back to Andover. I knocked on my in-laws' door. Evelyne was very cross and angry when she saw me." She asked, "What do you want, Billy?" Please Evelyne, I need to find Blanche. Please I beg you, to tell me where Blanche has moved to. Evelyne did not call me inside, "Billy if I tell you where Blanche is living, you must promise me that you will never treat our daughter in this shocking way again. Billy, you are fortunate that Alfred is not in. He has not seen Blanche, but Biddy has told him everything. How can you treat your wife in this despicable way? You'll be very lucky if Alfred ever speaks to you again. But after all, she is still your wife, so I will with reluctance tell you where she is now living. Billy, promise me that you will never do anything like this ever again."

"Evelyne, I swear that I will make it up to Blanche and I will never be cruel to her again. Evelyne wrote down the

244

address and gave it to me, she said, 'You go now and make sure you mend your bad ways.' I thanked her, then caught the train here to Peacehaven."

Billy sat with his head in his hands, "I am so dreadfully sorry, Blanche, this will never happen again. I do love you and the children, when I drink, I get drunk and totally out of my head. You know I am an alcoholic, but I promise I am going to stop drinking, so we can be a family again. I will change my job and instead of travelling from place to place trying to find work, I will try and get my job back by working on the local railways as a fireman. I made a promise to your mother and by the life of me, I will keep it! In future, I will make sure that you have enough money to pay the rent and buy food and other essentials."

Blanche started to cry, Billy took her in his arms saying, "Don't cry, my love, everything is going to be better from now on, you'll see."

If only Blanche could trust Billy to keep his word.

Billy looked in on Michael, he was sleeping peacefully. When he went in to see Eveline, she was not in her bed. Blanche told him she was staying with her grandparents for a while, "It is just until I feel better, also to give myself a well-needed break." True to his word Billy stopped drinking and life was good again. The first thing Billy did was to apply for his old job on the railways, but the only vacancy they could offer him was laying and repairing the railway tracks. He took the job and was happy to be working locally again. He knew this would please Blanche and hopefully forgive him.

Blanche sat down and wrote this letter to Biddy:

Dear Biddy,

I cannot believe how quickly and unexpectedly Billy turned up at the new house, he briefly told me how he had found out where I was living, Mama had told him, on account that he changes his bad ways and stops drinking. He has given her his word. He says he is going to find a local job working on the railways.

My darling, I cannot thank you enough for all the help you have given me. I do not know what I would have done without it. I love you so much and I thank you from the bottom of my heart. I must also thank you for taking Eveline to the hospital. I hope she has fully recovered now from her operation. I am missing her so much. I am sure she will be having a lovely time, enjoying herself at her grandparents' home.

Just to let you know that Michael is growing more lovely every day, he is now trying to talk. He goes through the night without waking up, laughs a lot and is a very happy baby. I am feeling so much better and happier now. Things have got to change, Billy has promised he will never treat me in this way again, maybe everything will be fine from now on, Oh I do hope so, Biddy, I will write to Eveline, Mama and Papa tomorrow.

All my love Blanche xxx.

Everything returned to normal, there was a big improvement in Blanche and Billy's relationship. Eveline had now settled into her new school, she loved being in a school with such nice teachers and her reading, writing and arithmetic were coming on in leaps and bounds. Her class teacher was very pleased with her, after such a short time, she would soon be top of the class. Her manners had improved, she was becoming polite and obedient. Alfred and Evelyne were very proud of her.

Eveline got very friendly with the Nightingale sisters, Daisy and Vivian. They would call for her in the morning and bring her home after school. She would come in from school, quickly change out of her school uniform, into her play clothes, have a drink and a snack, then out she would go next door, to join her friends Daisy and Vivian in their garden, they had a garden swing and a children's slide, all kinds of bats and balls and a skipping rope. If it was raining, they were allowed to play in their house and do jigsaw puzzles; Eveline had never been happier…Eveline had now been living with her Grandparents, for almost two months and this is where she wanted to stay. But unfortunately, it wasn't to be!

If the weather was good, Granddad would take Eveline on the ferry to Le Havre France to visit his son Alfie and Louise and for Eveline to get acquainted with her Uncle and Aunty. They had a large beautiful home, with a marble spiral staircase, where Eveline would sit and watch as Louise would arrange her dressmaker's models with all kinds of beautiful designs. While Eveline was there, Louise made her two lovely dresses, so different from the two she had. Alfie's perfume business was doing very well, his shop was always full of customers. Eveline did learn a few French words and started to say, my name is (Je m'appelle Eveline); (Bonjour) Hello; (Au revoir) Goodbye. She would love to play with their tiny whippet puppy.

Alfred only took Eveline there for short weekends, when it was sunny and warm, they would all go down to the beach, Eveline would paddle her feet in the water and splash about.

Then they would lay a blanket on the beach and enjoy a scrumptious picnic. Eveline and Alfred loved these times with Alfie and Louise in France. Alfie would entertain them in the Evening with his violin playing and he would play beautiful music, they all loved to hear him play. The French family were very kind and nice to her, but she couldn't understand a word they said, only when they spoke in English, did she get to join in their conversation. Because Louise and Alfie both had businesses to run, their children Evelyne and Philip spent a good deal of time close by at their maternal grandparents' home, the Beaulieus, during school term.

During the holidays, Louise had a nanny to look after the children. Eveline and Alfred saw very little of them. Eveline only got into trouble once, one afternoon while she was looking around the large garage, Alfie was busy changing a tyre on his bicycle. Eveline picked up a strange-looking glass ornament. It was a very old thermometer, she held it up to show him and said, "What's this Uncle?"

The thermometer accidentally dropped to the floor, the glass shattered and red stuff poured out of it. There was a mess everywhere, "Eveline, that was very clumsy of you, that thermometer was an antique, it belonged to my great grandfather." Alfie was very cross with her.

She said, "I am so very sorry, Uncle." He saw how upset she was and he forgave her.

Chapter Twenty-Nine

Biddy was doing all the things she dreamed of enjoying her life. She loved performing on stage with the Chorus girls, singing and dancing entertaining the audience, in London's West End Nightclub "The Windmill," the evening shows would start at seven into the late evenings. That meant she would be free all morning. All the girls would practise new routines in the late afternoon, around 4 o'clock. Biddy was now living in Soho W1. sharing a flat with her girlfriend Eileen, who at one time was an accomplished pianist and did very well.

We were now well into the late 1930s, Biddy was mixing with the Mayfair society, she made lots of rich friends, Biddy got friendly with Jean Kent, she too was with the Chorus Girls. Her real name was Joan Mildred Field and later went on to become a famous leading lady in Films. Her first film was in 1935 "Rocks of Valpre" some of her great films were "Waterloo Road" "The woman in Question." In 1952, she made "Before I Wake." There would often be film directors in the audience, looking for new talent to make the "Big Time" hopefully to become Film Stars. Biddy was now meeting other famous Film Stars, there was Margeret Lockwood and Patricia Roc, they were in the process of making a film called "The Wicked Lady." This film wasn't released until 1945, this film also starred James Mason and Michael Rennie.

When Biddy next met up with Jean, she asked her if she could get her into acting, she told Biddy that the first thing she must do was to enrol in drama classes. So she did. After six months, Biddy felt she was now ready to start a new career in acting.

When she next caught up with Jean, she said, "Jean I am ready now, can you get me an audition?"

Jean went to speak to her Director. A few weeks later Biddy got an audition at the Pinewood studios. Biddy turned up at the studio, her first audition went well, she was asked to go for yet two more. They liked her, she was very good, they started by giving Biddy small stand-in parts, in the big films. This was not quite what she wanted, she wanted leading roles, so she could become a film star! It was never going to happen. After four films, she realised it wasn't really what she wanted for herself, so she gave up acting, Then went back to what she loved doing best, singing and dancing live on stage. Biddy was selected to go to Paris to dance with a group. She was a great success performing extremely well. Until she became unwell, she was diagnosed with pulmonary T.B. Biddy was kept in hospital being treated with antibiotics, for about three weeks. Alfie and Louise came to visit her, as often as they could. After she had fully recovered, Biddy returned to the London stage and carried on with her dancing career. Biddy was told one evening while socialising with her friend Jean, that she probably did not make the big time in films, because she was small and petite, the film directors were looking for leading ladies, to be of average height!

It was now 1939, war was about to break out, Biddy was socialising with her friends Gillian and flatmate Eileen when two young handsome RAF cadets walked into the Social Club in their smart uniforms. The ladies watched as they walked towards the bar, Gillian recognised Jimmy Barton, he was once her brother's best friend. Gillian called them over to the table, Gillian got up and said, "Hello Jim, it's been a long time."

"Hello Gill, how are you?"

"I'm fine." He gave her a hug. "When did you join the RAF?"

Before he had a chance to answer, Gillian turned to the ladies, "Ladies, I'd like you to meet Jim Barton, he was a good friend of my brother's, we know each other well."

Jim then said, "Ladies, I would like you to meet my best mate Patrick, who likes to be known as Paddy." The ladies introduced themselves, then after they shook hands. Patrick asked the ladies what they would like to drink. Patrick ordered all the drinks and then sat down next to Biddy.

"I'm very pleased to make your acquaintance, Biddy."

There she was to meet the man of her dreams, she was attracted to him on their first meeting. He took Biddy out a few times after the shows. He told her he was born in 1904 in Ireland. "The family moved to live in Cambridge. I started working for Pest Control until I enlisted in the RAF. I joined the RAF because I wanted to be a pilot and serve my country. I am still training and have to return in two weeks' time. I am just on a short leave."

They started meeting up more frequently, they were getting to know each other well and loved being in each other's company. After two weeks together, they were gradually becoming very fond of each other, Biddy was falling head over heels for this very charming handsome man. Biddy felt sure he loved her as much as she loved him. He said, "I will very soon be going off to war, I will write to you. When the war is over, Biddy, I will return and we will be married."

Their last day together was very sad, he promised to keep in touch by mail. Before leaving that day, he got down on one knee and asked Biddy to marry him, the answer of course was "Yes." "Paddy, however long it takes, I love you dearly, I shall wait for you to return to me."

"I love you too, Biddy, with all my heart." They kissed and said their farewells.

Blanche was now missing her daughter, one evening while she and Billy were relaxing by the fire, she said to Billy, "I think it's time that Eveline returned home, I am missing her so much, she has been away for over two months. I think it's time we went and brought her back home."

Billy agreed and said, "This weekend is Easter, we shall celebrate the Easter Holiday altogether as a family. On Thursday, we will take the train to Yeovil and bring Eveline back home, Blanche."

They caught the early train to Yeovil and arrived at 11 o'clock. When Blanche, Billy and Michael arrived at their house, Evelyne was very surprised to see them. They were invited in to make themselves at home, with a warm welcome Grandpa picked up Michael and took him to the back room to play. He was nearly two and learning to talk. Grandma went to put the kettle on to make tea, she made some egg and cress sandwiches and put out her freshly made fruit cake, Blanche said to Mama, "You must have known we were coming," and they all laughed.

When they sat down to enjoy their midday brunch, Blanche said, "Mama, where is Eveline?"

"She is at school, but she will be home early today as it is the last day of term, they break up today for the Easter holidays. Tomorrow is Good Friday and we have invited our neighbours Mr and Mrs Nightingale around for dinner. They have two daughters, Daisy and Vivian. They are very nice girls, they take Eveline to school and bring her home. We are really good friends with them."

Mama filled Blanche in on everything that had been happening since she had last seen her daughter, the school she was attending was very good, Blanche was top of the class already. She was happy and doing very well. "You are going to see a big change in her, you will also notice a big difference in her manners, she is now polite and not cheeky anymore, she is loving her new school and has made lots of new friends."

"Mama, Billy and I have come here today to take Eveline home, where she belongs, we miss her and she should be with her parents. Thank you so much for taking care and looking after Eveline, dearest Mama and Papa, I am feeling so much better now, things are going to be alright from now on."

Papa heard the conversation, he was still angry with Billy, but he felt he could not interfere, but what he did say was, "Billy, Eveline is very happy here, she will not be happy leaving all her friends and leaving her new school, where she is doing so well."

Then Billy said, "Be that as it may Alfred, she is our daughter and we shall be taking her home today, that is final."

Evelyne then said, "Well, Billy, if you are set on taking her out of school when she is doing so well, she will be very unhappy, but she is your daughter and you have every right to take her home with you, we love her and we shall both miss her, so very much."

They all heard a knock on the door, mama went to answer it, Eveline was standing there smiling, "Guess what, Grandma? I got top marks for my maths exam today!"

"Well done, darling, you clever girl. There is a surprise waiting for you in the living room, now go and see."

When she saw her Mother and Father and her little brother Michael walking, she was not feeling altogether happy, but she smiled and went over to them saying, "Hello Mama and Papa."

They both answered, "Hello Eveline."

Mama said, "Darling, we have missed you, are you all better now, sweetheart?"

She hugged and kissed her mother, "Yes Mama, I am fine now," then she picked up her brother and kissed him too saying, "My, you have grown, Mickey!"

He looked at her and said, "Eveie."

"My little brother, you are getting heavy now." She put him down. He picked up his teddy and went to sit on the floor beside his granddad and cuddled his teddy bear.

Then Mama said, "Eveline, we have come to take you home, darling."

Just what she had thought. She then threw a tantrum, "Mama, I don't want to go home yet, I want to stay here with Grandma and Grandpa, I need to finish my summer term."

"Eveline my darling, I am sorry, but there will be no arguing, Papa and I are taking you home with us today and that's final. I am sure there will be a place at our local Catholic school, hopefully, you will start after the Easter Holidays." Grandma, with a heavy heart, sadly went upstairs and packed all of Eveline's belongings, she gave them to Billy, who said very little. Eveline was feeling sad, having to leave her Grandma and Grandpa, she had been so happy living here.

She gave them both a big hug, as she was saying her goodbyes, she said, "Please say goodbye to Daisy and Vivian for me, tell them I will see them again hopefully in the summer holidays and please would you kindly ask Mrs Nightingale to explain to the Head Mistress that I will not be returning to school to finish the summer term. Tell her that my parents have now come here to take me home, where I will carry on my education, starting at another school nearer to where I live, after the Easter Holidays." She went over to her Grandpa and Grandma, "I have been most happy here staying with you both, Thank you so much for looking after me, I love you both, so very much."

"Yes darling, we love you too, I will do as you ask and talk to the Nightingales tomorrow." Alfred had a tear in his eye as he said his sad goodbye.

Mother looked at Eveline and said, "Don't look so sad darling, you can visit your grandparents again in the summer holidays. We have a nice big chocolate Easter egg at home for you and Michael to share." Then they left to catch the next train home. When they returned home, things went well, Eveline started her new Catholic School, she settled in quite quickly, she liked her teacher and made some new friends.

Eveline became very close friends with a girl in her class, called Mary-Bell. She lived on the same street, she would call for her in the mornings and they would go to school together.

Billy had struck lucky. Someone had left, leaving a job vacancy for a railway fireman, he had already applied and got the job, he had started working the following week. He called it "being on the footplate."

Blanche was so happy, she would have money coming in to pay for expenses and rent. He was never going to get drunk again, for the sake of his job, dear wife and family, He was treating his wife with respect and kindness. Life was good and all the family were living happily together again.

It was a warm late autumn afternoon when Billy was on his way home, covered in dirt and sweat when he saw a big poster which read:

BERTRAM MILLS CIRCUS. STRONG MEN WANTED FOR MAINTENANCE WORK. PLEASE APPLY AT THE CARAVAN BEHIND THE ALE HOUSE IN THE FIELD BEYOND.

Billy stopped and read it, he considered the idea of working in a circus. If the pay was good, he thought it might be a better job, he at least would not be going home, filthy with coal dust and sweaty every day.

So he went home, washed and put on some clean clothes. As he sat having his meal, he then told Blanche about the Poster he had seen. "I would like to find out more about this job advertised for a maintenance man at this nearby Circus. What are your thoughts about me applying for this job, Blanche?"

Blanche was optimistic, "Well, I think it's a great opportunity for you, Billy, if you think you can handle it, give it a try, you have nothing to lose, but make sure you have the job, before leaving the railways."

At six that evening, he set out to try his luck. He knocked on the caravan door, he was invited in by a big burly man, who introduced himself, "I'm Mr Mills the manager; can I help you, sir?"

Billy said, "Good evening, Mr Mills, I am William Hancock, I would like to apply for the maintenance job."

"Do take a seat, Mr Hancock." He asked Billy many questions about himself, past jobs where he lived, had he ever been in trouble with the law?

Billy answered them as honestly as he could without incriminating himself. "Mr Hancock, I am willing to give you a week's trial." They discussed wages. "The circus will be in this area for about a month. Then we will be moving on, would you be prepared to travel with the Circus around Somerset? The work would only be seasonal in this country. You would have to share a caravan with your fellow workers. We travel to Europe and back to England each summer. We pay wages on a monthly basis."

He gave Billy an estimate of how much he would be paying him a month. Billy thought it was a good liveable wage. "We will review your wages after six months. You will be expected to fill in this application form. Your hours of work will be from seven thirty in the morning, until ten thirty at night. There will be a half-hour breakfast break, one hour for lunch and one hour for your evening dinner, which will be served at five o'clock. Our shows start at seven until ten at night."

Billy agreed to the working conditions, he was to be taken on a month's trial as a maintenance manager. After giving a week's notice at the railways, he started work a week later at the Circus. His vigorous training began with putting up tent poles and erecting the rigging for the trapeze acts. Securing all the safety ropes, clearing and cleaning up after performances. For the first few weeks, Billy found it very hard work, but he made some friends and he did enjoy watching the circus excitement. During the day, he would cut the grass, keep the outside clean and tidy. But most importantly, making sure everything was in good working order.

After a month with the circus, one morning Johnny Mills called Billy into his caravan and told him to take a seat. Billy sat down, wondering if he had qualified for the job, "Mr Hancock, I am very pleased with your work and I would like to offer you a permanent contract. In three weeks' time, the circus will be moving down to Cornwall. Would you be prepared to live in and share a caravan?"

"Mr Mills, I would be happy to sign the contract, travel with the circus and share a caravan. Thank you very much." Billy signed the contract and felt very happy. He knew Blanche would also be very happy that he now had a permanent job. Late that evening, when he returned home, he gave her the good news. She was overjoyed and said, "Billy, you will come home and see the family when you get time off?"

He said, "Of course I will, my dear, and I will send you enough money each week, to pay the bills, rent and buy food." For the next three months, Billy kept his word, he would return home to see the family, every third weekend off. Billy had never been happier and enjoyed working with the circus. He travelled around the West countryside, he made a close friend with a young man called Adam Gibbs, who offered to share his caravan with Billy. They got on well together, after the shows, they would play cards or darts in his caravan before turning in for the night. Things were going great. He would send Blanche a money order home, once a week, to pay for the gas, electricity, rent and enough to buy food for the family. Life was good while it lasted, but things were about to change for the worse!

Unfortunately for Billy, he became very friendly with one of the circus staff called Edward, who they all called Eddy, he was a very likeable chap, he was one of the lads who liked a pint of ale every night. After work each night, Edward would frequent the local pub across the road from the circus, with other members of staff, he asked Billy many times to join him, but Billy managed to refuse, by saying he was tired and needed his sleep. Then on Eddy's 25th birthday, all the working men were invited to his party at the local pub. Of course, Adam and Billy were also invited, it would have been rude to refuse. They put on their best suits and went along to the party.

Adam told Billy that he would not be stopping long as he did not drink alcohol, he would just stick to non-alcohol punch. Adam and Billy had both clubbed together to buy Eddy a pint glass beer mug, which they had inscribed, with his name on it. The party was in full swing when Billy and Adam arrived. Billy joined Adam in just drinking a non-alcoholic punch, but he was constantly being pestered to have something stronger, he refused several times. They gave Eddy his present, wrapped in fancy paper, he was really chuffed and said, "Thanks guys, you shouldn't have."

They wished him a Happy Birthday and someone shouted, "Everyone gets a drink to toast Eddy and sing Happy Birthday." The bar lady brought out a large birthday cake with lighted candles, placing the cake in the middle of a round table. Then plates of party food were placed behind. As Eddy blew out the candles, he then cut the cake. Pints of ale were handed around the room, everyone was given a pint, Adam refused and had a pint of non-alcoholic punch instead, how could Billy refuse one pint of ale, just to toast his friend. They all started singing Happy Birthday, as someone shouted hip, hip, they all cheered hooray, as they toasted Edward. The party was getting rowdy and the music became louder.

If only Billy had been stronger in mind, as the party went on, if only he had just kept to the one drink, he vaguely remembered his promise to Blanche, but as the evening went on, his willpower started to weaken when as his host came over and Eddy put another pint of ale in his hand, saying, "Just one more for the road, Billy, the circus is closed tomorrow, so we will all have a chance to have a sleep in."

That was Billy's downfall. He thought he would be OK if he was not going home, only to spend the night in Adam's caravan, so he could have a nice long rest the next day. Well, one pint led to two and three even before 11 o'clock he was drunk! He started singing than shouting along with the music and his friend Adam who he stayed with, was still only drinking punch, as he was a teetotaller. He saw how drunk Billy was getting, as a friend he said to him, "Come along, Billy, let's go back to the caravan now, I think you have had enough to drink tonight, we should leave now."

"Who do you t-h-i-n-k you're talking to, mind your own business." Billy slurred his words and suddenly, he just punched his friend in the face, which then started bleeding, a terrible fight broke out, many saw Mr Hancock start the fight until someone went and told Mr Mills exactly what had happened. Mr Mills broke up the fight, although Adam was not a big man, he had been taught self-defence, he could stand up to any man. Billy by this time was stumbling, he now lay flat on the ground. Mr Mills and another man put Billy in the back of Mr Mills' car and drove him back home.

They grabbed Billy from the car, holding him up, knocking loudly on his door. Billy was so drunk and in pain, that he could hardly stand up. Blanche opened the door and was in total shock when she saw Billy, his nose had been bleeding and his left eye was closed. His best suit was covered in blood and beer. "Mrs Hancock, is this your husband William?"

"Yes, whatever has happened to him?" she asked.

Mr Mills explained, "Mrs Hancock, I am the circus manager, Your husband William has been in a fight, several witnesses at the party tonight saw William punch one of my staff in the face, Billy being drunk and disorderly, had started a fight, hitting his friend Adam for no apparent reason. Mrs Hancock, my name is Johnny Mills, as William's manager, I cannot tolerate this kind of behaviour from my staff, under any circumstances. Would you kindly tell William from now on, he is no longer employed with Bertram Mills circus, I would be obliged if you can tell him not to turn up for work on Monday morning, as from this moment he is fired. He will receive his monthly salary delivered by post and a letter of dismissal will be sent forthwith. His contract will now be expired, I bid you goodnight, Mrs Hancock." He doffed his cap and left.

Billy was in a terrible state, he staggered into the house, he was black and blue. He stank of alcohol. "Oh Billy, what happened to the promise you made to me?" He was so drunk, badly beaten up, punched, kicked and looked in a very bad way, he could barely stand up. The worrying thing was that he had been sacked from his job. Where he was doing so well. What were they going to do now?

Blanche managed somehow to get him into the lounge then he just crashed out on the sofa. Blanche cleaned and patched him up, as best she could. Blanche could have cried, but she managed to stay strong. She did not want the children to ask too many questions. Billy stayed in bed for several days until his bruises faded. One morning he got up and told Blanche that he was going out to find work and would be back by teatime. He made his departure without another word.

Blanche was desperate, so what was she going to do now, her husband was out of work. How would they live, with no money coming in to pay the rent or buy food for them all? All Blanche could do was contact Biddy yet again. She could, but never would ask her parents for help, she knew what her papa would say and what his answer would be!

Chapter Thirty

One morning out of the blue, Eveline found her mother packing up all papa and her clothes and personal items. "Now Eveline, I want you to put all your clothes and belongings into bags, we are leaving this place and moving to another home." After all the cases and bags were packed, they were put into a van. Mama gave Eveline a shove into the back of this very large black van, while Papa was holding on to Michael, she did not know the driver of this large black van, but it broke down several times on their journey before they arrived at this lovely white bungalow called MAKINA in Ashford Common near Sudbury.

The place was pretty with all brand new furniture, Eveline had her own room with twin beds, with pretty green bed, covers Mama's room was decorated in pale blue, Biddy wanted Mama to stay with Blanche until Billy found a job, but Mama was unable to give Blanche her support this time because she was suffering from terrible pains in her leg. Grandma and Grandpa had now moved to London, Alfred would be caring and looking after her. Eveline was to start yet another new school, this time with her brother Michael, who would also be starting in the infants class. he had now turned five, Blanche took them both to their new school, they would soon be going to school together without Mama having to take them.

Once they had all settled into the bungalow, Billy said, "Blanche, tomorrow I am going back to see if I can have my old job back on the railways. I just may be gone a while." He left early the following morning, that was the last they saw of him for quite some time. One morning Eveline woke up with awful pains in her neck and throat, she could hardly swallow, Blanche thought she had the mumps, her kind neighbour called the doctor. After examining her, he told Blanche that she had the mumps and to keep her in bed. Blanche kept her in bed and gave her the doctor's medicine.

After a few days, Eveline began to feel a little better, she was missing school and her friends. Blanche was just outside the kitchen door, talking to her next-door neighbour when Eveline heard a terrible scream from the living room. She rushed out of bed to find that Michael had fallen into the fire grate. She started screaming, calling Mama to come quickly Michael had fallen into the fire. Mama who was just coming back into the kitchen, rushed into the living room and quickly pulled Michael out, she immediately put wet towels over his head, face, hands and arms, he was still screaming.

Mama told Eveline to hurry next door and asked her neighbour to quickly call for an ambulance and say, "Our Mickey has just fallen into the fire!" Their lovely neighbour immediately phoned for an ambulance and they rushed Michael to Middlesex County Hospital. Mother went with him, leaving Eveline with their lovely friendly neighbour, who gave her a warm chocolate drink and biscuit telling her, "Try not to worry, Eveline, he is in very good hands."

When Mama returned from the hospital, she was very distressed, she just told us that they were keeping Michael in hospital for minor burns to his face, head, arms and hands. She left the hospital after seeing Michael, with his head and hands all bandaged up. Tomorrow, Mama would take Eveline to visit Michael, but only if she was feeling well enough to travel. Mama adored Michael, he was a beautiful boy, with his blue eyes and fair curly hair, his cute smiling face. He was a happy little boy. Eveline and Mickey played well together, she was very worried about her brother.

The next day Eveline felt so much better, so Mama did take her to see Mickey at the hospital. It was strange seeing him with bandages all around his head. Mickey reminded her of a mummy that she once saw in an Egyptian picture book. Mama took Eveline a few times to the hospital. The following Monday, Eveline was so glad to be going back to school.

Biddy just happened to visit Blanche later that morning and she told her what had happened to Michael, she said, "Biddy, it is only minor burns, the Hospital informed me that his skin will heal in time and he will have very little scarring."

Biddy said, "Blanche, get your coat on, I want to see Michael in hospital, we should be back by the time Eveline finishes school, do you think you could ask your kind neighbour Lilly Straton to pick Eveline up from school in case we are late back?"

Lilly said she would be glad to help and pick Eveline up from school, just to let her know when they returned. They drove to the Hospital, Biddy was very concerned about Michael. But felt better after speaking to the Doctor, he told them both not to worry, Michael would be fine. They were home in time to fetch Eveline from school.

On Wednesday, just before lunchtime, Eveline was very surprised to see her Mama walk into the classroom, having had a quick word with the teacher, she then came over to her desk, grabbed her by the hand, saying "quickly darling you have to leave the school, we have to catch the next bus to London," dragging her out of the classroom, to the bemused looks of children in her class! Mama ran with her to the bus stop, where they boarded the Greenline bus for London.

It must have been about the 10th November because as they alighted from the bus, several people came up to them, wanting them to buy a POPPY for Remembrance Day, Mama shouted at them to get out of her way, she was in a desperate hurry, saying my Mother was very ill in hospital, so just go away.

Mama still held hold of Eveline, until they arrived at the Royal Infirmary Hospital where Grandma had recently been operated on. I just remember her letting me eat her apples. Everyone thought that her illness was the effect of her osteoarthritis. We were standing at her bedside, when Grandma said, "I am about to go to heaven." There was a very quick reply from Mama, who Eveline heard say, "Oh no you're not!"

It was less than a week later that Mother took me back to the Royal Infirmary Hospital. We started to climb the large staircase when Biddy came rushing down the stairs very angry, screaming at Mother for being late. "Blanche, why didn't you come yesterday, did you not get my telegram?" Biddy didn't know Michael was still in Hospital, but before Mama could answer, some friend of Biddy's was coming up the stairs behind them, she was carrying a large bunch of flowers for Evelyne. In Biddy's anger throwing her arms up in the air, she gave one swipe of her arm and all the flowers were strewn everywhere, her friend was staring open-mouthed at her, with a look of surprise in her eyes.

Biddy quickly grabbed Mother's arm and pulled her up the stairs, in turn pulling Eveline up with her, Biddy was still shouting and carrying on. They entered the room where Grandpa and Alfie were standing close by, with their heads down, they walked towards the bed and saw Grandma as she lay motionless on the bed, two nuns were starting to cover Grandma with a white sheet. Mother ran to her bed and pulled back the sheet and shouted, "Mama, Mama, Mama."

Grandma blinked her eyes twice, then brother Alfie pulled Blanche away saying, "Blanche, no calling will bring Mama back," he then let go of her. Grandma had passed peacefully away. Biddy and Mother started to have hysterics. Alfred tried to calm them both down. While all this was happening, Eveline was standing holding the rail at the foot of the bed, then on her right side, something made her look up and what she saw was so beautiful it's hard to describe. She was seeing something so bright and tall, this apparition then started to move towards the bed and as it did so, it became smaller and smaller, but its light stayed as bright, Eveline watched transfixed, as this ball of light became the size of a tennis ball, then it seemed to go into Grandma's chest, only for a second.

As the bright light came out of Grandma, it became two lights that now floated up and out of the closed window, into the sky! Biddy and Mother were both now calm and silent. Now everyone had their heads bent in silent prayer. (Saint Joseph had come and taken Grandma's spirit up to Heaven). Biddy and Blanche rolled Grandma over, they sprinkled her with some kind of powder.

The next day Eveline was taken to the mortuary, to see her Grandma one more time before the funeral. She did not go to the funeral. She was taken to stay with Biddy's new servant Marie at 45 Curson St London. Evelyne Jane De-rosa Knight was buried at Kensal Rise Harrow, aged 69.

Chapter Thirty-One

In 1939, the latest news was that Germany declared war on Poland from the west. Two days later, France and Britain declared war on Germany, then on the 17th Soviet troops invaded Poland from the East. War between USSR and Germany began on 3 September 1941. America became involved in the war when the Japanese bombed Pearl Harbour in Hawaii on 7 December 1941.

Germans started sending bombs, blowing up all parts of London and other parts of England, there was a curfew and blackouts. The Germans were sending V1 Flying bombs, destroying lots of beautiful buildings. Towns were being targeted blowing up London and all other parts of the United Kingdom. American troops declared war on Germany and Italy. They were the allies we needed.

Blanche had a disturbing letter from Patrick, saying that he had received his pilot's flying license. World war 2 was now imminent. From July to October 1940, the Battle of Britain had started. The Germans were attacking the British Channel. He said:

My part will be in defending our coastline. Please don't worry my darling, remember I love you with all my heart, one day I shall return to marry you. Take care, all my love Paddy xxx.

Biddy read the letter again, it was very worrying to think that Paddy was out there protecting our British coastline and the dangers he faced up in the sky. Biddy then wrote to Blanche telling her all this disturbing news. Blanche tried not to think about what the future held. She went around to her friendly neighbour's house to chat, taking with her a freshly baked fruit cake.

The year 1942 was to be the most terrifying, World War Two had started and for the next three years, the Germans would be sending more bombs to destroy our country.

Patrick was now flying planes and bombing the enemy, Thousands of men were losing their lives. Patrick's plane was shot down into the English Channel. He was so very lucky to have survived that mission. He was picked up by a British warship. He had very serious facial injuries and burns to his face and body. He was so badly burnt, they had to rebuild his face. Patrick had a miraculous escape, all the war details were lost, the doctors did some marvellous surgery on his face and body. He did have several operations but slowly he got over his injuries and was fighting fit again.

Biddy visited him several times in the hospital. They were still in love and one day they would become, Husband and Wife. When he had totally recovered, he returned to the Air Force to finish his time, until the war was over. He wanted to carry on and fight for his country. The next letter Biddy received was from Germany, He would be staying with the

Air Force until the end of the war. He was Biddy's real hero, all she hoped and prayed for was that he would return to her.

It was now late into the 1930s. Biddy was still living in a large flat above the hairdressers shop. It would be some time now before Patrick and Biddy would marry. Things were a little different now, as they were both busy with their careers, they would not be settling down just yet. During Patrick's time as a pilot, he was granted leave on medical grounds. He did manage to see Biddy, to plan their wedding day. While he was looking for a house, where they could call home when the time came for them to marry. He had been looking for a large house and had seen this lovely Georgian house for sale in the local housing agent's magazine in Cambridgeshire. He made inquiries as to this most fabulous-looking house. He picked up the keys from the agent and went to view the property and knew it would be just the right home for his beautiful bride-to-be.

He eventually went and bought this beautiful brick-built Georgian house with five acres of grounds in Royston Cambridge. This fabulous property was surrounded by high brick walls and a double wrought Iron gate, with its portcullis entrance. The house inside was just luxurious, it had everything a family could wish for; sheer luxury inside, it had a Finnish sauna bath. Large beautifully unfurnished rooms. One room had a built-in fine cocktail bar. It had a lovely Orangery leading out into the huge gardens and a large fish pond. Also had a garden pavilion which kept all their gardening equipment. It would need a lot of work and alterations on the interior and exterior, it would all have to be done before moving in. A balconied portico would be added.

Tennis courts and landscaping of the gardens were going to be a fine addition.

They were also going to have a fabulous swimming pool built, as another beautiful feature. There would also be an extended pavilion for all their tennis and squash rackets, croquet and games equipment. This superb house and gardens would become their family home after Biddy and Paddy were married. There was also a little cottage next to the main house, where their guests could stay Patrick would employ servants and a gardener.

When Blanche took Eveline on the train up to London to pick Michael up from the Hospital, Eveline was now feeling so much better, all signs of the mumps had gone. When they got to the hospital, Michael was still swathed in bandages, he was so happy to see them and very glad to be going home, after spending months in hospital. They went and did a little food shopping and caught the next train back home. After two weeks, Michael was to be returned to the Hospital to have all his bandages removed. Biddy came over to see how Blanche was feeling, after losing their dear mother. Both Blanche and Biddy were slowly coming to terms with the loss of their dear mama.

Biddy told Blanche that she had written to Agnes, telling her the sad news. Blanche asked Biddy if she would take Michael to the hospital, to have his bandages removed. Biddy said, "Yes, of course, I will, I also think it would do Papa good to see Michael and Eveline, it might cheer him up to see his grandchildren, He has not seen Michael for such a long time. I expect Papa is still feeling very low, slowly getting over the loss of his dearly beloved wife."

"I think that's a good idea, Biddy." She left, taking Michael and Eveline with her. At the hospital, they had to wait, while Michael was having all his head bandages taken off. His head was covered in red bald patches. The Doctor gave Biddy some special cream, he said "It must be applied gently to his skin, twice a day." The Doctor told Biddy not to worry, as all his hair would grow back. They also said that all the scarring would slowly fade, that it would completely disappear in time. That was very good news, they all left the Hospital feeling very happy. Now the children were both looking forward to seeing their granddad. They both chatted away in the car, as Biddy drove them there.

Grandfather was so very pleased to see both his grandchildren. He was sadly missing his lovely wife Evelyne, he had never felt so lost and lonely. It cheered him up no end to see both of them, he gave them some sweets and chocolate. He remarked on Michael's face and said how nicely it was healing. Biddy told her papa that she would pick Eveline up tomorrow after breakfast. She would be taking her up to London to do some sightseeing and also to buy her some new clothes. After spending a few hours with Papa, Biddy and Michael started to leave, Michael said goodbye to Evie, then to his granddad giving him a loving hug. "I love you so much, Grandpa."

"I am so glad you are now getting better, Grandson."

Then Biddy said her goodbyes, gave them both a kiss and cuddle and as she was leaving with Michael, she said, "I'll see you both tomorrow about ten o'clock." She then drove Michael home to his mother and stayed the night with Blanche. Mama was so very pleased to see her son, without his bandages, Biddy gave Blanche the medical cream and told her how to apply it. Blanche was so happy to see Michael, hugged him and gave him his favourite teddy bear.

The next morning Biddy left to pick up Eveline from Papa's home. Eveline said at breakfast, "Oh Grandpa, I am so excited to be going to London, with Aunty, she is going to buy me some new clothes and we are going sightseeing." Biddy arrived, Eveline was already. They said their fond goodbyes, then left for London. They did some sightseeing, Marble Arch and Buckingham Palace, then caught the underground to Shepherds Bush market, to buy her some new clothes. Aunty bought some nice dresses and cardigans to match. While they were busy browsing, looking on the ribbons stall, a lady standing next to them said, "What a beautiful daughter you have, my dear."

Biddy looked at the lady and smiled, "No Eveline is not my child, she is my niece."

"Oh well she is very lovely."

"Thank you," said Biddy. Holding a lead, sitting beside her, was a lovely big white dog with a distinctive black patch over the left eye, Eveline started to stroke the dog. Biddy studied it for a moment, she suddenly recognised the dog and the lady and said, "I think I know you by sight, I think we once met in the doctor's surgery, I think we had a little chat in the waiting room. Do you live in Whitehorse Street and is your name Pat Sanders?"

"Yes that's right, I have lived there for many years."

"Well, Pat, a few years ago, I lived in a flat just up the road to you, but moved away. I now live in Curzon street."

"What a small world!" Pat replied. "I still live in the same house." Pat Sanders and Biddy were to become very good friends, for many years to come.

Six months had passed. One day when Biddy arrived back at her flat, there was a letter waiting on the doormat. She opened the letter, it was from her Papa to say he had been very lost and lonely since Evelyne passed away. He said he had now joined a Bridge Club, saying how much he enjoyed playing once a week, he had made some new friends. He went on to say, "One of his new friends was a lovely lady called Florence; We have been dating for about two months. She likes to be called Florrie. We have such a lot in common, she is fun to be with, makes me smile a lot. She loves walking and we play all kinds of card games. Florrie has even taught me some new ones. She is patiently trying to teach me to play chess. I am very attracted to her. If by the end of the year, we are still together, I intend to propose to her."

Biddy wrote back to her Papa and said how pleased she was that he had found a nice lady friend, Biddy said she would love to meet her, they must arrange to meet up soon. They met up in a nice local pub near them both. Biddy took an instant liking to Florrie, she was warm and friendly and funny and with the jokes she told, Biddy was rolling in laughter, Florrie definitely got Biddy's approval.

Blanche received a letter from Biddy telling her all about this new lady friend of Papa's, she said, "I have met this lady Florrie, she is very nice and friendly, I think if Papa does marry her, he will be very happy, as they have a lot in common."

The next letter Biddy received was from her Papa, it was to say that he was planning to get married to Florrie and they would be honoured if she would be their witness. He said it would be a very quiet civil service in a Registry Office. He gave her the place and time. They would have a buffet at his home in Wandsworth. If she'd like to attend the wedding and be their witness, he asked her to let him know, then he will send her all the details: Date of Wedding, Time and Place. He also said he had sent an invitation to Blanche and the family. Biddy was delighted to be asked to be a witness when her Papa and Florence got married.

Florrie was the ideal lady for Papa, very softly spoken with a kind warm loving nature. She knew how to make Papa laugh. Papa would not be lonely anymore. Blanche sent a letter regretting that they could not attend the wedding as Billy could not have the time for work. Blanche and Billy sent their congratulations to them, wishing them both many years of happiness. They said they would love to meet Florrie very soon. Blanche received a letter from Papa and Florrie to say they would be most welcome to visit any time, just to let them know when. Florrie would love to meet Blanche, Billy and the children.

Blanche wrote back to let them know they would be delighted to come on Sunday 26 June, for the day. *It will just be the children and me, as Billy said he will not be coming this time, he likes to rest on Sundays, as his job on the railways is so demanding, he hopes you will understand and he will meet you when you pay us a visit. The children and I will be coming on the train. We look forward to meeting you Florrie and seeing Papa again, the Children cannot wait to see their Grandpa. Much Love, Blanche, Eveline and Michael. xxx.*

The meeting was good, Papa looked so happy to be with Florrie, Blanche found her to be a very easy-going lady, with a kind loving nature, she was generous too. Florrie had kindly bought little gifts for the children, an Enid Blyton's book for

Eveline and a football for Michael. It was all so new to Blanche and she found it a little hard to accept some other lady taking her mother's place. Eveline and Michael were so happy to see their Grandpa again, he chatted with them most of the afternoon. Blanche and Florrie sat and talked about life in general, Blanche tried to find out a bit about Florence's background. Florrie said she did not really like talking about herself, as it was very upsetting. But she did tell Blanche a little about her upbringing. What she did reveal was that she liked school and did quite well, just before leaving school, her life changed completely.

When she found out that her parents were splitting up, her father had been having an affair with her mother's best friend, it was heart-breaking for her mother and herself. Her mother, Jane, divorced her husband Raymond. A year later her mother was out with her close friend Brenda they had joined a bridge club and her mother Jane met a male bridge partner who she liked, they started dating and after six months he asked her to marry him.

"My father had remarried and moved away. I never saw him again, he did write to me but I never answered his letters. He then stopped writing, lost touch with me and I never heard from him again. Mother married Steven. She was happy enough, but I did not like or get along with my Stepfather, he was very strict with me, never showing much love, kindness or affection towards me. I left home at sixteen and joined the Women's Land Army and made lots of friends. I dated a few boyfriends, but never found a man that I wanted to marry and settle down with, not until I met your father."

Blanche felt very sorry for her and said, "Florrie, once you joined the Land Army, did your life improve and were you happier?"

She said, "Yes Blanche, I have been very happy since. When I heard that my stepfather had passed away, I would go and visit my mother quite often. She was always pleased to see me. She is getting very frail now, she employs a lady who comes weekly to do the housework. The district nurse comes in daily to help wash and dress her and administer her medicine."

Their train back to Sudbury was due at 4.30 pm. It was soon time for Blanche and the children to leave, they had spent a wonderful day with their granddad and were reluctant to go, they said their goodbyes and Blanche invited them to come for a visit as soon as they were able. The children said a big thank you to Florrie for their gifts, they said their fond farewells and caught their train back to Sudbury.

On the train home, Blanche was deep in thought about Florrie; she seemed very nice and friendly, it was so good to see Papa happy and content with his new wife.

Chapter Thirty-Two

When Biddy was driving Eveline back home, after spending the weekend together in London, she saw Eveline was looking sad. "Eveline why do you look so sad, didn't you enjoy your time with me?"

"Oh Aunty, I love being with you, It's just that Father and Mother are so strict with me, I am always getting into trouble with them, I do not seem to make them happy. Father stays away for long periods, then when he does come home, Mother and Father are always fighting and shouting at each other. I scream at them to stop as it keeps me awake at night. Aunty late one evening I thought I heard Mama screaming downstairs when I looked over the banister, I saw Mama being held up against the wall and Papa banging her head against it. When I shouted for Papa to stop, he did, then he just shouted at me saying 'Get back to bed or you will get a good spanking,' he then stormed out of the house."

Biddy did not know what to say about this and thought that Eveline was exaggerating a little. "Don't worry darling I will speak to your Mother."

"No Aunty please don't say anything, it will just make things worse, she will tell me off for telling tales."

"OK if that's what you want darling, I shall not mention it."

"Thank you, Aunty, so much for giving me such a wonderful time, for the lovely clothes and things you have bought me, I love the Indian doll dressed in national costume. I love you so much."

"You are welcome, sweetheart," Biddy replied.

When they arrived back, Blanche was in a very bad frame of mind. In a meek voice, she said, "Hello Biddy."

"Blanche, whatever is the matter with you?"

Blanche then broke down and said, "Oh Biddy I am expecting a baby in less than six months' time, I went to see the Doctor today and he confirmed that I am pregnant."

"Why, that's wonderful news, Blanche, you should be very happy!"

"Biddy darling, I think we shall have to move again, as this bungalow is going to be too small, I'll need a three-bedroom house."

"Well, Blanche, I met up with Patrick, while he was on a short leave from the RAF, Patrick and I are now officially engaged, we hope to be married as soon as Patrick can get time off from the Air Force. We plan to be married in London. Do you like my diamond engagement ring?"

"Oh it is so gorgeous, Biddy, have you set a wedding date yet?"

"We have not arranged a date yet, but Patrick is buying a large mansion house in Cambridge. I was thinking that I could perhaps find you a council House in Hertfordshire. I shall make some inquiries for you. So come on dear Blanche, cheer up things are going to improve you'll see."

Time passed quickly and the months flew by.

"Blanche started to become extremely aggressive with Eveline. Maybe it was all the worry and her state of mind, being abused at times by Billy, living without the support of her husband for most of the time, it was just getting to her and being pregnant again was not helping her at all." Eveline was becoming very disobedient and cheeky and not doing as she was told. Sometimes it was for not doing her homework or not doing her chores, Mama would shout at her and discipline Eveline, for being so untidy. Blanche's pregnancy was making her lazy and lethargic; she just didn't feel happy about bringing another child into the world, she was so worried about her situation, would Billy bring in enough money to support another child? What would Billy say when he came home and still had not told him, but it was obvious as she was now showing a large tummy. Blanche knew they were struggling to pay the bills now. How were they going to afford another child to clothe and feed? It was making Blanche so depressed and unhappy she was unable to sleep.

She was taking her anger out on Eveline. She would lose her temper and she made her do extra chores. She prayed that she could control her feelings and temper, but she just could not. She would often send her off to bed early, but she would just play with Michael, then Mama would come up and say she was sorry afterwards. Telling her she must do as she was told and not answer back. She didn't put much food on the table and they were both losing weight. Blanche was not cooking much either, ham, bread and cheese and soup and a piece of fruit. She hated herself for being so unkind to her daughter, Mama never raised her hand to Eveline once.

When Billy did make an appearance, he was sober and in a good mood. Which was a change as he was often drunk and hostile to Blanche. She told him that they were going to have another child in five months' time. It was strange, but Billy was very happy about another child in the family. "Blanche my dear, don't look so sad, I will try and get more overtime, we will manage somehow, we always have before my dear." Sometimes when Billy came home drunk, he would be hostile to Blanche when they were alone, but they never hit or smacked the children.

To Eveline, it was such a relief when school started again, after the long summer holidays. She would be at school during the day, with good school meals, no chores to do, then after school, she would take her brother Mickey out to play with the other children in her street. He was now almost five years old. That way she could get away from her mother's wrath.

One day Biddy happened to call in unexpectedly, to find this lovely new bungalow in such a mess, that she lost her temper and gave Blanche a good telling off, shouting and screaming at her, saying, "Look at the state of this place, Blanche, you haven't tidied up or washed or cleaned the place for weeks; it's disgusting! What has gotten into you? I have had enough, sister! It's time you got your act together and started taking pride in yourself and your home. After all I have done for you! Good riddance." And she left. While all this shouting and nastiness was going on, Eveline went and hid under her bed, Biddy had left, in such a very bad temper, she didn't even say goodbye to her. Eveline was doing so well at this new school, she hoped that this would be the last school she would attend. It was very unlikely…

Biddy drove home feeling sorry, she never should have spoken to her sister in that way, maybe she should be more understanding, after all, she did have an abusive husband who treated her so badly. Oh dear poor Blanche, it had slipped her mind that Blanche was now pregnant. She would write and apologise to her, after all, she had taken the biggest responsibility anyone could take on, looking after and bringing up her son. She decided to make it up to her, the best way she knew how.

When she got back to her penthouse flat in London, she telephoned the office at Hertfordshire County Council to ask if there were any available three-bedroom houses in the Hatfield area to rent. She was told by the rent office that there was a three-bedroom house for rent in Astwick Avenue Hatfield Herts. She agreed to the rental payments on a weekly basis. They would write and tell her when she would be able to move in, the keys would have to be picked up from the Council Offices in Hatfield. Biddy said she would send them a month's rent in advance when she heard from them. She had to give her name and present address and she gave it as Mrs Blanche Hancock at the address where Blanche was now living.

Forms would have to be filled in, terms and conditions would apply. Rent book and details would be forwarded in two weeks. She hoped this would make Blanche happy and show her how sorry she was and prayed she would forgive her. The next day she made a point of going to see Blanche very early, with her humble apologies. Blanche was so happy to see her, that she forgave her sister. She said, "Biddy, I deserved that, I needed you to see what state I had got myself into and I am so truly sorry. I also have a confession to make, I have been so unhappy lately, that I have been taking it out on Eveline. I love her and yet I have treated her so badly. I swear to you now, I will never be a bad mother to her again, I shall pray for God's forgiveness."

"If you are truly sorry, Blanche, God will forgive you. If it was me, Blanche, I would talk to Eveline and explain that you have not felt well lately, tell her you are so sorry for being so strict with her. Tell her how much you love her, that you did not mean those things you said, it was very unkind of you, take her in your arms and say, 'My darling Eveline, I love you, it will never ever happen again'."

"Now Blanche, what I am about to tell you is something that is going to make you so very happy." Biddy told Blanche that she had secured a three-bedroom house in Hatfield. "Hertfordshire County Council will shortly be writing to you, with forms for you to fill in, there will be details about the house. They will also give you details on where to pick up the Keys, enclosed will be a rent book and where to pay along with your terms and conditions that will apply. The rent must be paid weekly and when you hear from them, you must contact me, then I will send you the first month's rent in advance, which you must send to them with your signed contract letters. Do you understand all that, my dear?"

"Oh yes! I will contact you as soon as I hear from them, Biddy, you are wonderful, you are my saviour, I can never thank you enough. You are the kindest loving sister, whatever would I have done without all your help, over the years. We must never fall out again, because we're sisters and we love each other."

"Blanche, it is what you have done for me, my dearest sister, don't you ever forget that!"

Chapter Thirty-Three

Two months later, Blanche, Billy and the family moved into their three-bedroom Council house, in Astwick Avenue Hatfield, behind the De Havilland Aircraft Factory. They were living there for less than six weeks when Blanche started to have signs that she was going into labour. Billy, who had just returned home that evening from work after recently finding a job as a local tractor driver, found Blanche in labour, he quickly called the local midwife from a nearby phone.

Blanche gave birth to a healthy baby girl, Caroline June Jane, on 5 June 1939. Billy gave Blanche much more love and attention he had ever given her, they started getting along a lot better without them rowing and arguing. Blanche was happy to nurture her new baby girl, she was now looking forward to being together as a happy family once more. Billy liked the house, everyone was more than happy, living in this spacious three-bedroom house. Michael loved watching the planes coming and going. But Mother's only complaint was that the house being so near to the airfield was noisy, but she would soon get used to it.

They did not stay living there very long, because Biddy found them another house in Selwyn Crescent, Hatfield, with a big garden in a much quieter area. This was not a council

House but was privately owned, where they paid a very low rent to the landlord. The next three years were good, everyone liked their new home, with a large garden. Life was good, things were so much better for them all. The year was early 1942, Blanche was pregnant again, the baby was due in August and Blanche was happily looking forward to the birth of her baby. Billy had found a more permanent job, working as a General Labourer. He came home every day when he could, but sometimes he was sent to work in areas away from Hertfordshire, he was on a good wage and was able to pay the rent and buy food for the family. With a regular wage coming in each week, Blanche was so happy, she did not have to worry about being behind with the rent payments or paying fuel bills any more.

Biddy often came to visit Blanche, to make sure everything was going well and that there were no problems. The house was clean and tidy, Blanche was taking a pride in her home and herself, Carol was growing fast and would soon be starting school, already she was showing signs of being very bright and would try reading her children's book, that Aunty Biddy had brought her for her fourth birthday. Blanche seemed like a different person. She said to Biddy, "I have made really good friends with my neighbours and Eveline will soon be leaving school, she has already made up her mind that she wants to find a job at the Ballito stocking factory at Fleetville, she is going to apply for an interview, as soon as she leaves school, at the end of the summer term."

Biddy said, "Well, that's good; she will be bringing in an income, which will help everyone, I do hope she gets the job, now Blanche, I will call again soon." They hugged and Biddy waved as she drove away in her posh car.

The next time Biddy paid a visit to Blanche, she told her that she had been to see Papa and Florrie, she liked to see them from time to time, but after four years of marriage, Florrie's health was not so good. Biddy said, "I thought that she did not look very well, she looked very pale, Blanche, so I asked her if she was unwell and Florrie said, 'Biddy, I have been feeling under the weather lately but I am feeling much better now'."

"I think she was putting on a brave face, but I felt that there was something wrong with her, anyway I will call and see her again soon Blanche, but for now I must make haste and get back to London." Blanche watched and waved, as she drove off in her white limousine car. The following week Blanche received a letter from Biddy:

My dearest Blanche,

I have to tell you that Patrick has been sent out to Germany to fight, so we have postponed our wedding plans. I will let you know more when I hear from Patrick. I enclose ten pounds for you to buy the family fish and chips for the children's supper, fill up your cupboards with food. I'll be over to see you again soon. Love Biddy xxx.

After Blanche had read the letter again, it was very disturbing to think that there was another world war going on. She tried not to think about what the future held and went around to her friendly neighbour's house, for a cup of tea and a chat. She had baked a fruit cake that morning and took some with her.

The year 1942 was to be the most terrifying, World War Two had already started and for the next three years, the Germans would be sending their bombs to destroy our

Country. There would be no wedding plans as yet, as to when Biddy and Patrick would be getting married. Patrick was desperate to get back and marry Biddy, so he asked his officer for a special two weeks' leave to get married. Billy was to get a very upsetting telegram, letting him know that his brother had been killed as a prisoner of war on a Japanese warship that was destroyed by the United States American Navy in 1942.

Billy never got over losing his older brother in this dreadful war, he was later informed by his parents that his younger brother had also lost his life when a British Naval Ship was targeted by a German warplane. Losing both his brothers had a profound effect on Billy's mental health.

That night Blanche had a bad dream, she dreamt that she was in labour and there was no one to help her to give birth. She woke up in a sweat, relieved to find it was all a bad dream. The baby was due on 23rd August and she was already six months pregnant. She did hope that her sister's wedding date would be after the birth of her child. But the war was on, only time would tell.

On 5 June 1942, there was a lull in the bombing and a chance for Patrick to return to Britain, Biddy was more than ready now to marry her fiancé Patrick. He was at last given special permission he needed, but he was told that he must return to his flying duties in two weeks' time. Their honeymoon would have to wait. The wedding date was all set for Saturday, 12 June 1942. Biddy kept her word and took Blanche and the family out, to buy them new clothes for her wedding, Her Wedding dress and the bridesmaid dresses had already been made. The caterers would start making her wedding cake. All the wedding invitations were sent out, friends were notified, the wedding would take place at the Catholic Church in London, the reception was all booked.

Biddy drove Blanche and the family to Cambridge to do the shopping, she bought them all lovely outfits. Eveline chose a full-length dress with matching long cotton gloves, they bought Michael a light grey suit, short trousers with jacket. Caroline chose a very pretty puff sleeve dress and bonnet in shades of pink. Blanche chose a full-length puff sleeve dress with a loose flowing skirt, also a fur wrap collar and flowers to wear in her hair. They also bought matching shoes. On the way back, they stopped outside the house called "Brantwytch" where Biddy would eventually live, just to take a look in at the gates. She did not have the keys to enter. But they all loved what they saw from the front gates. Patrick would be renting a house in Hunting Forbury, until after the wedding.

Brantwytch, their beautiful home in Royston, would be ready and waiting for the happy couple to move in. The wedding day arrived all too soon, Mother and Eveline went to the hairdressers to have their hair done. Biddy sent a large wedding car to pick them all up and take them to the Church and on to the reception. Did Billy not want to go or was he not invited to the wedding? The wedding was to take place in the Roman Catholic Church, all the Knight relations were there. Alfie, Louise, their daughter Evelyn and son Philip had travelled over from France. Alfred and his wife Florrie managed to make it there. Biddy looked stunning, her bridesmaids also looked beautiful. When they entered the reception hall, the live music played and there was dancing. Patrick's and Biddy's close friends came.

It was a lovely wedding, everything looked so beautiful, all the tables were decorated with flowers and garlands. The buffet lunch was excellent, there was something for everyone to eat and enjoy. The band played and the guests danced. They were waltzing, then changed to a foxtrot and then the quick step. The speeches were said and everyone toasted the bride and groom. Their wedding cake was three tiers high, after the cake was cut, soon they had to depart, as their taxi was waiting outside. Blanche and the family gave the happy couple their very best wishes. Mother, Michael Eveline and Caroline were chatting all the way home about their Aunty and Uncle's lovely wedding. It was a really grand day for them all!

Blanche was very soon to give birth to Philip, Mrs Chapman, the kind lady who lived opposite, had a telephone, when Mother went into labour, Eveline went over and asked her if she would call the midwife. Mrs Chapman stayed with mum until the midwife arrived. Mother gave birth to a healthy boy. Philip was born on 25 August 1942. Billy at this time was back working on the railways. He seemed happy enough with his job and had settled, at last, living as a proper father with his family.

They were soon to have some bad news from Biddy, that she would be coming to see them shortly. When Biddy arrived, she said, "Florence apparently has been fighting cancer for a long time. The sad news, Blanche, is that she recently lost her fight against the disease, Florrie sadly passed away just over a week ago. I did attend the funeral, but there were only about a dozen people there. They were mainly Florrie's relations and friends. I really did not know anyone, but they were all very friendly. Father was strong, but he did have tears in his eyes."

"Biddy, I didn't really get to know Florrie that well, I am so sorry to hear this sad news, Papa did write and tell me she was sick, but he never mentioned that she had cancer, I remember she looked ill when they last came to visit us. It is always sad when a member of the family dies, I will say a prayer for her."

Biddy said, "I did go around to see Papa yesterday and he was bearing up after losing Florrie. He told me that he had just joined a Bridge club, as he was finding it lonely living alone, he had made friends with a lady called Bridgette Acrid, who was his bridge partner. He invited me to his house last Sunday for lunch, to meet her. Well, Blanche, I found her to be pleasant enough, friendly, father seemed very relaxed in her company. They seem to get along very well. Bridgette said she would like to meet you and your family, so we will have to arrange something soon, Blanche."

Chapter Thirty-Four
The War Years

In 1939, Germany declared war on Poland from the west, two days later France and Britain declared war on Germany, on the 17th Soviet troops invaded Poland from the East, War between USSR and Germany began on 3 September 1941. America became involved in the war when the Japanese bombed Pearl Harbour in Hawaii on 7 December 1941. By 1942, the Germans had already started sending bombs blowing up all parts of London and other parts of England, there was a curfew and blackouts. Germans were sending V 1 Flying bombs and destroying lots of beautiful buildings. Towns were being blown up all around London and all other parts of the United Kingdom.

American troops declared war on Germany and Italy. They were our allies and we needed them. The bombs were so terrible, destroying so many buildings and killing millions of people. As we were living near Hatfield Aerodrome, where the warplanes were being made. That's where the Germans were now targeting their doodlebugs. These flying Bombs were now being dropped in our area of Hertfordshire. Living in Selwyn Crescent, our mother would watch and listen for the constant sound of air raids when the sirens would go off.

People in this area would make their way to the nearest air raid shelters. Everyone was given a gas mask to wear.

Many people were being evacuated to different parts of the country after their houses had been bombed. How the people lived like this, from day to day, there was no way of knowing, with the blackouts, the noise of flying bombs overhead, Nobody knew the outcome of this terrible war. Things were about to become disastrous for the whole family, life for them was about to change, in more ways than one...

It was on a Sunday morning in early July 1942 when Michael and Eveline left home in Selwyn Crescent to take the two-mile walk towards the Catholic Church in Old Hatfield. They had made this trip to Church a few times, without their Mother when she was unwell. They would take a shortcut through the farmer's field, to be closer to their destination. On this particular morning, while walking across the field, Eveline suddenly had a strange feeling, something was very wrong. She later told her mother after their terrifying encounter, that it was called "Extrasensory Perception." Eveline said nothing to Michael, who was seven years old, she was just thirteen at the time and they continued on their way.

Just as they were entering the main town of Hatfield, Eveline heard the sound of an aircraft coming up behind them, the noise sounded very odd, it was getting closer to them! On a sudden impulse, she quickly grabbed Michael and pushed him into a tall hedge which was growing alongside the footpath. She then fell over him, mainly to hold him down, telling him to stay very still and not to utter a sound, waiting until the plane passed over. It was then they heard the most deafening sound of machine gun fire, strafing the road with pelts and bullets, just beside the footpath where Michael and she had been walking. Too afraid to move, they stayed there, until it became quiet.

The plane was a German fighter, which was shot down after straying into our territory, the pilot was looking for somewhere safe to land. On landing in nearby fields, the plane crashed and burst into flames, killing the pilot. Michael and Eveline then got up and once again headed for the Catholic Church. They were five minutes away from the Church when they heard the sound of horses coming up close behind them, they stopped to see who it was. One of the riders was a man, who looked down at them in amazement, then said, "What on earth are you two doing here? Didn't you hear the air raid sirens?"

Eveline was too frightened to answer. Then she noticed the other rider was a lady, shaking her head in disbelief. "Where do you live?" the man asked. "We'll take you home, there is no need to be afraid, we will get you home safely."

Michael spoke for the first time and told the rider where they lived. He dismounted, lifted Eveline up and placed her in the saddle in front of the lady, then he did the same for Michael on his horse. It was the first time they had ever been on a horse and enjoyed every minute of it. The riders headed towards Selwyn, which was a relief, as another thought struck Eveline, at least they were not taking them down to the police station, where they would have been in very big trouble with their parents.

When arriving at their home, the gentleman lifted Michael off his horse. He then lifted Eveline down. He tethered his horse to the lamppost and walked up to the front door and knocked, with them following close beside him. Our mother opened the door and was startled to see them with this strange man. "What the hell!" seeing her frightened children, Mama pulled Michael and Eveline inside. Even before the rider had time to explain, Mother called Billy to the door. She ushered the children into the back room and went to make some tea.

Father came and spoke to the riders. The gentleman told father what had happened. The rider started to tell father off, saying "Why did you let your young children go out alone when there is a war on, enemy aircraft have been dropping bombs in this area, your children could have been killed, sir! We could have you arrested for the negligence of your children."

Father then lost his temper and started shouting at him, "How dare you, my children were going to church, as they did every Sunday, with or without their parents." Father, still suffering from his hangover, lost his temper and punched the man, then a fight started. The lady rider must have phoned the police, they soon arrived and took Father off in a paddy wagon. He was bound over to keep the peace. The wardens never brought any charges.

Evelyne just shuddered to think how easily they could have been caught up in that gunfire and been killed. Oh yes, Mother was furious shouting at them, "Look at the trouble you have caused us." When Eveline tried to explain, she was told not to answer back, Mother was very cross and wouldn't give Eveline a chance to explain, but shut her in the coal shed for being disobedient, telling her, "how many times have I told you not to speak to strangers, let alone go off with them. Those people could have taken you away, we may never have seen you or Michael again. I hope this will teach you a lesson." She was shut in the shed for what seemed like an hour, in actual fact it was only twenty minutes. She then opened the shed door and said, "You must never go off with strangers again, your father has been arrested for assaulting a warden and taken to the police station. I am very worried about him."

Michael was not that bothered about his ordeal, it was like an adventure to him. Michael later told Eveline what had happened to their father. It was only later that evening, Eveline had a chance to explain to her mother exactly what had happened to them. She said, "Oh my darlings, I had no idea, I am so very sorry, I did not know all these facts, how awful and traumatic it must have been for you both. It was all my fault, I should never have let you go to Church without me, Thank the good lord you are both safe. Eveline, the reason I shut you in the coal shed was to teach you a lesson, that those riders could have been child abductors, taken you both away and I may never have seen my darling children ever again. I should have known better about this war going on. I am so sorry children, please, please, forgive your Mummy."

They never again saw or heard from the riders again, but they will always be remembered, they most probably saved both their young lives. Eveline just shuddered to think how easily they could have been caught up in that gunfire. There were two reasons why our Mother never took us to Church that particular Sunday, the first reason was that she was almost six months pregnant and not feeling too well. The other reason was that father had come home very drunk the night before and was sleeping it off. Mother could not leave him alone in his condition with a heavy hangover. Mother was a strict Roman Catholic and would never miss Mass unless she or one of her children were ill. Father never went to Church, as he was not religious.

When Father did return home, he told Blanche that he had been bound over to keep the peace, the warden never brought any charges against our father. Mother explained everything to Billy, he then said, "Blanche, I must learn to control my temper, I am truly sorry. The man was not in any kind of uniform, the police informed me he was on Warden Street Petrol. Blanche, I know I am to blame for my own stupidity. Our poor children must have gone through a terrible ordeal, I will make it up to the children and take them to the zoo next weekend."

One evening in early October 1944, Mother was asleep in the front bedroom with baby Philip, who was sleeping in his cot beside her, in the back bedroom eldest sister Eveline, was sleeping in the back bedroom in a double bed, brother Michael and sister Carol slept in the small box room at the front of the house. This room contained just two small single beds. Father was not at home that night, as he was working on the railways doing his night shift. Mother was awakened by a loud droning noise, she looked out the window and saw that a flying bomb was heading in our direction, towards the house. The noise was so loud that everyone woke up.

Eveline, feeling frightened, left her room and got into the bottom of Carol's bed; she often did this when the sirens went off in the night. Mother was a very pious lady, she just prayed with Philip in her arms, watching from the bedroom window, the doodlebug was constantly dropping height as it came, suddenly it changed direction and was heading directly towards their house! It was nearly midnight, Mother held Philip praying, she was feared for all their lives.

There was suddenly a loud bang, the whole house shook, as the bomb suddenly hit our chimney, As the flying bomb came down, there was a terrible explosion, hitting the two semi-attached houses adjacent to our gardens, where both houses were flattened to the ground. The force from this massive explosion shook all the houses around the estate. The damage in the area was massive! Our house had all the windows and doors taken out, there was so much damage to the exterior brickwork, also to the interior, the house was wrecked, there was, plastering and ceiling dust everywhere, the wall at the back of the house was missing and Eveline's bed layout in the garden! The beautiful oak extending dining table and chairs, the bureau and sideboard were all broken and destroyed. The damage to our home was heart-breaking. All they could hear was the noise of the people in the street, panicking and shouting. It was total chaos, as Eveline was crying that she had bits of ceiling dust in her eyes and could not see.

Carol was saying, "We all have, Eve, don't cry."

Mum shouted, "Are you children alright? Everyone just stay where you are, do not move."

"Yes mum, we are all OK, just plaster dust in our eyes."

Just then they heard a loud voice come up from below stairs, saying, "Is there anyone up there?"

Mother shouted back, "Yes we are all alive."

Eveline then gently made her way to the landing, from the banister she said, "Yes sir, we are all OK."

He said to her, "I'm the air raid warden, I will just check the staircase to see if it is safe or damaged."

She watched him as he came slowly up the stairs, checking each step to make sure they were safe, then Mother came out of her room with Philip in her arms. The warden said, "Yes, the stairs are safe for you all to come down. Do you have a husband, madam?"

"Yes, he is working on his night shift, he will be home in the morning."

"Don't worry, we will inform him on his return, what's your name, madam?"

"My name is Mrs Blanche Hancock, my husband's name is William Hancock."

"Well, Mrs Hancock, we will be taking you and your family to the hostel where you will sleep tonight and be fed. Tomorrow I make arrangements for you all to be evacuated, to a safer place or you may want to make your own arrangements when you see your husband in the morning. All your details can be given tomorrow before you leave, we will bring Mr Hancock to the Hostel in the morning. Your house, Mrs Hancock, will have to be rebuilt and that could take a long time, but we will keep you informed."

Mother and Eveline packed up a few necessary belongings, Mother found two suitcases on the top of the wardrobe and packed clothes for everyone. While Eveline went downstairs and found what documentation they might need. Though much had been destroyed or in the rubble. She picked up the money tin from the back of the kitchen cupboard. When they finally had what would be needed and could carry. The Warden who had been waiting for them put the cases and bags in his truck. Michael and Carol went around the back of the house, to see what damage it had caused to their home.

Carol said, "Tell Mum, I am going to spend the night with our friendly neighbour Jill Baker's, to pick me up in the morning."

There was so much debris and glass everywhere, Michael had to be very careful not to fall over. The stars were out, it was a clear night. Looking across the back-to-back gardens all Michael could see was the remains of Eveline's bed. The two houses that backed onto us were completely flattened, he could see fire and smoke coming from them. A sight he would never ever forget! With only two back-to-back gardens separating us, it could so easily have been our family killed Those people who lived on the other side of the Crescent were all killed, the two semi-attached houses were totally demolished. In house Number 2 lived Ruth Knight and their eight-year-old daughter Irene, their bodies were found huddled together, their father was away working at the time. In the house next door Number 4, lived Mr Earnest Woodcock and his wife, they both lost their lives. Michael was called, they had to leave the house open, front and back doors were gone. For anyone to come in and take whatever they wanted, which they probably did, they lost most of the entire contents of their home! Mother wanted to know where Carol was.

Michael said, "Mum, she went to spend the rest of the night at the Baker's House, which was still intact and we can pick her up tomorrow morning." They all got into the Army truck, which took them to the hostel, for the remainder of that terrible night. When their father returned home from work the following morning, he could not believe the devastation of his home and that the family were all gone, he didn't know if they had been killed or taken to hospital. He looked around and saw his daughter's bed in the garden. He was on the verge of breaking down when a Warden put his head around the corner and said, "Are you, Mr Hancock?"

"Yes please tell me where my wife and children are."

"It's all alright, Mr Hancock, your family are all safe and well, but in shock, they are staying at the hostel waiting for you." Just then Blanche appeared to collect Carol, she was just leaving her neighbour's house when they both saw father talking to the Warden.

When father saw them, he came to them, looking so happy, they all needed a really big hug, all father could say was, "Thank the Lord you are all safe." The Hancocks had lost their home, they would most likely lose all their personal belongings and contents. But at that time, they were just so thankful to be alive. The warden then drove them in the Army truck to the Hostel, where they all met up. Father told the Warden that he would be taking his family to his parent's home in Plymouth. The Hancocks were taken to the Salvation Army for a change of clothing. The Warden then drove them to Hatfield Station. Billy said to Blanche, "I will just pop into the Station Cafe and get us all a drink."

"No Billy, don't do that; the train is due any minute." Father took no notice of mama, just as the cafe door closed behind him, the train pulled in. Everyone boarded the train, the guard blew his whistle. The Station Master waved his flag, the train moved off, leaving Billy on the platform holding a tray of cups! Seeing the look on their father's face made Eveline and Michael giggle with laughter. Even Blanche had to laugh, saying, "Your father never listens to me." They had already decided to head to Billy's parents in Plymouth, but they had to change trains in London, where they waited for Billy to come in on the next train. Mother had words with Billy saying, "I told you, Billy, the train was due in, why didn't you take any notice of me, Billy, you are such a stubborn man!"

"Oh do leave off, Blanche, I really thought I had enough time to get everyone a well-needed drink." There the matter was closed...

When they arrived in Plymouth, they ordered a taxi, which took them to Billy's parents' house. Their grandmother was very surprised but pleased to see them, she invited them in, making them all welcome. Then father explained their dire situation that their house had been bombed and had to evacuate their home.

Grandma Rose told them, "I am afraid you are not at all safe here, the Germans are bombing here constantly, as we are next to the Naval Base, this is a prime target for the Germans to bomb! Your grandfather is not here at the moment, as he is working at the docks, we will discuss your situation when he returns, you are welcome to stay here for a few nights. Our son Sidney is away fighting, so we do have a spare room. You will have to double up as there are five of you, I do have a cot in the basement where Philip can sleep. I think Grandfather will agree that tomorrow I must start making arrangements for you all to be treated as evacuees and organise for you all to stay in a much safer place, it will most likely be in the Devon countryside."

Rose arranged their evacuation giving them all the details they would need. They said a big thank you to Rose and William, saying their fond farewells and they waved goodbye. They then caught the next train to the lovely village of Mary Tavy in Tavistock, Devon. They got a cab to the Old Rectory at Crapstone, where they ended up. They were met by the Vicar of the Church and the evacuation officer in charge, giving them accommodation in a school hut. It reminded them of a dormitory, as it had lots of beds.

The school was split into two parts, next door was the children's school room, on Sundays, it became the Church Hall. After six months, father found them accommodation in nearby Peter Tavy, Tavistock. They remained living there reasonably happily for over two years. The children loved Devon, they found it so beautiful with winding country lanes, the wind whistling through the trees, making a sound on the electric wires above. After school, they would all go exploring the countryside, with fields of primroses. They would find abandoned tin mines, where the children would throw stones down, but being so close, it was a very dangerous place for them to be!

Life carried on and after two years, they had an official letter to let the Hancocks know that their house had been rebuilt and it was safe for them to return. It was now 1946. The war was over! The family returned home to find the house in Selwyn Crescent had all been rebuilt; what a relief to return home at long last!

Chapter Thirty-Five

After the family returned home, mother contacted Biddy, just to say they had all returned home safely. The house had been rebuilt and was looking good, but the house needed to be refurbished, she said a lot of their household goods were put into storage and had been returned. "Please come over. We are all looking forward to seeing you, as it has been a long time and we miss you." Biddy came the next day to see what needed replacing, she bought them all new furniture including carpets and curtains, which was needed. Any personal belongings that had been found, were taken to the Police station to be claimed, nearly all their old photographs were damaged or lost, some were of them taken in India with the dogs and some in Canada taken of Alfred's relations, other personal things that belonged to their grandmother and grandfather were missing, some of great-grandmother's pictures were also missing. Grandmother's precious jewellery which was in an ivory inlaid box was also missing. They just had to accept this and be grateful for what they got returned, most importantly that they were all still alive!

Life carried on until late May 1946 when Mother found she was pregnant again. Charmaine was born in one of the worst winters of 1947. Eveline was sent out in very deep snow, on Saturday 22nd February to fetch Mother's close friend Mrs Toms, a very kind jolly lady who owned and ran a little shop, which sold all kinds of foods and sweets, in Roe Green Lane. Mrs Toms had once worked as a nurse. Her daughter Edna Toms was one of Eveline's closest friends. Mrs Toms walked quickly back with Eveline, she was just in time, as Mother was starting labour to give birth, this lady helped bring Charmaine Rio-Linda her third daughter into the world.

Patrick O'Neil-Dunne had a distinguished war career with the RAF as a Flight Lieutenant. He served in the Battle of Britain to V.E. Day. He took part in the Dam-Busters Raid, D-Day and the crossing of the Rhine. He was mentioned in despatches and was one of the few RAF crew to survive the three tours of operations. While serving his time in the RAF, his plane was shot down, Patrick had a miraculous escape, as all the war details were unfortunately lost. Although he was badly burnt, he managed to make it alive, what a lucky man Patrick was, to survive this dreadful war and having to have his face rebuilt. Patrick loved sport, racing and gambling. He would one day make his fortune, he did this by falling into the tobacco trade by accident.

After he graduated in architecture in America, he started up the Rembrandt Tobacco Company. Later he went on to become world director of a cigarette conglomerate which included Rothman's and Dunhill. He went on to become company director for Rothman's and travelled all over the world. He played a leading role in changing the smoking habits of millions, by the 1950s and 1960s Mr O'Neil-Dunne always maintained that cigarettes were good for you. In later years, he went on to invent the filter tips and the flip-top packet for cigarettes. Patrick and Biddy had many happy years together, they had two sons and a daughter and in later years, they adopted a little girl from Hong Kong.

In 1971, he wrote his autobiography and chose roulette as the subject for his book. It's called *Roulette by the Millions*. He had many books published in America. He also wrote a book about his daughter called *Sally, The Diary of a Waaf*; his last book was called *Sweet and Sour*.

The prime minister of the UK was Clement Attlee (Labour) from 1935 to 1955. He improved Social Services, creating the National Health Service. Over in USA, the president at that time was Harry S Truman (Democrat).

Our father was not living at our house at this time, sometime after I was born, he was sent away to Arlesey Mental Hospital. He had a severe mental breakdown in health, beating up our mother and pushing her out of the house. Blanche had managed to knock on her neighbour's door, they called the police and they called the local doctor, Mr Jones came and certified our father, he was taken away and put into a mental institution. While in the hospital, they gave him electric shock treatment, he was kept in Arlesey Mental Hospital for the next seven years.

When he was released from the Hospital, he came home and lived with us. He helped around the house, he even fixed Philip's bicycle. After a few weeks, he started to look for work. He left home yet again, leaving our poor mother to bring us up alone. Philip and Charmaine lived most of their childhood without him.

On 10 January 1948, Alfred Frederick John Knight married Bridgette Acrid at the Catholic Church St Gregory, Garratt Lane Earlsfield London. They were very happily married and lived at Daphne Street Wandsworth. They were only married for three years when Alfred Knight died of a sudden stroke in 1950. He was 84 years of age, on the day of the funeral, our Mother took Eveline and Charmaine to see their granddad, Charmaine was only three years old and she still remembers that day so well. She recalled seeing her dear granddad laid out in his coffin in the front room. Someone lifted her up to see him, he had a white lace cloth over his face, it was taken off. She said he looked very pale and was not breathing, Instinctively, she knew he had passed away!

They did not take Charmaine to the cemetery, but they did take Eveline. He was laid to rest at St Mary's Catholic churchyard in Kensal Rise Harrow Rd. London. Charmaine stayed with her grandmother's sister, playing in their tiny back garden. Until Mother Eveline and Bridgette returned. They went home in a London taxi cab. The years flew by. It was now 1950. Eveline had left home long ago. Now married to her husband David. In later years, Michael also left home to join the Army. When Michael returned home, things were not good, Mother and Father were arguing most every night, keeping Charmaine and himself awake. One morning Michael lost his temper, for abusing Mother yet again, she had a black eye and her face was swollen.

In the kitchen that morning, there was an awful fight and Michael beat up father and threw him out of the house. Father left and he never returned to our house again. Carol was also away, she was still attending boarding school, when she left the Grammar school she never returned home. Carol went off to live with her married sister Eveline. Then she found a job at Boots the chemist as a pharmacist.

While working at Boots, she met and later married Bill Reeley. Philip had also left home to join the Army, to serve his National Service.

Things soon got back to normal, our mother was happy again. She took real good care of Michael and Charmaine. Biddy would often come to visit Mother, one day while Michael was out at work, it was half term holidays, Charmaine was at home. Grandfather Knight had left Blanche his Sword as a small legacy. Biddy and Blanche were in the front room having tea and cake. Charmaine heard Biddy ask Blanche, "Do you still have Grandfather's sword?"

"Yes Biddy, it is hanging in the alcove in the back room. I will show you." Mum took it off the wall and showed it to Biddy, she said, "Blanche, this sword needs a really good professional clean, leave it with me and I will have it restored."

So Mum let her take the sword. Mum and I went outside to see her off, she got into her Rolls Royce, Mum and I noticed a few curtains moving, across the street, no doubt they were wondering who that was, as Biddy was all dressed up to the nines.

When Michael came home from work, he asked Mother where the sword was. She told him that she had given it to Aunty Biddy to be professionally cleaned. Michael was very cross, "Why did you let her take the sword away, we could have had it cleaned up, Mother, the sword looked fine in its sheath, don't you realise Mother that it was our only family heirloom of Grandfather. I don't think Biddy will ever return the sword."

Mother had already promised it to Michael in writing. He knew in his heart, they would never see Grandfather Knight's sword again, and we never did. Mother believed all his war medals for bravery were given to her brother Alfie Knight in France, but now we will never know for certain.

In 2019, Charmaine's son Marcus drove her up to Kensal Rise, to see her first grandmother Evelyne Jane Knight and her grandfather Alfred Knight's graves. The number of Evelyne's grave plot number was in Alfred's little red diary dated 1948 that Charmaine found. The graveyard was huge and it took us twenty-five minutes to find Evelyne's, but finding Alfred's was more difficult to find. After searching in this massive churchyard for over an hour, most of the Headstones had sunk into the ground, plus the inscriptions had faded over the years. We gave up looking and drove to where grandfather had once lived in Daphne street. Marcus parked the car at the end of the street, I got out and walked up the road to find the number of the house.

I built up some courage and went to knock on the door. But there was nobody in, as I walked back to the car, another car came down the street and stopped outside the house. I waited and watched to see what house he went to, my luck was in, I walked up to the man as he was now on the doorstep, I said, "Excuse me, but may I talk to you?"

The man turned, smiled and said, "Yes."

I then explained who I was and that my grandfather lived in this house for many years. I showed him the wedding certificate of their wedding. I told him my son and I was not able to find my grandfather's grave. I went on to tell him when I was aged three, I saw my grandfather laid out in his coffin, in this very house in the front room. I described what I remembered of that day and quick detail of what I remember of the inside. He was very interested and asked me if I would like to come inside.

I said, "Thank you, but I'd better go and tell my son, he is waiting in the car."

He said, "Tell him to come in as well." What a very kind gentleman he was. It was the strangest feeling standing there in the same place where I had last seen my grandfather, laid out in his coffin. He showed us around, nothing had really changed. We very kindly thanked the gentleman; he said, "My name is Terry Thomas." I will always remember him and be grateful to Mr Terry Thomas, we all shook hands, thanked him kindly and left.

Alfred Fredrick John Knight was an amazing man, he always walked tall and was courageous. He left a small legacy to all his grandchildren in his last Will and Testament.

Mine was left in trust with the Barclays Bank until I reached the age of eighteen. I do believe he helped Carol financially, by paying her school fees while she was at the Grammar school.

Epilogue

In 1961, after Michael had thrown father William out of the house, our father somehow made his way to Worcestershire, where sister Carol and her husband Bill lived. It was very late when he arrived at their home, Carol was asleep in bed, Bill did not want to wake her, as she had a demanding job as a pharmacist dispensing assistant at Boots and needed her sleep. Bill took charge and patched William up, he gave him food and drink, William told Bill what had happened to him, he made him comfortable, letting him rest for the remainder of the night.

Early the next morning, Bill gave William a packed lunch and drove him to the main road going North. He dropped him off and he wished him well, William told Bill to tell Carol that he was making his way to Scotland to stay with a friend he had met while he was in Arlesey Hospital. He thanked him. William managed to hitchhike to Scotland, where he stayed with this friend was a mystery, but if he did arrive at his friend's place, we never found out. My mother found out some years later that he had become an inmate of Woodilee Mental Institution at Lenzie Glasgow, for a long time. He was admitted to the Stobhill Hospital Glasgow, less than twenty-four hours before he died. The cause of death was Bronchial

Carcinoma, aged 68 years. My mother was notified of his death when the letter arrived at our home, with a copy of his death certificate, registered 23/2/1970.

After Charmaine was married, Aunty Agnes came over from Canada to visit Biddy at her family home in Royston. While she was there, Biddy brought her over to see Blanche Charmaine and Michael. Sadly, Charmaine missed Aunty Agnes's visit because no one told her Agnes was coming. If she had known, she would have liked to have met her. Charmaine had recently given birth to her daughter in 1976. They were living in their new council house in Hatfield. Charmaine was so sorry she missed the only opportunity she would ever have of meeting her Aunty Agnes.

The last time our mother heard from Aunt Agnes was in 1977 when she sent her a birthday card from Whitby Canada. Agnes Wilbur lived in the Cottage Hospital Whitby, Canada, until she passed away.

Alfred Frederick John Knight's Family and Siblings,

Amelia White (mother of Alfred) married George Knight in 1865. Born in 1843 and died in 1923 in Somerset England. Age 80.

George Knight (father of Alfred). No evidence of a divorce from Amelia (married Frances Taylor) (Stepmother of Alfred)

Frances (Taylor) Knight (stepmother) fostered Alfred, born 10/6/1846 in Somerset England and died on 12/1/1920 in Kearney Ontario, Canada.

William Thomas Knight (Alfred's stepbrother) was born on 21/10/1869 in Wales England and died on 8/2/1929 in Orillia Ontario, Canada.

312

George Henry Knight (Alfred's stepbrother) was born 1/4/1873 in Hallow, Worcestershire, England, and died on 18/9/1905 Perry Twp. Parry Sound. Ontario, Canada.

Charles Knight (Alfred's stepbrother) was born 27/7/1877 in Hallow, Worcestershire England and died on 1947 in Orillia Ontario, Canada.

Walter Knight (Alfred's stepbrother) was born 24/6/1881 Hallow, Worcestershire England and died on 30/12/1945 Hutcheson Cemetery Huntsville Canada. Married Ida Jane Hoover in Bethune, Canada.

Mary Ellen Knight (Alfred's stepsister) was born 30/3/1884 Hallow Worcestershire England and died on 18/3/1968 in Hutcheson Cemetery Huntsville Canada (married Thomas Byron Clark) on 5/2/1902 Emsdale Parry Canada. John Knight (Alfred's stepbrother) was born 28/4/1889 in Quebec Canada and died on 31/3/1927 Chaffey Twp. Cemetery Canada. Married Phoebe May Finley on 1/7/1913 Huntsville Ontario.

Alfred Frederick John Knight's Children,

Son Alfred Lionel Philip Knight (Alfie) (married name Louise Beaulieu in France) born 7/2/1896 in Subathu Nr, Shimla, India, died on 10/15/1965 in Le Havre, France.

Daughter Agnes Evelyn Maud Knight (married name Wilbur) (divorced) born 7/3/1901 in India and died date not known. Ontario, Canada.

Daughter Blanche Emily Constance Millicent Knight (married name Hancock) was born 28/9/1905 in India and died on 17/4/1979 in Watford Hertfordshire England.

Daughter Cecelia Ivy Virginia Knight (Biddy) (married name O'Neil-Dunne) was born 6/10/1910 in India and died on 29/5/2009 in Melbourne, Cambridgeshire England.

Alfred married three times:

Alfred Fredrick John Knight (first marriage) married Evelyne Jane De-Roza in 1892 in India. Grandmother died in England in 1937.

Alfred Fredrick John Knight (second marriage). Married Florence Arkill in 1942. Died in 1946. Alfred Fredrick John Knight (third marriage). Married Bridgette Acrid in 1948. Bridgette outlived Alfred.

Husband of Cecelia (Biddy) Patrick O'Neil-Dunne was born in Ireland on 1/12/19 08 and died on 19/3/1988 in Royston Cambridgeshire.

(Husband of Blanche) William James Dicker Hancock was born 30/3/1901 in England and died on 16/2/1970 in Glasgow Scotland.

(Husband of Agnes) Neil Macmillian Wilbur (Divorced June 1944).

(Wife of Alfie) Louise Beaulieu (married in France) was born in 1890 and died in 1893.

Acknowledgements

To my deceased sister, Tara Evelyn Knight (formally Eveline Rose), for all her written memoirs of her childhood and growing up.

To my dear sister, Carol Reeley, for her help with grammar and editing my book.

To my dear brother, Philip Knight, who helped me with the protocol of life in the Army. Along with an Army song!

To my daughter, Maria Leto, for her help getting me on to the correct app for writing my book.

To my son Marcus Hale who gave me help with my computer problems.

To my genealogist Mathew Homewood who gave me all my vital information about the history of my ancestors.

To my cousin, Darren Vivian in Canada, with the Knights Canadian Family Tree he sent to me, family names and dates of my distant cousins and long-lost relatives now passed on.

To my cousin Brigitte Knight for her French input into Uncle Alfie's life in France.

Many thanks go out to everyone who helped me with writing this book. Memories of all the Knights now told; for this, I am truly grateful. My story will be left as a legacy to my five grandchildren and for future generations to come.
I would like to wind up my story with an old Army song, my brother Philip Knight sang to me when he came home, after serving his time in the British Army.

They Say that in the Army

They say that in the Army the food is mighty fine
The bread rolled off the table and killed a friend of mine
Oh, I don't want no more of army life
Gee ma I wanna go, but they won't let me go
Gee ma I wanna go home.
They say that in the Army the beer is mighty fine
But how the hell do they know, they haven't tasted mine
Oh, I don't want no more of Army life
Gee ma I wanna go, but they won't let me go
Gee ma I wanna go home.

They say that in the Army the girls are mighty fine
You ask for Betty Grable, they give you Frankenstein
Oh, I don't want no more of Army life
Gee ma I wanna go, but they won't let me go
Gee ma I wanna go home.

They say that in the Army the pay is mighty fine
They give you thirty shillings and take back twenty-nine
Oh, I don't want no more of Army life
Gee ma I wanna go, but they won't let me go
Gee ma I wanna go home.

They say that in the Army the beds are mighty fine
They should sleep on my bed, the springs dig in your spine
Oh, I don't want no more of Army life
Gee ma I wanna go, but they won't let me go
Gee ma I wanna go home.

Note from the Author

My only legacy I have of my grandfather Knight is finding his tiny red diary, as I would never have dreamed of writing a book. I am so glad I learned to type, as it has made writing this book so much easier.

With delving into Grandfather's life and times, and finding a good genealogist, I have managed to put this story together.

My grandfather's life was meant to be written. I now have contacts with relatives in Canada. Long lost cousins, I never would have known. Also, my cousin Brigitte still lives in France.

Alfred Fredrick Knight will always be remembered for being a great gentleman and soldier; he was brave and gallant all the way to the end. He always stood straight and upright. He had a tattoo on his left leg, maybe to cover his deep scar, which he had since he was a young lad of thirteen. He was at my christening in 1947 and I still have a lovely picture of him holding me in his strong arms.